RENEGOTIATING RURAL DEVELOPMENT IN IRELAND

Renegotiating Rural Development in Ireland

JOHN McDONAGH
National University of Ireland, Galway

LONDON AND NEW YORK

First published 2001 by Ashgate Publishing

Reissued 2018 by Routledge
2 Park Square, Milton Park, Abingdon, Oxon OX14 4RN
711 Third Avenue, New York, NY 10017, USA

Routledge is an imprint of the Taylor & Francis Group, an informa business

Copyright © John McDonagh 2001

All rights reserved. No part of this book may be reprinted or reproduced or utilised in any form or by any electronic, mechanical, or other means, now known or hereafter invented, including photocopying and recording, or in any information storage or retrieval system, without permission in writing from the publishers.

Notice:
Product or corporate names may be trademarks or registered trademarks, and are used only for identification and explanation without intent to infringe.

Publisher's Note
The publisher has gone to great lengths to ensure the quality of this reprint but points out that some imperfections in the original copies may be apparent.

Disclaimer
The publisher has made every effort to trace copyright holders and welcomes correspondence from those they have been unable to contact.

A Library of Congress record exists under LC control number: 2001094267

This publication was grant-aided by the Publications Fund of the National University of Ireland, Galway.

Typeset in *Times New Roman* by Password, UK.

ISBN 13: 978-1-138-72383-2 (hbk)
ISBN 13: 978-1-138-72377-1 (pbk)
ISBN 13: 978-1-315-19280-2 (ebk)

Contents

List of Figures   vi
List of Tables   vi
Preface   vii
Acknowledgements   ix

1   Rural Change and Development   1

2   A Plurality of Irelands: Changing Discourses of Economy, Society and Space   10

3   Thoughts on Rurality and Rural Ireland   47

4   Deconstructing Development – Irish Style!   74

5   Retrospect and Prospect – the Role of Church, State and Community in Rural Ireland   111

6   The Emergence of Rural Governance in Ireland   162

7   Recasting the Rural in Ireland   202

Bibliography   211
Index   231

List of Figures

Figure 2.1	The provinces and counties of Ireland	11
Figure 2.2	The 1963 planning regions of Ireland	13
Figure 2.3	The new planning regions of Ireland	14
Figure 2.4	The health board regions of Ireland	15
Figure 2.5	The tourist board regions of Ireland	16
Figure 2.6	Ireland's regional authority areas	17
Figure 2.7	Gross Value Added (GVA) change 1991–1997	28
Figure 2.8	The new face of the Irish economy	30
Figure 5.1	The animation of local development	121
Figure 5.2	Monsignor J. Horan and Knock Airport	125
Figure 5.3	Canon J. Hayes and Muintir na Tíre	126
Figure 5.4	Father J. McDyer and Glencolumbkille	127
Figure 5.5	Developing the West Together study area and associated core groups	135
Figure 5.6	The terms of reference of 'A Crusade for Survival'	138
Figure 5.7	The cover of the Western Development Partnership Board Report	154
Figure 5.8	Proposals submitted by the WDPB	155
Figure 6.1	Reconfiguring Ireland's regional status	170
Figure 6.2	The spatial distribution of LEADER I areas in Ireland	185
Figure 6.3	The Gaeltacht regions of Ireland	196

List of Tables

Table 2.1	SFA, National Employment Survey, 1999	41
Table 4.1	Economic and social infrastructure investment by region	101
Table 4.2	Economic and social infrastructure investment by sector	101
Table 4.3	Employment and human resources investment by region	102
Table 4.4	Employment and human resources investment by sector	102
Table 4.5	Productive sector investment by region	103
Table 4.6	Productive sector investment by sector	103
Table 4.7	Productive sector investment by category and region	104
Table 6.1	County/City Development Board	193

Preface

Rural areas clearly have a 'geography'. Some expand and prosper while others decline through depopulation, unemployment and emigration. This 'geography' of rural change has moved the arena of rural development firmly into the political, social, economic and cultural domains of regional, national and EU policies. The changing commodification of the countryside and the movement away from agriculture provide a complex future of rural change in Ireland. Recognising this complexity, this book attempts to explore the processes and outcomes of rural development and change during a period of major restructuring in rural Europe. It is not my intention to encompass within this book all the wide-ranging debates that surround this arena of study nor do I claim to provide a definitive text on rural development in Ireland. It is hoped, however, that those with an interest in the rapidly changing geography of rural Ireland will herein find a number of issues that will stimulate their interest.

This book explores the relevant concepts and theories of rural change but it does not adopt a specific definition of rurality or development and neither does it adhere to a particular theoretical framework. Instead, the intention is to utilise the diversity of approaches and understandings of rural development to explore, Ireland's commitment, understanding and attitude toward this increasingly significant issue, in terms of government, community and citizen. Exploring the basic assumptions and philosophies that underlie this arena, this expression of ideas is important as it comes at a time when there is notable emphasis placed on rural development and on partnerships between the state (national and European) and the local community.

The main aim is to question the concept of rural development; to investigate the progress of rural development and to explore the emergence of new forms of rural governance in Ireland. The central debates include the need:

- to examine whether there is a transition from centrally controlled, top-down development strategies to more locally-designed and integrated frameworks;

- to explore whether effective community leadership can be an important contributor to local economic and social development;

- to determine the type of relationship which exists between the local and the national, and how this relationship determines and/or affects local capacity for rural development;

- to discover the extent to which the process and practice of rural development have evolved in terms of the changing relations between the state and the private sector;

- to evaluate how far the rural agenda is, or is not, set by local interests, and

- to explore the emergence of new forms of rural governance in Ireland.

A critique of the current transformations taking place in rural Ireland is provided through an analysis of the events that have instigated profound change, in the combining of traditional and modern forces, in Ireland's search for its own model of modernity. Addressing the renewed interest in developing alternative and integrative approaches, rural Ireland is explored spatially, that is, in terms of its contested mappings; historically, in terms of the rural development paths pursued; and theoretically, in relation to the imprecise and contested discourses surrounding 'rural' and 'development'. This book endeavours to occupy the space between theory and practice, and, rather than seeking solutions to rural decline, will focus on an attempt to determine what is (mis)understood by rural development; what are seen as 'problems' and, what may be future strategies. The overriding concern of this work is an attempt to assess the renegotiation of rural development in Ireland through the representation, reproduction and repackaging of suggestions, ideas and alternatives for rural renewal.

It is hoped that this work will be of use primarily to undergraduate and postgraduate students studying rural geography and other social sciences, and also to those with an interest in the rural affairs of Ireland.

John McDonagh

Acknowledgements

I wish to gratefully acknowledge the contribution and support of many individuals and organisations in the preparation of this book.

My extreme appreciation goes to Paul Cloke, Micheál Ó Cinnéide and Tony Varley for their advice, contribution of ideas and beneficial comments on initial drafts of this book. I am also thankful to Mairéad Corr and Mark McCarthy for their support and comments and to all those organisations and groups who gave so willingly of their time. My thanks also goes to those people who took the time to talk with me, to provide me with information and who were so forthcoming in their opinions and observations. I am also grateful to the Geography Department at the National University of Ireland, Galway for their support and patience through the compilation of this book. Special thanks to Siúbhan Comer for cartographic assistance; to Róisin Kelly for her research help, to Maura MacNamee for proof reading the text and Peter Simmons for typesetting an excellent CRC. Any remaining errors or omissions are however strictly my responsibility. Further, whilst every effort was made to trace copyright holders, in some cases this proved impossible. As such I also take this opportunity to apologise to any copyright holder whose rights have been unwittingly infringed.

Writing this book has been an enjoyable experience particularly because of the support I have received throughout. In this regard I want to thank my father, my family and Maria's family for their interest, support and help during the writing of the book. I wish to specifically thank my wife Maria and my daughter Rachael, both of whom give me a whole new and exciting perspective on the world. Without Maria's help and support this book would never have been started or finished. I particularly wish to thank her for all her truthful comments, her contribution to the layout and bibliography; her never-ending patience as the piles of reports and boxes invaded her home and her honest feedback on each chapter. I will be forever grateful for her unwavering belief in my capabilities, and never allowing me to give up!

Finally, it is with great sadness that my mother never got the chance to see this finished work. Her belief, support and encouragement will, however, always be with me. This book is dedicated to her.

1 Rural Change and Development

There is general acceptance that there is such a thing as 'rural', that this differs in some way from 'urban' and without too much difficulty people can differentiate one from the other. So what makes this unconscious acceptance of the rural so easy? Is it tradition, history, culture, or merely part of our make-up? When do we recognise something as being non-rural? If we describe ourselves as being from a rural area, does this description change and, if it does, under what circumstances? How do the policy makers think of rural areas? Are there instant images created and, more importantly are there 'striking contrasts between the description of rural life preferred by various government officials and [that of] the rural people themselves' (Matthews, 1977, p.120). These are the questions that permeate this attempt to explore the renegotiation of rural development policy and practice in Ireland.

Rural development can be described as a complicated, sophisticated, technical and dedicative process that involves personalities, politics, negotiations and vested interests. Also, rural development clearly has a 'geography'. Some rural areas thrive, expand and prosper, while others suffer unemployment, depopulation and ultimately terminal decline. The nature of rural change is therefore becoming a key dimension of political, social, economic and cultural understandings. The dynamism of rural areas and the multi-dimensionality of the changes that occur in this arena have projected rural space; the increasing demand on rural resources, and the alternative use of rural areas to the forefront of regional, national and European policy. The social and economic changes that are currently being experienced in the Irish countryside (decline in agriculture, changing commodification of the countryside, the 'Celtic Tiger') are giving rise to a multiplicity of social spaces and thus a proliferation of different constructs, ideals and lived experiences.

This study of rural development in Ireland is centred on four main theses. The first attempts to understand the changing constructs of rurality that mould Irish rural development policy, process and perception. The second thesis deconstructs the paths of development pursued, and critically assesses the main practices of reports, committees and pilot programmes (strategies now synonymous with rural development in Ireland). The third consideration addresses the way in which rural areas are governed and, specifically, explores the complexities of a shift from government to governance. The fourth argument concentrates on whether a highly centralised, political system dominated by sectoral interests, such as exists in Ireland, can accommodate the changes needed to achieve the multi-sectoral, flexible and co-ordinated approach (and the decentralisation of authority implicit in such an approach) currently favoured in the rhetoric of government policy (Cuddy *et al.*, 1990; Commins and Keane, 1994; Department of Agriculture and Food, 1999).

Interweaving these four foci throughout the book, it is possible to examine a number of related factors that invariably affect the way people act or think, as well as the way in which policies and strategies are drawn up in relation to developmental discourses in Ireland. The accumulation of theoretical knowledge that guides the type of rural development policy being suggested, considered and, in many cases implemented, is also evaluated. This deconstruction involves the exploration of popular conceptions of rurality and community, of different discourses of development, and of the lack of understanding (conscious or not) involved in partnerships and developmental practices. In terms of perception, with the argument advanced for a new form of rural governance, which would allow greater sharing, rural Ireland's slow transformation is traced from its early association with agriculture and with physical space, to a perception determined more by the new social processes at work in these spaces. Further, the nature and structure of Irish democracy are challenged with the argument advanced for a new form of rural governance which would allow greater sharing in the decision-making process between the state and the voluntary/community sectors. Overall, a picture of the uncertainty affecting rural Ireland is assembled, the future development paths explored, and the type of objectives, policies and processes being pursued in relation to rural development, questioned.

Why this book?

The fundamental changes that have taken place in the rural economy, have led some authors (Healy, 1968; Varley *et al.*, 1991; Varley, 1991b; Euradvice, 1994) to refer to a 'rural crisis'; indeed intense debate has raged 'about the concept of the rural and what reality, if any, is its referent' (Gray, 2000, p.30). This debate (see Cloke, 1985; Hoggart, 1990; Halfacree, 1993; Pratt, 1996) and the current process of rapid rural change provide an opportune time to determine, through government, community and citizen, Ireland's attitude to rural development. As the issues of rural development become even more complex, the assumption of a greater role by local communities and a diminishing dependence on central government seems critical. Rural development policy is now recognised as having been too long an appendage of agricultural policy and, to a lesser extent, regional policy (Commins and Keane, 1994; Shortall, 1994) with no clearly formulated or consistent set of policies emerging. There has been a tendency to conflate rural with agriculture, safeness, friendliness, community and family - but also with backwardness, isolation, poverty and a pre-modern society (see Gray, 2000). The rural is being redefined in the context of modernisation pressures as well as pressure from market forces, increased mobility, spatial diversity, new rural dwellers and differing uses of the countryside. The development of a theoretical insight into rural development processes (Hoggart *et al.*, 1995), the conceptual shift from the mechanistic and reductionist view (Sheeran, 1988) and the call to interpret different constructs of rurality (Cloke, 1995) are becoming increasingly significant in forming strategies for the future of rural areas. There is a growing need to examine how rurality is constructed and deployed in a variety of contexts (Murdoch and Pratt, 1993), which necessitates a move toward looking at the rural as a construction made up of a whole set of meanings (political and socio-cultural) and as a lived experience rather than merely as physical space.

A number of elements are significant in the changing role of rural Ireland. These include the inevitable decline of the traditional agrarian system, challenges to the patriarchal and religious dominance in Irish culture, and the reduction in isolationist attitudes following Ireland's accession to the European Union (EU) (Girvin, 1993). The tendency is still commonplace however, to view spatial problems as problems in their own right - that rural problems are specific to rural regions and that such difficulties can be dealt with exclusively through some kind of specifically regional or rural-oriented planning. Rural development initiatives in Ireland are seen to be reactive rather than proactive and while policies claim to be part of an integrated framework, they are in practice, implemented in a fragmented and sector-specific way. The Irish Government therefore seem far 'more at ease with an approach that focuses on supporting individual projects' (Ó Cinnéide, 1996, p.10), rather than with the encouragement of community development and enterprise.

A further focus for debate surrounds the understandings of 'rural development'. Is rural development a government-initiated programme or a process of endless variety? Something which has a start and endpoint, or something which deals with quality of life issues that are 'everybody's business, not simply the business of the world's small, weak cadre of rural advocates' (Wilkinson, 1992, p.25)? From this complexity of debate, this book raises the notion of development in Ireland as 'spectacle'. That is, development that is designed to pacify the rural populace, by colonising reality and becoming reality (Escobar, 1995) with images displayed in programmes and projects pursued by successive Irish governments. Essentially this 'spectacle' stems from the unwillingness of government to alter the administrative and institutional capacities of the state, providing instead the 'spectacle' of development through various EU-derived initiatives like LEADER or area-based partnerships. Such initiatives are represented as 'development' although often the withdrawal of funds has meant the initiatives are incapable of sustaining improvements and have merely achieved a short-term improvement in certain conditions (see Hoggart and Buller, 1987). While there has been however, a perceptible shift in recent years from the top-down sectoral policy to a more bottom-up partnership arrangement, rural communities in Ireland still have only limited influence on the development process. Nevertheless, whether from a top-down or bottom-up perspective, it is becoming increasingly apparent that 'the most effective path to rural development involves the integration of the top-down functional approach with the bottom-up territorial approach' (Ó Cinnéide, 1992b, p.12). While this is a compelling prospect, to create an egalitarian institutional framework that could facilitate such integration provides the real challenge. To reconfigure the structures of governance in rural areas would seem the starting point for such a challenge.

The highly centralised system of government in Ireland creates a sense of powerlessness at local level and leads to dependency on the state (Ó Cinnéide, 1993a). It is therefore one thing for 'government administrators and social scientists to declare that the locals are in charge and quite another to provide the kinds of intervention and assistance that would increase the possibility of success in local actions' (Wilkinson, 1992, p.33). As the EU leans more towards a regional policy, the state is under increasing pressure from the top-down and bottom-up to recognise the role that local communities can play. Within this role, it is also important to understand what 'participatory development' is and how it differs from the more conservative process of simply trying to involve people in development projects that have already been decided. The argument is that a disparity of approach often develops between the disadvantaged and the professionals, where 'too many professionals unconsciously believe that rural development will be achieved through the efforts of governments and development agencies' (Burkey, 1993, p.xiii). The resulting danger is that voluntary organisations are co-opted as instruments of government policy. The isolation of government from citizen is therefore a major stumbling block to development, and the 'gap between the state and local communities under present structures [in Ireland] is too great for interaction to lead to success' (O'Núanáin, 1992, p.82). The critical move is to build towards an intermediate position, where the development of the human capacity (knowledge, research, innovation, education and training), is paramount. This intermediate position must also recognise that local communities can not be empowered sufficiently to take on this task alone but need partnership with the government and the EU. The challenge is to create a structure or organisation that will bridge this gap and create a system of governance with a balance that enhances the power of the state in favour of rural development while limiting its role sufficiently to ensure that local communities have control over their own development path (Heelas and Morris, 1992).

To say then that this book is about democracy, and its lack, in Irish state and community sectors, might be to over-simplify the issues of concern. To suggest that Ireland is not a democracy might raise eyebrows in many quarters, but this suggestion is made, albeit rather tentatively. The fundamental question, when exploring the types of development discourse being employed in rural Ireland, is whether Ireland can be judged a true democracy. Is there a need to lift off the mantle of dependency, loosen the strings of centralised control and create an environment that gives credit to people's ability to run their affairs without authoritarian control from the state? The premise of this book is that rural Ireland does not have a democratic ethos where local communities can participate genuinely in the decision-making processes, nor under which they can develop greater self-reliance. A major contributory factor to this inability is the centralised decision-making process and the political clientelism that forms a central part of the political process creating 'an unfriendly environment in Ireland for participatory democracy' (Varley, 1992, p.52). Therefore, the need is for new forms of rural governance that are not merely a partnership between governmental and non-governmental groups to produce some service or to fulfil some funding criteria, but a form of governance that is about achieving a 'collective benefit' unobtainable by government and non-governmental forces acting independently (see Stoker, 1997).

My approach

People experience and act on the world at multiple points, times and places (Cook and Crang, 1995), and thus, no matter what precautions are taken, this book is influenced by my own perceptions and background. The reasons for accepting the challenge of exploring rural development in Ireland stem largely from my rural background, my academic background, my involvement in community development projects, and, rather simplistically, a desire to understand why? Why is nothing substantial done when just about everybody is calling for the participation of local communities in rural development? In compiling this book, my approach has drawn on my academic experiences in Ireland and Britain and most importantly my experiences of rural living. Born in the western part of Ireland, growing up on a small farm in a tightly-knit community and subsequently emigrating (and returning in the era of the 'Celtic Tiger'), I have experienced the ups and downs of rural life. Some rural communities are thriving while others are dying away; busy family farms become redundant because of their inability to compete with imported produce; local shops can no longer compete with out-of-town superstores; families move out in search of more secure employment, local primary schools are downsized or threatened with closure; 'holiday homes' are built by those living in cities or different countries (with the lack of community this engenders) and, new rural dwellers arrive with differing perceptions and ideals of rural living (see McConnell, 1993). This book was born from these experiences and the need to answer why this happens – whether the answer lies in politics, culture, history or geography, or whether in some inevitability and we must 'take our medicine'.

The overall moulding of this work has involved coalescing lay and academic experiences and allowing the lack of preconceived ideas on rural development to infiltrate its theory in the search for direction. This research therefore occupies the 'manoeuvring space' (see Keane, 1996) between theory and practice, and, rather than seeking solutions to rural decline, is focused on an attempt to figure out what is understood by rural development, what are seen as 'problems' and what are seen to be future solutions. Essentially, this undertaking pursues these ideals through academic and lay discourses, while having no expectation that people's perceptions of rural development will in some way fit together with clear well-structured images for the future (Halfacree, 1993).

The format

The format of this book is based on conceptual, theoretical and empirical frameworks. Sequentially, the chapters set the research in context; explain the contested constructions of the 'rural' in Ireland; explore development discourse and the rural development strategies and reinforce the argument through use of empirical study.

Chapter 2 determines the 'plurality of Irelands', in terms of changing discourses of economy, society and space. This provides a background to the current transformations taking place in rural Ireland, that have brought profound changes, in the combining of traditional and modern forces, to Ireland's search for its own model of modernity. This chapter introduces the key themes of 'history', 'change' and 'culture', and show how they interconnect to form the somewhat contradictory character of Ireland. The emerging issue of the functionality of rural space is also addressed. Specifically this is explored in relation to the creating or maintaining of rural economies; the operation of the labour market, and more crucially, how the human resource deficit experienced in rural areas has a significant role to play in future strategies for rural Ireland. This chapter sets the tone for the book, indicating how these factors provide a framework of contestations within the country, giving rise in turn to contested mappings, versions of change, notions of 'problems' and 'needs', and constructions of identity.

Chapter 3 begins from the premise that the 'rural' must be considered in terms of a complex range of activities and there is a need to re-evaluate much of what is taken for granted in terms of the 'rural' in Ireland (McDonagh, 1998). This chapter also takes into account my own positionality, both as coming from a rural background, by looking at 'what it means to be rural' and/or attempting to understand 'how rural I am'. The changing definitions of, and approaches to, the rural are explored, using ideas and conflicts from Irish and English legacies. The redefining of the rural from physical space to a more social construction bound up with a whole set of different political, social and cultural meanings, is stressed (rural as areas of lived experiences rather than defined spatially or territorially). This shifting emphasis form the rural as a physical landscape implies a whole new set of meanings in socially constructed ideas of communities, kinship and nature. The consequence of this argument shows how the rural impinges on almost every aspect of Irish life, socially, economically and, in influencing the decision-making process. Examination of the symbolism associated with rurality and how these symbols or myths have become attached to the term rural through everyday social practice is therefore crucial.

The theoretical constructs that underpin Irish rural development policy and practice are outlined in **Chapter 4**. Employing First and Third World development discourses, this chapter explores the theoretical framework that development provides for comprehending and evaluating rural change. The 'power-development' connection is paramount in determining whether development in Ireland is more 'spectacle' than substance, designed primarily to attract funds and to placate the rural masses. The Irish understanding of rural development and the creation of a rural development 'spectacle' raise a number of questions. This 'spectacle', pursued in Ireland particularly in the last decade, is critically assessed and the level of understanding of the so-called 'new approach to rural development' (Commins and Keane, 1994), from centrally planned sectoral approaches to locally focused inputs, scrutinised. The contested concept of 'rural development', and the so-called 'new approach to development' is consequently probed to show their integral part in forming understandings, judgements, and answers about rural development in Ireland. Tracing the transition from rationalist centralised planning, to negotiational local planning (a system influenced by delegation, decentralisation and deregulation) (see Kearney *et al.*, 1994), the argument is made for exploring alternative channels between state and community to raise economic, social and political productivity (see Uphoff, 1993).

Chapter 5 draws together a number of the debates explored in the previous chapters and sets in motion a debate continued in Chapter 6. The remit of this chapter is to explore in particular, the representations and strategic partnerships being forged at different levels in rural Ireland. The promotion of integrated rural development and the growing responsibilities being placed on the voluntary sector to create its own rural economies are questioned. The nature of this rural development discourse is explored through the unique combination of Church, state and community. This chapter helps contextualise the role of communities in development and explores the distinct position of the Church, and key members of the clergy, in influencing rural development in Ireland. This argument is supported through the utilisation of the 'Developing The West Together' group, formed in 1991, as a vehicle to investigate the critical partnerships being forged between local communities, the state (national and European) and the private sector in the promotion of an alternative model of rural development. This approach allows exploration of the interface between partnership and integrated development, as well as enabling the reader to become aware of the emergence of new types of governance and the barriers to regional devolution (even responsibility) endemic in the Irish system.

Building on the empirical study of Chapter 5, the changing way in which rural areas are governed and the emergence of new forms of rural governance are the central concerns of **Chapter 6**. The way in which rural communities function, how classes, interest groups and personalities holding various degrees of power, combine to influence community affairs (Sorensen and Epps, 1996) all underpin this newly emerging discourse. The EU continuously promotes the importance of the local and regional level, and this has yielded (albeit slowly) a reconfiguration of rural development policy and the administrative nature of these policies. The complex set of relationships between different actors and networks that is emerging signifies this shift from local government to local governance (see Stoker, 1997; Marsden and Murdoch, 1998; Goodwin, 1998). This chapter therefore explores the rhetoric of 'community participation' and contributes to the debate on the search 'for an efficient and effective blend of governmental and non-governmental forces' (Goodwin, 1998 p.5) involving its range of new agencies and institutions with public, private and voluntary sector inputs.

The final **Chapter 7** reiterates the notion that rural development has a 'geography' and endeavours to draw a conclusion on the current process, practice and understanding of rural development in Ireland. This chapter summarises the current discourses affecting rural Ireland and determines whether there is a changing relationship between state and citizen arising from the emergence of new forms of rural governance. Further, the need to recognise the emergence of the region as a powerful political and economic factor providing a new 'space of engagement' for rural development is promoted as is the greater recognition of the role of local actors in rural development discourse commended.

Finally, any book with rural development in its title leaves itself open to the criticism of being too ambitious. Accepting the validity of such an argument, I find myself using rural development in the title of this book in any event. This is not in any vain attempt to deal with the myriad of debates that can be found under this banner, but more an effort to explore the fundamental questions and understandings current in rural development policy and practice in Ireland. Also, the book deliberately concentrates on certain aspects of rural change, at the expense of others. This approach is warranted as it helps to deepen our understanding and unconscious acceptance of things 'rural' and, raise questions for future debate in the Irish rural development arena.

2 A Plurality of Irelands: Changing Discourses of Economy, Society and Space

The Irish mind has been fashioned by Church, climate, colonialism and geography [and] offers an incredible variation in scenery and an almost equivalent variation in character (Coogan, 1975, p.21).

Variations in cultural, demographic and social features within Ireland produce a diverse amalgam of identities. Merging contestations and contradictory configurations, this chapter explores how these identities indelibly mould the 'character' of the Irish and play a determining role in rural development discourse. These interconnected discourses form contested mappings, contested constructions of place identity, contested versions of change, problems and needs. Discourses of development, rural regeneration, history and culture are therefore drawn together to deconstruct, what is termed the renegotiation of rural development in Ireland.

Issues of national identity are of particular interest in a contemporary Europe undergoing processes of political fragmentation on the one hand and unification on the other (O'Connor, 1993). Just as individual identities are shaped and influenced by outside perceptions and representations, so too are the national and cultural identities of regions shaped by those both outside, and inside, that culture. For all its complexity of imagery, Ireland, situated on the north-west perimeter of Europe, is small in relation to its neighbours. The Republic of Ireland has a land area of approximately 70,282 sq. km, and stretches 274km from East to West, and approximately 483km from North to South (Figure 2.1). Ireland consists of two States, the Republic of Ireland, an autonomous republican democracy, and Northern Ireland, part of the United Kingdom. The population is approximately 3.7 million with an average density of 50 persons per sq. km, ranging from less than 20 persons per sq. km in Co. Mayo, to 1147 persons per sq.km in Co. Dublin. There is a movement away from the peripheral underdeveloped 'region' that was Ireland's lot, to a more developed, outward looking and advanced economy that characterises Ireland in the twenty-first century. Peripherality however is still relevant and is recognised economically and spatially, with notable differences between the East and West of the country.

The identities and regional expressions of Ireland are far from clear-

Changing Discourses of Economy, Society and Space   11

Figure 2.1 The provinces and counties of Ireland

cut. In a study of twenty-four state agencies and semi-state organisations in 1992, it was revealed that 'fourteen had different numbers of regions [and] even where two or more bodies had the same number of regions, in no instance was the geographical borders the same. In other words, of the twenty-four organisations reviewed no two had the same geographical region' (Rural Development News, 1992, p.1). This would seem to be a major achievement in a country the size of Ireland. Johnson (1994) suggested that any discussion of regional matters in Ireland will also run into problems due to the 'remarkable sensitivities about names'. Trying to avoid a political statement (but in the eyes of many, inevitably making one), Johnson settles on referring to the 'British Isles ... that archipelago off the north-west coast of Europe in which Ireland is second largest and which is dominated by Great Britain'(p.3). Murphy (1991) recognised this uneasy identity also, and explored the number of expressions and interpretations employed. Eire is included among Murphy's interpretations and though constitutionally correct, is rarely used by Irish people except when speaking Irish, as it is more often seen as a rather patronising anglicism. He also lists the Republic; the Free State; the Twenty-Six Counties; the Nation, and the country and further suggests that '(t)he 'Republic' is coming only slowly into popular speech, being too formal, too controversial or too sacred! The 'Free State' is constitutionally outmoded by fifty years but is used widely by Northerners, mostly out of colloquial habit, but in the mouths of Provo (nationalist) supporters out of contempt. The 'Twenty-Six Counties', while geographically correct and politically neutral, is in diminishing use. The 'country' and the 'nation' are popular and journalistic synonyms for the state, though the use of 'the nation' in this sense is deplored by those who regard the nation as coterminous with the un-united island' (ibid., p.83).

The term 'Ireland' therefore, is not without its difficulties, and to the political purists, its 'implicit implication is that its writ should run over the whole island', leads to frequent footnotes that 'Ireland' in the published figures refers only to the twenty-six counties (Johnson 1994, p.3). Moving from this nebulous nomenclature, the regional divisions of Ireland also create an uneasy identity. The twenty-six counties that constitute the Republic, are one of the few recognised identities within Ireland. This identity is not of a political or cultural nature but is seen more in terms of sporting relationships, the enthusiasm for gaelic football and the GAA inter-county competitions. The four provinces - Connaught, Munster, Leinster and Ulster which are also part of the configuration, have less 'identity' and little or no administrative use (except in the case of the six counties of Ulster which make up Northern Ireland (Figure 2.1)). In the earlier part of this century, the twenty-six counties and the five county boroughs formed the basic administrative units of the country, having responsibility for Local Government and planning (see Chapter 6 for more detail on this topic). As effective planning units, their boundaries were restrictive (Brunt, 1988), and following the Local Government Act of 1963, nine planning regions were established (Figure 2.2). The IDA (Industrial Development Agency) used these official regions as basic spatial units, but they were not successful in creating or maintaining a viable regional administration due to various other organisations operating across different boundaries (Johnson, 1987). Further confusion to the regional 'melting pot' has been added in recent years, creating further divisions. These include planning regions (Figure 2.3), Health Board regions (Figure 2.4), Tourist Board regions (Figure 2.5), Education Board regions, Regional Circuit Court structures, and Regional Authority Areas (Figure 2.6) the majority of which bear no relationship in terms of their geographical boundaries. These form a series of administrative groupings, which do not amount to any real coherent attempt at regional streamlining or regional policy. More recently the creation of two 'super regions' was brought about as a result of Ireland's subsidy shopping in Europe. These new regions are the Objective One Region consisting of the Border, Midlands and West Regional Authority areas, and known as the BMW region; and the Objective One Region in Transition consisting of the Mid-West; South-West; Mid-East and South-East, and known as the South and East region (Figure 5.9).

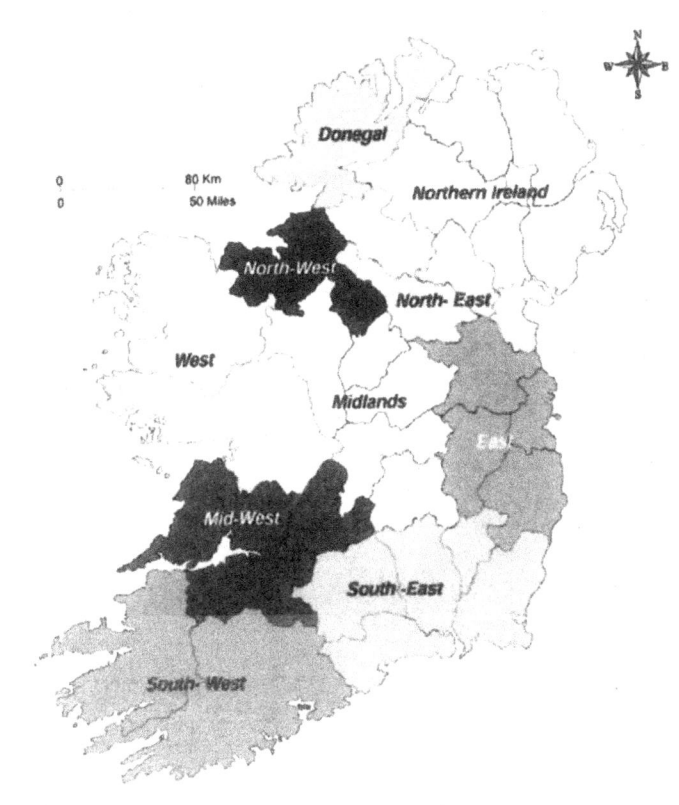

Figure 2.2 The 1963 planning regions of Ireland

14   Renegotiating Rural Development in Ireland

Other images and perceptions of Ireland abound. The 'Ireland of the tourist', a 'Land Brimful of Riches' (Kavanagh, 1996) with rugged mountains and golden beaches, sprinkled with generous helpings of churches, castles, thatched cottages, quaint villages and friendly pubs. There is the 'Ireland of the people', where in some places, the beauty of the landscape masks the poverty and degradation being suffered through emigration, depopulation, unemployment, and decline of the Irish language. There is also the Ireland of the 'Celtic Tiger' with its prosperity and employment masking the growing gap between rich and poor. Further, there is an Ireland struggling with new ideals, beliefs and values, with the old Ireland battered by changing attitudes towards sex, religion, work, consumerism and education (Finnegan, 1983). Finally, there is an Ireland that is divided politically (Northern Ireland and the Republic of Ireland), by an international boundary, which provides a division not only in

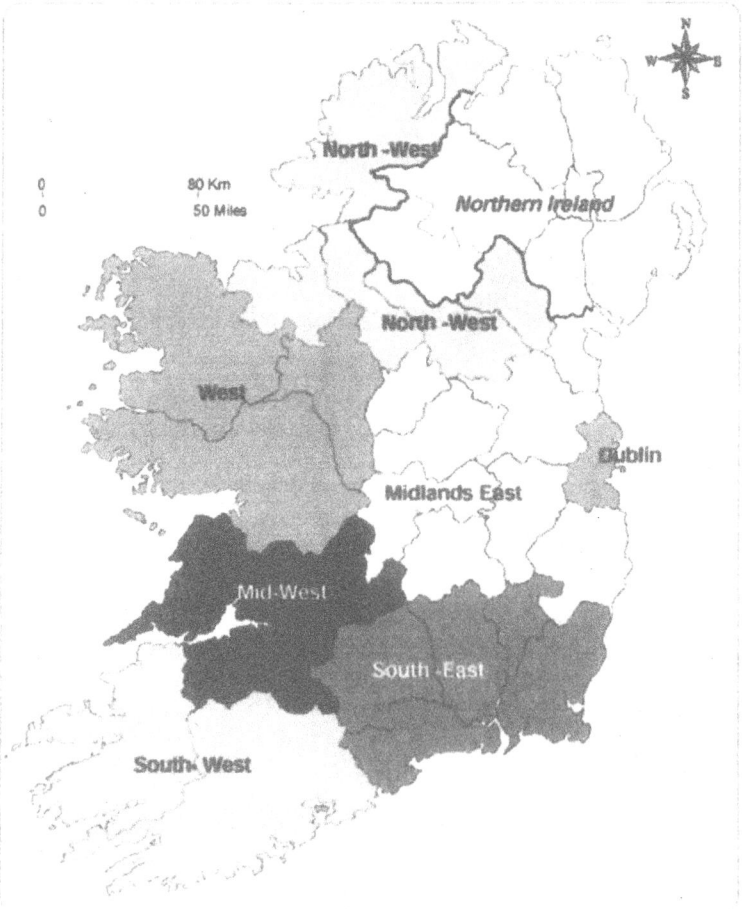

Figure 2.3 The new planning regions of Ireland

Changing Discourses of Economy, Society and Space   15

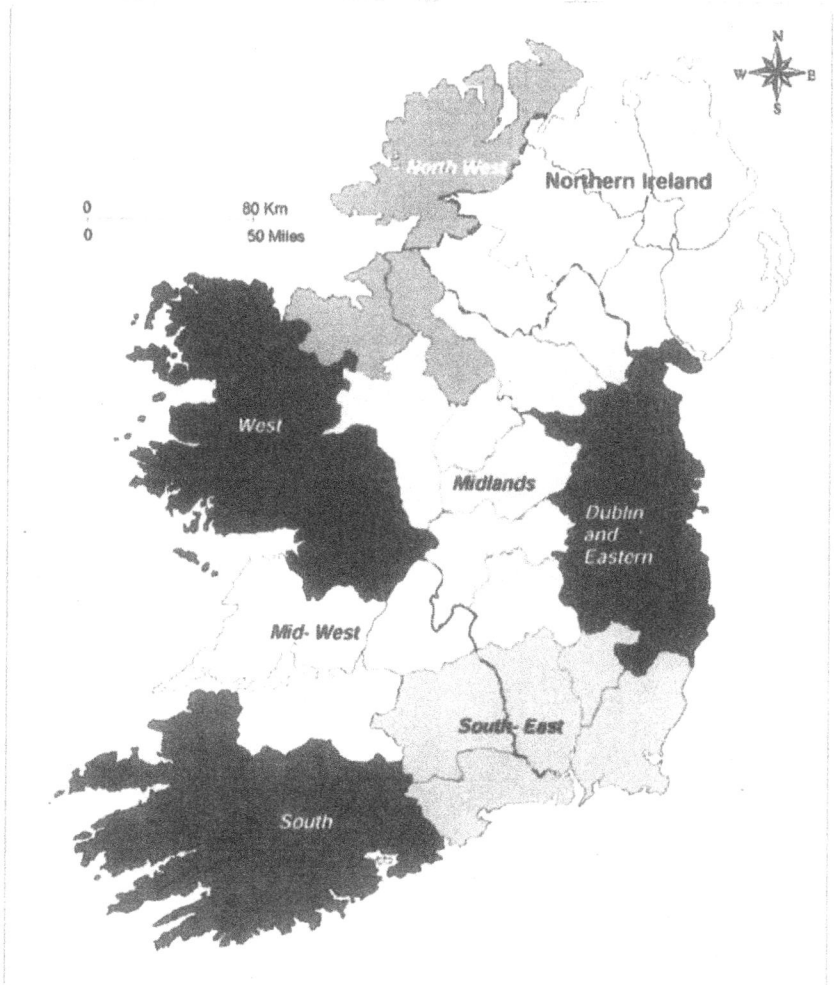

Figure 2.4 The health board regions of Ireland

geographical space but in terms of community, where Catholics and Protestants live in a persistent state of tension and conflict.

The changing constructs of Ireland and the evolving human landscape are therefore formed by everyday events and, as such, they 'reflect our tastes, our values, our ideals, our prejudices, even our fears, in clear tangible form' (O'Connor, 1992a, p.9). In an era of unrivalled potential for Irish tourism (Flanagan, 1994), Irish culture is becoming important not only in relation to maintaining a region's identity, but also as a well-recognised economic asset. In fact, it is often suggested that 'symbols give us our identity, our self-image, our way of explaining ourselves to

16   Renegotiating Rural Development in Ireland

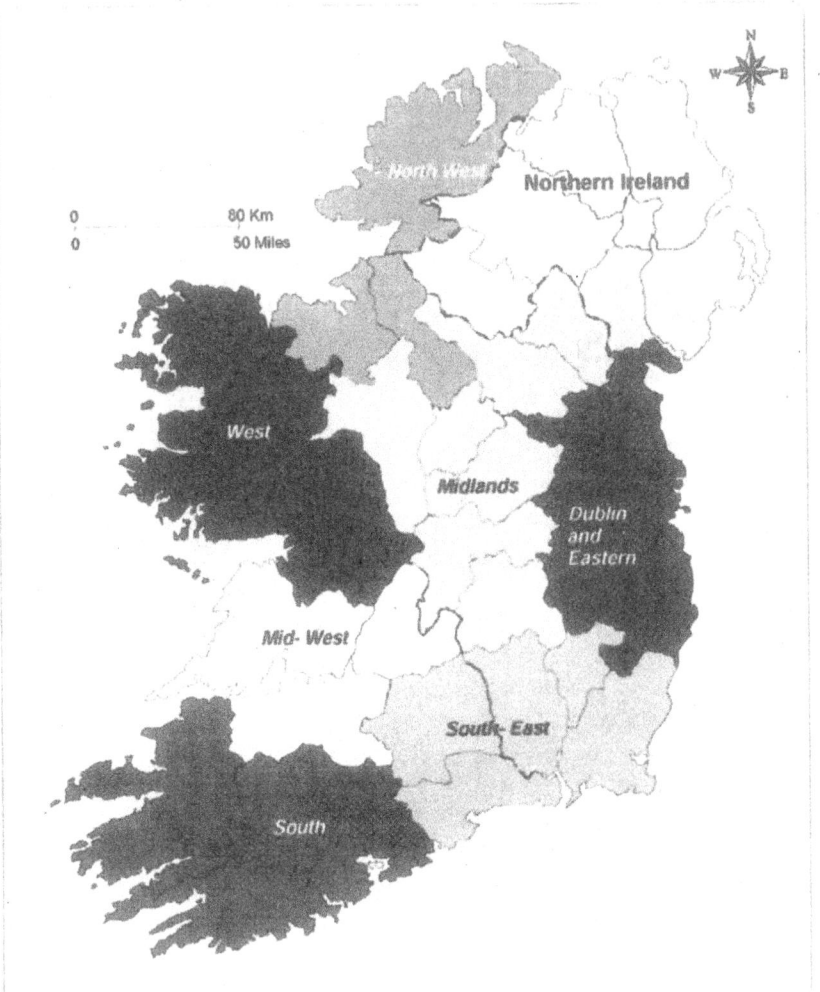

Figure 2.5 The tourist board regions of Ireland

ourselves and to others' (President Robinson, 1990, cited in O'Connor, 1992a). The predominant association of landscape with identity is promoted nowhere more prominently than in the West region, where the distinctiveness of its landscape, and its identification with national identity, has led to its use as a representation of true 'Irishness'. Such perceptions of the West have given rise to different identities. In fact the western region can be conceived as having two faces, that of Ireland at its most picturesque, and at its most melancholic. The West tends to mean 'all those rugged and ravaged areas' which hug the wind-swept Atlantic coastline, where life is lived on a mere subsistence level, where the farms are too small, the soil too poor, and the conditions too defeating, to hold out much hope of improvement (Healy, 1968). Parts of Connemara, may well offer 'a particularly scenic touring area', but it seems that 'half the rocks in the world had been hurled into this single knob of Ireland and that a race of men had been condemned to piling them up as walls to enclose an occasional cow or a patch of potatoes' (Connery, 1968, p.63). On the other hand, the West is also popularly regarded as a place of great natural beauty, an Emerald Isle that is a richer green than you could imagine, where the waters seem clearer, the air fresher, and where the people are friendlier and the way of life is steeped in past traditions. In short, a pre-modern society, where a 'process of spectacular inversion of modern industrial society ... has turned parts of Europe into a museum of authenticated remnants of past cultures' (Horne, 1984, cited in O'Connor,

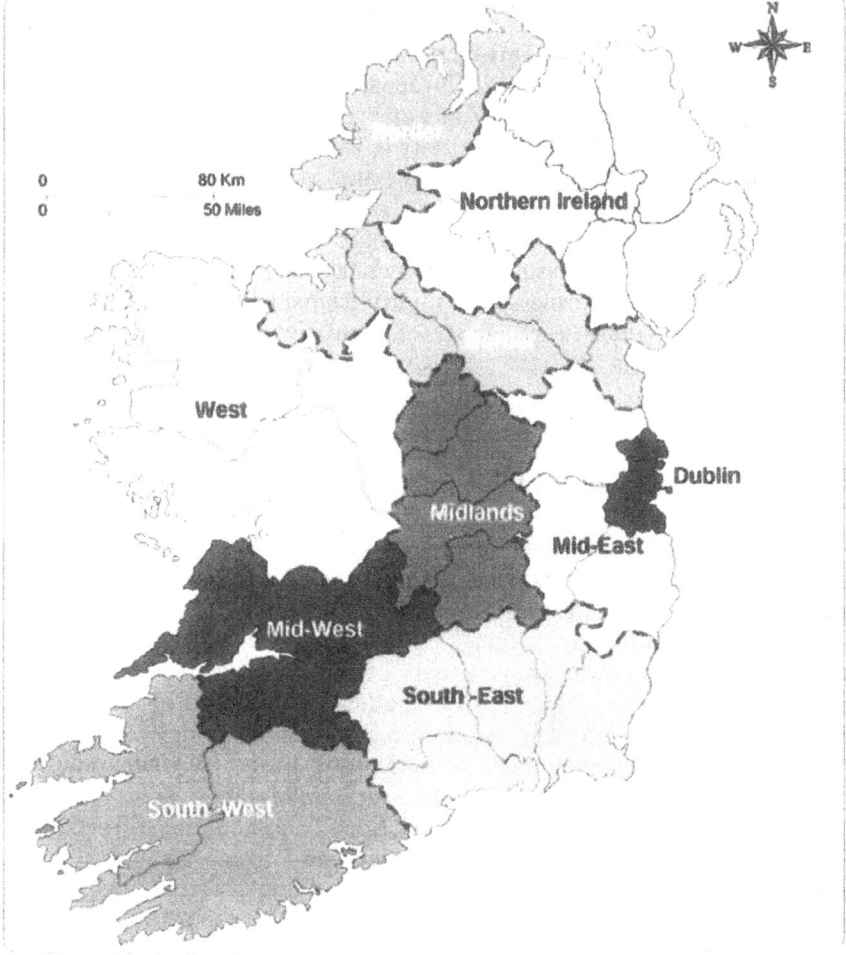

Figure 2.6 Ireland's regional authority areas

1993, p.70). Work, an apparently secondary and leisurely affair, is often presented in a romanticised view of man in harmony with nature, where people have a 'penchant for enjoyment - for talking, drinking, laughing and playing music' (O'Connor, 1993). Tourist brochures often refer to the region as the 'Wild West', boasting dramatic landscape, sweeping coastlines, and rugged mountains. One can 'step back in time' and visit the relics from 5,000 years ago preserved at Céide Fields, in Co. Mayo, or the Folk Village at Glencolumbcille, where 'a huddle of small, thatched cottages furnished to represent the lifestyles of the 1720s, 1820s and 1920s provide a unique opportunity for visitors to witness the 'speed' of progress' (Cresta, 1995). This 'untamed region' is depicted as the perfect antidote to the stresses of modern life. Smith (cited in Nash, 1993, p.89), has even suggested that the construction of the West's identity could be viewed both in the 'context of Irish history and culture and within a broader context; the context of the anti-modernism and romantic primitivism of early modernism, the context of European discourses concerning racial degeneration, eugenics, evolution and environmentalism, spiritualism and rural regeneration, and the particularity of these discourses in the context of Irish nationalist attempts to revitalise and revivify the nation'.

These images form the foundations of Irish development discourse. Ireland tries to embrace a folksy image to attract tourists, while simultaneously shunning such images in favour of a more modernised face for its European partners. The multiple constructions, from physical landscapes to symbolic and cultural identities all contribute to the (mis)understandings and interpretations of rurality and development in Ireland.

Agriculture: still a key to Irish rural identity?

Traditionally Ireland has had an agriculturally based economy and even today the Irish landscape remains distinctly rural. In fact, the importance placed on farming and agriculture was such, that to talk of things rural was synonymous with talking of things agricultural. The importance attached to farming and land ownership created a people with a strong rural identity (see O'Hara, 1998) - an identity, that while undergoing change, is nevertheless still a significant economic, social and ideological construct. Since the 1960s the importance of agriculture to the Irish economy has been in decline with the result that rural areas have experienced a haemorrhaging of their communities. Nationally, agriculture still accounts for 15% of employment, with only Greece and Portugal having a higher percentage in the EU; this reflects the degree of importance it possesses in comparison to other EU countries. However, the proportion of people employed in the agricultural sector has fallen from 37% in 1960 to 8% in 1998 (Sweeney, 1999, p.11). The sector has become more commercialised, specialised and intensive with a clear and distinct divide growing between the south and east where agriculture accounts for a low 3.5% of employment and the north and west where it accounts for a high 31.1% (Ó Cinnéide, 1992d). In the south and east, farms are larger, farmers are perceived as young, educated and married, the land is more fertile and tillage is more common (Brunt, 1988, p.101). In the north and west, there is a greater proportion of smallholders and farmers are more likely to be elderly and single. Diversification and pluri-activity are seen as a way in which agriculture can continue to be important to the national economy. The number of acres under forest has increased from 1% to 8% (compared to the EU average of over 30%) with a target of 17% by 2030 (Department of the Environment, 1997), the role of rural tourism is expanding and alternative types of farming are growing in popularity. Even so, the financial situation of Ireland's farm holders has continued to deteriorate in the past two years. Aggregate farm income fell 6.2% in 1997 and 5% in 1998, implying that average income per farm probably declined for two years in a row, even taking the decline of farms into account (OECD, 1999). Approximately 56% of Irish farm income was due to the Common Agricultural Policy (CAP) in 1998, up 30% since 1995, and approximately 30% of farms had incomes below £9,000 per year (on average only half of farm household income comes from farm activities). In terms of size, 70% of farms are less than 100 acres and it is probable that only about 30,000 farms out of the total of 148,000 farms will be economically viable in the medium term (OECD, 1999). Only 12% of farmers are under the age of 35 and 46% are over the age of 55.

In explaining how things have come to be the way they are, it is useful to touch on some of the events which have sculpted the landscape of rural Ireland, and which I would suggest, have contributed to the current rural deterioration. In 1890, the British launched the Congested Districts Board to redistribute smallholdings in Ireland. In the West of Ireland for example, demand far exceeded supply, and the hope of increasing farm sizes from about thirty acres in the 1930s to approximately two hundred acres for a viable holding today (see Curtin and Varley, 1991), has proven a persistent impediment to radical land reform. The most notable attempt at reform was initiated by the Fianna Fáil government in the Post-Independence era. Fianna Fáil (still Ireland's largest political party), regards itself as the champion of the small farmer, and in the 1930s their leader Eamon de Valera (who later became President), spoke of his vision of a country populated by families living on thirty-acre farms. This idyll was most vividly portrayed in de Valera's oft quoted speech of St. Patrick's day 1942 in which he spoke of 'the Ireland which we dreamed of would be the home of a people who valued material wealth only as a basis of right living, of a people who were satisfied with frugal comfort and devoted their leisure to the things of the spirit; a land whose countryside would be bright with cosy homesteads, whose fields and villages would be joyous with sounds of industry' (cited in Moynihan, 1980, p.466). More than anywhere else, this ideal was realised in the western region, where a 64% decrease in the number of farms over 200 acres occurred between 1901 and 1960, while a 92% increase was recorded in the number of 30-50 acre holdings (Curtin and Varley, 1991). Support for family farms still remained a significant aspiration in Irish public policy, despite the imminent failure of such a policy, and the inevitability of emigration from such holdings. Irish governments systematically continued to give allowances, including unemployment assistance and exemption from rates, to help small farmers' incomes. Governments however, have been caught in a catch-22 situation where policies have sought to encourage people to stay on their farms in an effort to stabilise population, while advocating the merging of uneconomic small farms into larger more productive units. Higgins (1986) showed that by 1980 almost 44% of incomes in rural communities relied on money transfers from the state, while Pratschke (1984, cited in Brunt, 1988) suggested that despite this biased fiscal system which benefited rural households, their position relative to urban households had disimproved.

A brief examination of the contesting discourses within the agricultural sector reveals that a combination of post-colonialist hangovers, a mistrust of international markets and the need to assert an Irish 'rural-based' identity has in many ways led to the demise of many rural areas in contemporary Ireland. Ireland's historical legacy of landlords and large estates, along with the notion of a countryside dotted by small farms 'joyous with sounds of industry', and the onset of the CAP and the need for large-scale intensive farming methods, have combined to place the future of the small farmer and the survival of the rural community very much in doubt. The limited success of programmes to aid a rural recovery led in the 1990s to a new rural discourse and the importance of the 'rural custodian'. The desire to maintain rural populations as a cornerstone of the overall fabric of society has subsequently been brought firmly into the political arena. Commissioner Ray MacSharry, speaking at a conference in 1990, commented on the injustice of having 20% of the farmers consuming 80% of the CAP price support. He pointed to the environmental threat posed by intensive, large-scale farming, and the foolhardiness of a policy that resulted in huge surplus production. In a positive stance in favour of small farmers, he highlighted their association with the preservation of the 'social fabric' of society, and the more environmentally friendly and custodial nature of their farming methods (MacSharry, 1990b). While these comments may be dismissed as rhetoric, the important role that small family farms still play in many rural communities is undeniable and action to secure their future crucial. If, as has been suggested, the small farmer will not be able to 'feed off the intervention truck forever', then it is necessary to introduce structures and policies which help ensure the long-term survival of rural communities. Brunt's (1988) contribution to this debate is to suggest that farms must be operated in a manner which best preserves the quality and distinctiveness of the countryside for the benefit of non-farming communities. Brunt also recognised the attendant dilemma of there being little tradition within Irish farming communities of viewing the countryside as amenity (the land is seen as family territory, a means of achieving social prestige and a factor of production, irrespective of the level of efficiency attained), but argued nevertheless that 'farmers will have to try to adjust to the fact that rural economic and social progress in future will increasingly depend on [such] a multi sectoral approach' (ibid., p.103).

Where small farmers do survive, they are very much dependent on state financial support, EU funding, or in some cases what Carter and Parker (1989) describe as 'money from America'. Most significantly, whatever the future holds for rural Ireland, it seems likely that farms and farming practices will only survive for the tourist's gaze. A contemporary example of this is the new and potentially lucrative Rural Environmental Protection Scheme (REPS). The REPS can be seen by the cynical observer as 'farmers playing at being farmers' or more generously as an important change in agricultural policy towards conservation and sustainability. Introduced in June 1994, the REPS are an agri-environmental plan to ensure participants farm in an environmentally friendly way. The REPS are policy-driven from the EU, a fact which highlights the 'chasing after funds' that the Irish government engages in, and which also underlines the lack of a national policy for the sustaining of the rural environment (unless outlined by Brussels). The controversy which surrounds the REPS seems also to reinforce Coogan's (1975) image of a country 'looking over its shoulder towards the possibility of a government grant', while confirming the lack of innovation or forward-thinking on the part of farmers in rural Ireland. Still firmly leaning towards reliance on the welfare cheque; the need for a 'new approach' to rural development in Ireland would therefore seem all the more critical. The role of agriculture despite inevitable change is still an important force in the Irish psyche. The movement away from traditional farming practices may have detracted from the visual character of rural areas but the creation of regional brands and rural specific products have all asserted the strength of rural identity and helped to redefine it. The recognition of different types of farmers from the maximisers and satisfiers identified by Strijker (2000) to full-time and part-time farmers have witnessed the future of agricultural change from a uni-linear to a multi-linear development. The role of women in agriculture (see O'Hara, 1998), the role of agriculture in nature conservation and the role of non-farmers in rural areas all combine to (re)construct different identities of rural Ireland.

The changing economies of Ireland

The buoyancy of the Irish economy in recent years reflects a move from 53% of the EU average GDP per capita in 1973 to being in excess of the EU average in 1998. While this is true for the country as a whole, geographical imbalances still remain. In the post-war years Ireland was characterised by a mainly rural-based and traditional society similar to that of the 1930s. Its context for development centred on the importance of the small farmer, self-sufficiency and cultural integrity. This ideology followed the policies of neutrality, nationalism and economic autarky adopted by the Irish in an attempt to release themselves from the clutches of the long-established political and economic dominance of Britain. While the rest of Europe rebuilt their economies, Ireland took the road of self-sufficiency and independence, but its policies 'were not adequate to achieve the national goals of raising living standards and increasing job prospects, and throughout the second quarter of the twentieth century Ireland continued to rely on emigration, as it had since the 1840s, as a solution to internal deficiencies' (Brunt, 1988, p.xi).

The industrial history of Ireland since it gained political independence in 1922 can be divided into a number of phases. In the 1950s the policy was one of self-sufficiency, where Irish manufacturing remained predominantly small in scale, technologically unsophisticated and almost exclusively focused on a small home market (Kennedy et al., 1988). It became clear that such a protectionist policy was insufficient, and a watershed in Irish economic development was marked by the publication in 1958 of the Programme for Economic Expansion (Department of Finance, 1958) which involved the modernisation and mechanisation of agriculture, and the development of an export-oriented manufacturing programme based on the attraction of foreign capital. The judgement of this programme was that 'with virtually the whole country underdeveloped it seems wasteful to subsidise remote areas' (Programme for Economic Expansion, 1958, cited in Brunt, 1988, p.18). The 1960s emerged as a decade of unprecedented growth, with national output increasing annually by 4%, industrial output by 7% and industrial exports by 18% (ibid.). The euphoria of this new-found growth was short-lived, with the dependence on foreign investment highlighting a number of problems including 'reduced domestic control over economic performance, profit repatriation, the predominance of assembly type plants with relatively little research and development capacity ... and frequent closures of branch plants associated with adverse market trends' (Ó Cinnéide, 1993b, p.210). Irish industrial output did increase substantially, but the resultant high export levels did not result in increased employment, or higher incomes. In reality, employment in manufacturing declined by almost 20% (NESC, 1993). O'Raghalaigh (1993, p.23) investigating the part played by foreign-owned firms, described Ireland as the 'end of the rainbow for multinationals', and suggested that it was:

> a tax-haven ... a magical island at the end of a rainbow where foreign companies can legitimately hide profits from the greedy gaze of their domestic tax authorities. Internationally accepted legal principles of taxation - rules against 'double taxation' - make it possible for us to be tooth-fairies to multinationals. Our politicians are addicted to the policy. It entices foreign companies to Ireland, makes us look like an export power-house and does bring an awful lot of jobs to the country. The political argument was that it would bring enough jobs (which it has not).

With an ever-increasing national debt, it became evident that despite the undoubted impact of the world recession in the 1980s, a significant part of the economic downturn in Ireland was due, in no small part, to the 'unsustainable level to which Exchequer borrowing had been raised by extravagant public spending policies' (Fitzgerald, 1993, p.38). Irish governments subsequently moved away from attempting to spend their way to prosperity, and instead began to focus on the European 'gravy train'. O'Raghalaigh (1993, p.23) argued that 'politicians care(d) little about any of this [and had] a dependency culture ... consumed by the myth that being the island behind the island, on the so-called periphery of the Community, [was] central to our poor job performance and economic difficulties'. O'Raghalaigh (ibid.) further suggested that the majority of Irish politicians believed that 'living off American enterprise and Euromanna falling from Brussels [would] solve [the] employment problems - and the occasional rural revolt'.

Predictions about Ireland's economic future envisaged further problems at this stage as it became increasingly difficult to attract mobile investment to the country due to low cost factors of Eastern Europe and the more innovative policies of other European countries (Amdam, 1996). It was increasingly suggested that too much emphasis had been put on a 'jobs target' (as opposed to the quality of skills required for the jobs created), with an over-dependence on an elaborate system of state support (O'Tuathaigh, 1993; Walsh, 1993a). The review of industrial policy published in 1982 reinforced this picture of a lack of progress when it indicated that the Irish system suffered from a high dependence on foreign-owned firms, low-skilled employment, little research and development commitment, a poor indigenous sector and limited linkages with the rest of the economy (NESC, 1982). This is a situation, which could easily be juxtaposed with that of the 1990s. Many parts of rural Ireland, it could be argued, were acquiring a business and entrepreneurial community, but there were still strong traces of what Coogan (1975, p.11) called the 'gombeen-man class', which kept the 'country cautious in commerce' and continually looking towards government grants and/or protected markets. Curtin and Varley (1991) also suggested that developments in industrial policy swung sharply against the peripheral counties of Ireland.

This was indicated, not only by the *White Paper on Industrial Policy* (Department of Enterprise and Employment, 1984), which suggested that resources were to be devoted increasingly to high technology industry and internationally tradeable sectors, but was also reinforced by the IDA priority areas. These areas had the greatest growth and job creation prospects, the highest unemployment levels and job losses, and the highest prospective labour force growth. Gillmor (1986, p.32) also suggested that the emphasis was now shifting toward 'solving national problems and emphasising productivity', with priorities favouring the East and South at the expense of the marginal regions of the West and North-west.

During the 1960s and 1970s, there emerged a decade of significant expansion for industrial employment within Ireland (Gillmor, 1982, cited in Brunt, 1988). A preference for a more dispersed pattern of industrial location became evident, reflecting government policy and locational preferences on the part of private investment (Brunt, 1988). During this period, industrial development became synonymous with regional development, but it was not until 1972 that the government issued a statement which advocated a policy of industrial dispersal to 'minimize population dislocation through internal migration' (ibid.). It is a mark of the government's lack of commitment to the regional problems within Ireland that no other definitive statement on regional development has appeared since this date. The 1970s were nevertheless seen as one of the most successful periods of regional development in Ireland (see Walsh, 1989). The IDA was given the power to initiate a suitable location policy, with the acquisition of sites, and the building of advance factories. Their jobs target was aimed at forty-seven towns scattered throughout Ireland, with a positive discrimination towards the more marginal regions. The consequences for many parts of rural Ireland however, were that the growth in manufacturing and services, which had a significant impact in the more urbanised parts of Ireland, did not compensate fully for the heavy losses in agriculture. Total employment subsequently continued to decline.

Throughout the 1980s there was a steady decline in regional development interests. This, partly due to the economic recession, was brought about by increasing dependence on EU investments, especially in agriculture. Walsh (1992b) argued for priority to be given to efforts to reduce regional disparities, through defined regional systems, and the facilitation of local and regional involvement in the implementation of development strategies. The reduced political commitment to regional development and a reduction of dispersed industrial policy adversely affected many parts of rural Ireland. A concern for the creation of greater spatial equity was again replaced by concern for aggregate national performance, primarily in response to a rising national debt and the need to control inflation (Brunt, 1988). It was no longer possible to divert mobile resources to the Less Favoured Areas (LFA), with the creation of jobs in any part of Ireland becoming the main priority. This policy led to a drop in international investment in rural areas, and with a poor indigenous development, the vulnerability of the industrial sector was exposed.

From the oil crisis of 1973 up to 1987, Ireland's economy suffered from a severe recession. Unemployment increased by over 33,000 to 109,000 by 1977 and by 1981 inflation had risen to 20%. In 1981 a national economic plan *Building on Reality, 1984-87* offered some hope for economic growth although it did not anticipate an immediate increase in employment. In 1987 the economic downturn ground to a halt (Ó Gráda, 1997), as public spending was slashed, with the result that government spending fell from 50% of GDP in 1986 to 37% by 1988. Borrowing fell to approximately 2% of GDP and as a result foreign debt rose far more slowly than GDP. The correction of government finances in 1987 introduced a period of steady growth (Haughton, 1998). The economic upturn really took off in 1994 with the emergence of the 'Celtic Tiger' and between 1994 and 1998 output growth based on GDP has averaged over 9% per year (OECD, 1999).

This economic upturn has been fuelled in the main by Foreign Direct Investment attracted by industrial and fiscal policy and by favourable demographics. The net flow of direct investment in Ireland between 1986 and 1990 was US$96 million increasing to US$1,124 million between 1991 and 1997 (Danson, 2000). US companies were originally attracted by highly skilled cheap labour and the fiscal and industrial policies designed to make Ireland more attractive. Ireland, in contrast to the rest of Europe, had a high birth rate until the early 1980s. This has resulted in a relatively young population and a low rate of old-age dependency (OECD, 1999). There has also been an increase in the return of emigrants, both skilled and unskilled, further fuelling growth in certain sectors, particularly in Information Technology (IT) and sectors where language skills are necessary. The increase of female participation in the workforce and the fact that the Irish labour force is also highly educated, with 28% having completed third level education compared to the OECD average of 26% (OECD, 1998), has also proved attractive. The majority of the fiscal policies introduced stabilised Ireland's economy with one of the most important being the low corporation tax rate of 10% (to be raised to 12.5% in 2003 (Smyth, 1998)). Since the 1950s, when Ireland opened its economy and no longer operated on the protectionist principle, foreign investment has become increasingly important. The country's commitment to a free-trade environment and its location as a gateway to Europe has been an advantage, particularly with respect to the software industry. Ireland's EU membership, good telecommunications infrastructure, and cheaper wages than core European countries make it an attractive export base for US Multi National Corporations (MNCs). The use of Community Structural Funds has also given Ireland a major boost in improving infrastructure and providing training and retraining, and continues to yield positive externalities.

Overseas companies have been the main contributors to Ireland's economic boom and its reduced unemployment levels. However, the majority of companies are engaged in low-level translation and localisation work, with very few engaged in high value Research & Development (Ó Riain, 1997). Although Ireland is the second largest exporter of software in the world after the US, the large MNCs such as Microsoft and Intel account for most of the exports. The Irish government have however invested hugely in technology-orientated education to provide a trained labour force for such international giants, with a by-product of this investment being the growth of an indigenous software industry. Employment in the software industry consequently is divided between the multinationals and the indigenous companies. The pharmaceutical industry has also had a great effect on the Irish economy. Nine out of the top ten companies in the world are located in Ireland and they make up 25% of total exports (IDA, 2000). More recently one of the latest trends in foreign investment in Ireland has featured the establishment of service industries such as call-centres and back offices. Both can locate anywhere there is a high standard of communications and trained staff. Call centres and data-processing centres are located in such diverse places as Castleisland, Co. Kerry and Mullingar. The Irish Financial Services Centre (IFSC) in Dublin, founded in 1987, also provides huge tax returns for the Irish Exchequer. The IFSC focuses on back-office banking and corporate treasury and there are over 270 companies certified to operate under the programme. In 1992, 59% of the labour force was employed in the services sector compared to only 28% in industry and 13% in agriculture (Ó Gráda, 1997). There is no evidence to suggest that this figure has dropped, in fact it is probable that it has risen.

There has been considerable expansion in the tertiary sector in Ireland in recent years. The significance of this growth is in its wide geographical dispersion, and the added benefits it gives to struggling rural areas. Part of this growth has been due to the increased demand for producer services from the productive agricultural and industrial sectors (Ó Cinnéide, 1992a), while the strong growth of tourism, especially rural-based tourism, has been another factor in the creation of new service employment opportunities within the private sector (ibid.). In the 1970s an important aspect to the expansion of tertiary services was the enhanced provision of health and education facilities to all areas of Ireland. This provided new sources of employment and gave rural residents a high level of access to these services (Cuddy, 1991). The expansion had the knock-on effect of stabilising rural populations by improving their quality of life and providing them with better employment opportunities. Throughout the 1980s there was continued growth in the services sector in most regions. The heavy dependence on state borrowing led to this growth being short-lived (Crotty, 1993). This 'false growth', and the subsequent reduction of services in remoter rural areas, has been strongly resisted by rural residents, who face 'growing problem(s) of inaccessibility as service provision becomes more geographically concentrated in the interest of economies of scale [and a] growing trend towards the privatisation of the delivery channels of many rural services is likely to exacerbate this problem' (Ó Cinnéide, 1992d, p.91).

One striking feature of the geographical concentration of services is the way in which population loss leads to the withdrawal or curtailment of necessary services, like the post offices, banks, Garda (police) stations, clinics, the absence of which accelerates the process of depopulation (see Carey, 1995a). Politicians and local communities alike have recognised the consequences of such closures, specifically from the threat of deregulation, an eventuality which is felt would spell disaster for small rural areas. In an effort to combat this decline, the then Minister for Rural Development (1995), proposed the introduction of a number of pilot programmes to demonstrate how essential public services could be organised more flexibly, and with a greater degree of integration, so that an essential range of services could continue to be provided even where population is low (Carey, 1995b & c). This concept involved service agencies co-operating together and with local communities to share premises, overheads and technology in what could essentially be described as a 'one-stop-shop'. Fallon (1995) suggested that this advance would at least ensure that people get as good a service as possible, without having to travel miles to avail themselves of it. What constituted 'travelling miles' however was left open to debate.

In making the connection between the plight of rural Ireland and the importance of service provision, it would seem to be contradictory (even absurd) to talk of achieving population stability in rural areas while allowing services to be downsized or terminated in smaller communities (as envisaged in the remit of the Western Development Partnership Board (1996), and also stated in the *Rural White Paper* (Department of Agriculture and Food, 1999), in terms of maintaining the maximum population in rural areas). The subsequent reduction of services in remoter rural areas, although strongly resisted by rural residents, reflects a trend towards privatisation and a growing dependence on voluntary organisations to provide alternative delivery channels (see for example, Commins and Keane, 1994; and the workings of Forum). Boylan (1992, p.16) subscribes to the notion that 'much less attention ... is directed at providing insights into why ... service provision in rural areas are curtailed in the first place, by whom and why?' The use of the term 'reorganisation' in relation to many of these rural services would in many sceptics' minds also set the alarm bells ringing, as would the concept of 'partnership' and the understanding of its role in successful service provision (see Chapter 6). Although examples of the one-stop-shop (as envisaged by Carey), are not yet fully operational, some reservations can be expressed at the level of partnership between the service agents (Local Authorities, Electricity Supply Board, Eircom, An Post) and the local communities. In most cases when service agents meet the community sector, the community sector is

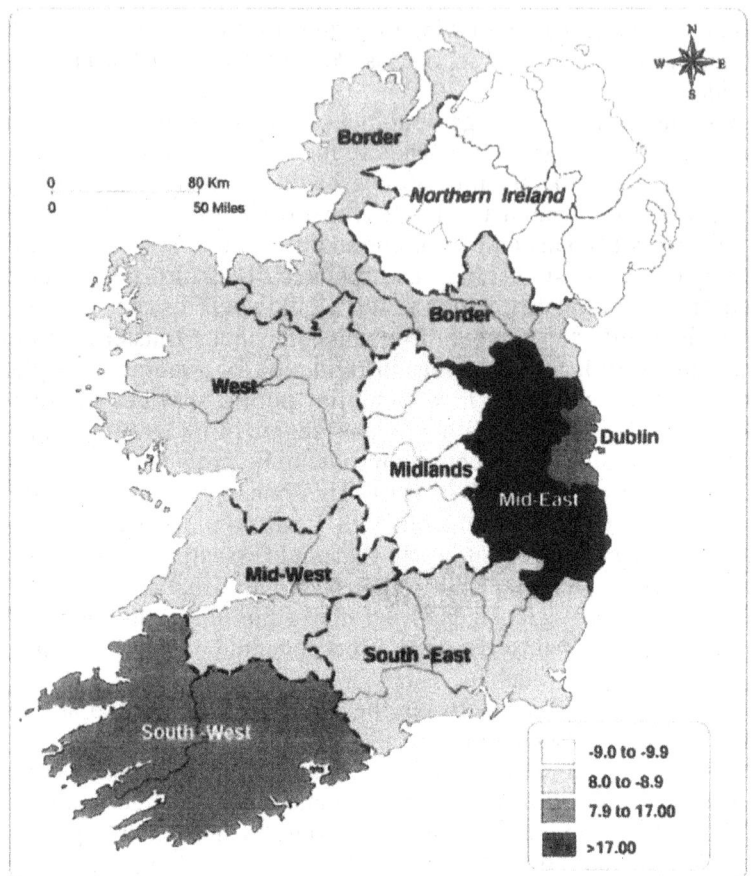

Figure 2.7 Gross Value Added (GVA) change 1991–1997 when the Ireland average=100

not seen as an equal partner, nor even as a potentially equal partner (Dillon, 1989; Healy and Reynolds, 1992). This would certainly have to change for the one-stop-shop concept to be successful. It is therefore fair to suggest, that the real 'policy' which may help stem rural decline, is a commitment by the state and private sector to 'partnership' (see Chapter 6).

Although Ireland's economy is continuing to grow, there are several factors that take from the Irish economic miracle: high long-term unemployment, lack of tax reform, a housing crisis and widespread poverty. There have been several indications of overheating of the economy. Labour force growth has increased from 2% per annum in the 1993 to 1995 period to 3% per annum since then. This strong demand for labour has resulted in skills and labour shortages, particularly in the software, engineering and technology sectors as well as the hotel and catering sector (OECD, 1999) (see later section). The concentration of employment in urban areas coupled with increased speculation in the housing market has pushed house prices up dramatically. Annual inflation recently hit a ten-year high of 6.8%, putting the Programme for Prosperity and Fairness at risk (Coughlan, 2000). There have been increased demands for pay rises which would put Ireland's reputation as a low-cost supplier of skilled labour at risk. Since Ireland committed to the Euro, the power to introduce deflationary measures has largely passed into the hands of the EU. Interest rates are closely connected to European interest rates and Irish policy makers are not equipped to control demand.

The economic boom has increased average living standards but it has also increased social polarisation (Figure 2.7). In 1997 over one third of the population was living on the poverty line, that is on 60% of the average income (Sweeney, 1999). In relation to children, 17% are described as living in abject poverty deprived of basic necessities (O'Morain, 2000). In fact, poverty levels did not fall between the 1980s and 1990s, and depending on the measures used, they either remained static or rose. Among those most at risk from poverty are small farmers, lone mothers, the long-term unemployed and people with disabilities (Sweeney, 1999). These risk factors are consistent with the drop in income levels experienced by small farmers and their dependence on EU aid. Although social exclusion is more an urban phenomenon, particularly in larger cities where ghettos have developed, rural poverty has risen in relation to the size of the population. It is highly possible that many rural households are not classed as poverty stricken because more than one member of the household works for marginal wages and the collective wage of the house keeps it above the poverty line (O'Hearn, 1998). This would suggest that the problem of rural poverty is far more widespread than previously thought. This inequality is still a significant force within this now prosperous economy. While political rhetoric advocates promoting balanced regional development, there has been little specific action (Ó Cinnéide, 1995). Income estimates for Ireland in the mid-1990s further indicate regional variations. According to the Central Statistics Office (CSO) figures of 1995 income per capita is lowest on the Border (£5,985 per capita) and in the West (£6,040 per capita) and highest in Dublin and the Mid-East (£10,499). The Midlands, the South-East and South-West have an income per capita of £6,800, £7,375 and £8,106 respectively (O'Leary, 1999). The more rural areas have the lowest income per capita in the country. The strong argument that Ireland makes in favour of regional intervention at EU level does not carry the same conviction domestically. Subsequently, it is inconsistent to claim 'special treatment for Ireland as an under-developed Community region if we do not apply the same principle to the distribution of Structural Funds and other development supports within Ireland' (Euradvice, 1994, p.22). While the new regions being created (Objective One and Objective One in Transition) were a case of subsidy shopping rather than a response to this

Figure 2.8 The new face of the Irish economy (Watt, 1997)

Changing Discourses of Economy, Society and Space 31

situation, they may be instrumental (by default) in restoring some equity in relation to current regional imbalances.

The economy of Ireland has suffered from extremes, in relation to its public debt, dependency syndrome, 'chasing' of European funds and the emergence of the 'Celtic Tiger'. The Irish economy has vacillated between crisis and euphoria. As recently as 1992, a report published by the European Commission *The Regions in the 1990s*, suggested that the Republic of Ireland was the most seriously disadvantaged region in the northern periphery of the EC (Walsh, 1992a). Having one of the highest unemployment rates, at almost twice the Community average, it was one of the few countries in the EU to experience population decline. In the year 2000 this picture has been hugely changed. Ireland's performance in recent years has lead to 'the highest economic growth rates and lowest inflation rates among the EC countries. It is a highly profitable and desirable location for foreign investments, with annual repatriation of profits now amounting to over 10% of GNP' (Walsh, 1992a). Further, in a complete turnaround from previous generations of Irish emigrants, Watts (1997, p.8) described the 'Army of navvies cross(ing) [the] Irish Sea in search of riches', where large numbers of British labourers descended on Ireland to take up well-paid jobs in the construction industry. This industry, growing at about 6% a year, compared favourably with the British growth of about 2.5%. In fact, the shortage of construction workers in Ireland, lead to the Irish Construction Industry Federation conducting a Lord Kitchener-style campaign which declared 'We need you back in Ireland' (Figure 2.8). These two issues, that of emigration and skill shortages, and their continuing role in the changing constructs of rural Ireland, will be investigated more closely in the next two sections.

Emigration and rural identity

Emigration has played a large role in the psyche of rural communities in Ireland. For generations, Ireland's greatest export has been people and more often than not the youngest, most educated, and ambitious of the population. In rural Ireland the unconscious acceptance that young rural dwellers would inevitably emigrate was very much part of rural identity. In fact, it was largely accepted that a rural Irish person will just as easily travel to another country for work, as perhaps those living in parts of England or Scotland, will travel to another town. In historical terms (pre-Famine era, before 1845) Ireland boasted a population of over eight million people and had it continued at that rate of expansion it would now perhaps be one of the mostly densely-populated islands in Europe. The loss of over four million people to starvation and emigration during the Famine (especially in rural areas) started a trend of decline that continued to the 1990s. For much of the latter part of the eighteenth and the nineteenth centuries, Ireland's population continued to wax and wane, while in the twentieth century, its demography was still seen as somewhat at odds with the trends of most other western European countries. Following a brief respite in the 1960s/1970s, allied to the economic growth of that era, the deteriorating performance of the economy in the 1980s resulted in a resumption of high levels of emigration. Between 1981 and 1991 it is estimated that total net emigration amounted to approximately 208,000 persons (Walsh, 1992a). The difference between these emigrants and those of the 1950s was however the greater education and skill levels they possessed, and despite continued emigration, there were areas where the population rose or at the very least remained stable.

In 1986, the total population of the country fell for the first time in almost twenty-five years and marked what many economists regarded as a watershed in Irish economic history. It was estimated that the decline would continue until 1996, by which time a projected 242,000 people would have emigrated (see NESC, 1986; Brunt, 1988). The prediction was recently reiterated in the report commissioned by the Developing The West Together group (Euradvice, 1994) which suggested that the West stood to lose almost 110,000 in population by 2011. These predictions are now seen as an exaggeration particularly considering the turnaround in immigration. There has been agreement however that continued population decline did adversely affect the economic situation of rural Ireland (see Brunt, 1988; Walsh, 1992b; Walsh, 1993a). Coward (1989) argued that the economic implications for rural areas of continued population decline, not only 'limited the domestic market and act(ed) as a deterrent to economic growth', but was also significant in that emigration (largely responsible for the declines) had been a selective process. In other words, it has been implied (but not explicitly demonstrated), that emigration removes those individuals who are more innovative (Kennedy, 1973; Ó Cinnéide, 1995), leaving a residual population that is more conservative, less likely to question established authority and less receptive to social change in general. During the vacillations of population increase and decline throughout the nineteenth and twentieth centuries, emigration continued to act as a safety valve for poor performances in the Irish economy. Although Coward (1989) suggested that, in some cases, emigration had beneficial effects, by reducing the size of the labour force and the number of people unemployed, the overall economic, psychological and social consequences have been adverse.

While there has been this tendency to focus on emigration as one of the major causes of Irish rural problems, its selective culling of the younger generations, and those more innovative and open to risk-taking (see Walsh, 1993a), there is also evidence of two different outlooks on, or at the very least new images for, emigration. The most notable of these changing discourses are the attempts to dispel the 'fatalistic connotations ... and substitute the euphemism of outward social mobility for emigration'

(Healy, 1968, p.45). No longer, it is suggested, would it be necessary to express sorrow at what is seen as a kind of national blood-letting; instead, the Irish people are encouraged to 'be proud of our emigrants [and] regard them as part of a global generation of Irish people. We shouldn't be defeatist or pessimistic about it. We should be proud of it' (Lenihan, 1988). This new found 'acceptance' is also reinforced by what is (affectionately) referred to as the 'Irish Diaspora', with its 'exciting and audacious idea of locating a national and international Irish Diaspora Centre in Galway city' (Anon, 1995c, p.18). The contribution of the Irish Diaspora is (allegedly) sufficiently significant to be identified as a world culture in its own right. A group of Galway people, (including professors and city managers) has with this brief but provocative observation, sought to challenge perceptions of the whole emigrant experience. They propose a more positive approach so that the:

> Irish Diaspora, in other words, is no longer seen as something that has leaked away from Ireland, instead, we are to see our Irish forebears as bringing with them to their new homes the seeds of vital culture strong enough to survive uprooting and transplanting, that over the last two centuries has produced a strong new culture that yet has unbreakable links to the old which gave it birth (ibid.).

The second image is that of campaigns to encourage emigrants to return (and to entice other nationals to come and work in Ireland) typified by the Lord Kitchener-style campaign, which declared 'We need you back in Ireland' (Figure 2.8). This new-found optimism contradicts the doom and gloom scenario (as signified by Euradvice's study of the West, 1994); and suggests a brighter future for rural Ireland. In a report prepared for the state training agency FÁS, the pattern of emigration from Ireland was seen to be undergoing major changes (Yeates, 1996). Fewer people are emigrating (and usually by choice rather than necessity), and because the economy is so buoyant, many emigrants are returning to Ireland (Watts, 1997). In fact this turnaround in Irish emigration has its own problems, particularly the issue of a lack of personnel to fill vacancies. Even though there is a greater number in the labour force, there are still vacant positions being left unfilled. These positions range across a wide number of sectors and tend to exacerbate with increasing distance from urban centres. This is of such growing concern that state agencies such as FÁS and Údarás na Gaeltachta have specifically designed campaigns to try and entice emigrants back to Ireland. However it must also be recognised that not all areas undergo the same change and in many parts of rural Ireland there is still population decline and withdrawal or curtailment of services. Of particular concern in these rural areas is the human resource deficit and the barrier this creates for the survival of many rural communities.

The hidden challenge for rural Ireland[1]

The landscape of European rural areas is changing. Agriculture is no longer dominant in most regions of the EU. Some rural areas are experiencing increased levels of in-migration while others are suffering from increasing levels of population decline. The sustainability of the Irish rural economy and community is intrinsically linked to a mix of occupations, services and infrastructure. The Irish rural economy has faced a number of well documented problems including lack of employment opportunities, unemployment, low incomes, poverty, inadequate levels of amenity and service provision, environmental decay, under-utilisation/over-utilisation of productive resources and absolute population decline (see NESC Report No 97, 1994). Many of these problems are interrelated as, for example, an area with poor service provision generally experiences population out-migration. Employment policy (particularly that of the IDA) has to date focused on creating jobs and encouraging multinational investment. This policy has been successful in dealing with chronic unemployment rates. However, it has failed to reproduce and/or retain the range of skills, professions and services needed in rural areas and thereby has contributed to the decline of rural areas and to the human resource deficit which now exists. McGreil (1999) argues that this 'laissez-faire' policy has consolidated the growth of strong population centres while simultaneously undermining vulnerable rural areas.

In Irish rural development policy, concern with demographic issues, unemployment, under-employment and access to resources, while important in terms of job creation, has neglected to focus on the attraction and retention of human resources in rural areas. In this context the operation of the labour market in rural areas and, more particularly, the human resource deficit experienced in rural areas provide a very definite (if somewhat hidden) challenge to the future of many rural areas. Despite a background of increased participation in the labour market and current unemployment figures of 4% in Ireland (as compared to 10% in Europe) there is increasing evidence of skill shortages in rural areas (IBEC, 1998, 1999; Department of Enterprise, Trade & Employment, 1997, 1998; SFA, 1997,1998; McGreil, 1998; Mernagh and Commins, 1997; FORFÁS, 1996; Ferrao, 1995; McIver Consulting, 1995; Finnegan, 1994; Bowler *et al.* 1992; Keeble *et al.* 1992). This shortage is set against a background of national unemployment to the order of 150,000; a scarcity of skilled personnel to fill vacant positions in rural areas; depopulation in selected rural areas, and economic and social decline in rural areas.

From a human resources perspective, rural areas face a number of structural weaknesses. These include an ageing demographic structure; (CSO statistics on the number of births since 1980 indicate that the number of 18-year-olds in the population is likely to fall from 74,338 in 1998 to 47,929 by 2012); an exodus of young people and skilled workers; a predominance of jobs in the type of work undergoing deep-reaching changes, and ongoing cultural under-valuation of formal types of education and training (OECD, 1995, p.95). Further, it is recognised that these skill shortages are a widespread multi-disciplinary, cross-sectoral phenomenon affecting a range of skilled, semi-skilled and non-skilled occupations. This 'problem' is also notable by its lack of recognition in policies and operational programmes designed to promote rural and regional development, and the lack of research on the extent, nature, causes and effects of skill shortages in rural areas.

Before delving into the issue of skill shortages as they relate to rural Ireland, there are problems associated with such an investigation. Primarily, much of the evidence compiled on skill shortages is drawn from large-scale surveys which are invariably important in quantifying this issue but too widespread in nature to explore the complex and ambiguous problems of the shortage (Causer and Jones, 1993). As Meager (1986) suggests, the evidence of skill shortages reported may often be a measure of an employer's reported difficulty in recruiting particular types of staff rather than a guide to the actual availability of given skills within a population. Causer and Jones (1993) recognising this, suggest that 'surveys which simply require employers to indicate their perceptions of whether recruitment has become more difficult are open to the criticism that they rest upon subjective impressions rather than objective data' (p.4). Likewise a more objective way of assessing skill shortages can have drawbacks, leading us to conclude that there is no simple way to identify recruitment difficulties. In this discussion, skill shortages are seen to exist where there are not enough people available with the necessary skills to do the jobs that need doing! However, it is also recognised that not all recruitment difficulties will be due to a lack of skills, for example, jobs may be unattractive due to poor pay or long hours. The perception that some unemployed people do not want to work as they are better off on Social Welfare with the occasional job on the 'black market' is also an issue. It is therefore suggested that problems of attracting and retaining skills in rural Ireland needs to be viewed both from the vantage point of agencies/organisations/employers as well as from the point of view of the prospective employee or person moving to a rural location.

Policy objectives

The tailoring of rural development policy around demographic issues, unemployment, under-employment and access to resources has been instrumental in creating the human resource deficit now being experienced in rural areas. The deployment of new production technologies, partly in order to make the major agricultural commodities more competitive, greatly increased productivity per farmer, per hectare and per person engaged in agriculture throughout the EU. Not surprisingly, large labour surpluses, leading to out-migration and population decline, became common features of rural areas in all developed countries. It was against this background that the creation of new employment opportunities in rural areas became a major focus of rural policy initiatives.

In European social policy the primary emphasis is on employability and maximising labour resources already available. Examples of these policies include early and systematic intervention programmes with unemployed people, which provide the necessary skills to improve employability. The Amsterdam Treaty includes an employment chapter relating to the condition of Member States' employment policies. For this purpose the European Commission draws up annual guidelines and, the National Development Plans, prepared by each Member State, must take account of these guidelines. The Guidelines agreed for 1999 at the Vienna European Council in December 1998 are:

Improving employability through:

- Improving youth unemployment and preventing long-term unemployment;
- Transition from passive measures to active measures;
- Encouraging a partnership approach;
- Easing the transition from school to work; and
- Promoting a labour market open to all.

Developing entrepreneurship by:

- Making it easier to start up and run businesses;
- Exploiting new opportunities for job creation; and
- Making the taxation system more employment friendly.

Encouraging adaptability of businesses and their employees through:

- Modernising work organisation; and
- Supporting adaptability in enterprises.

Strengthening equal opportunities policies for women and men through:

- A gender mainstreaming approach;
- Tackling gender gaps;
- Reconciling work and family life; and
- Facilitating reintegration into the labour market.

The European Commission's White Paper on Education and Training, *Teaching and Learning: Towards the Learning Society* (1995), identified three factors of upheaval in modern European Society, that is, 'the

Changing Discourses of Economy, Society and Space   37

internationalisation of trade, the dawning of the information society and the relentless march of science and technology' (p.5) all of which emphasise the challenge of providing skills, ensuring employability and, promoting economic growth in rural areas. In terms of sustainability, the European Commission in its seminal paper, *The Future of Rural Society* (1988) laid down a sound strategic policy thrust for the sustainable development of rural areas. The delivery of sustainable development, however, ultimately depends on the capacity of human resources in the rural areas concerned. Any limitations with respect to human resources are likely to affect adversely the competitiveness of rural areas and retard the full exploitation of local potentials to the detriment of the quality of life and the sustainability of rural communities. The National Employment Plan for Ireland (1998) includes policies and actions to promote a framework for lifelong learning to encourage individuals to access quality education and training on an ongoing basis and enterprises to invest in human resource development,to meet new and rapidly changing needs.

Why do people move into or out of rural areas?

There are no easy answers to this question, only deductions and generalisations. Some people are undoubtedly attracted by the perceived idyll of rural living – an idyll which is bound up with ideas of community, kinship, family, safeness, values and mores, a particular way of life, culture and closeness to nature. It is also clear however, that many others are deterred by factors such as the limited range and quality of services and amenities readily accessible in dispersed rural communities; limited employment opportunities for one's spouse; restricted opportunities for career advancement; isolation from professional peers and the associated difficulties of making suitable substitution arrangements during periods of absence (such as holidays, illness). Out-migration from rural areas also emanates from attachments to other (mainly urban) places developed during periods of extended stay, as for example, while undergoing training or third level education. Other potentially influential factors in the decision to leave (in preference to availing of local employment opportunities in rural areas) relate to the relative anonymity afforded by large urban centres and to the desire to join friends (and family) who may have already emigrated. Such considerations, beyond the death of employment opportunities, are looming ever larger over the fate of rural communities.

What are the implications?

Human resource skill deficits have an impact at a number of levels from the local to the national. For example, a human resource skill deficit has obvious implications for education and training both at policy and implementation levels. Finnegan (1994) recognised the difficulties for rural communities, and suggested that in Ireland young graduates between the ages of 18-25 were highly mobile and as a result were unlikely to contribute to their native community in the short-term. In the Department of Education's Green Paper (1998) it was suggested that 'the well-educated and flexible workforce which has been a central part of Ireland's current economic growth is itself a wasting asset, unless renewed on an ongoing basis through a continuous drive to upgrade and re-skill'. The OECD report (1995, p.28) emphasised the intrinsic link between job creation and the enhancement of human resources suggesting that from a social standpoint rural areas face the problem of 'how to ensure at least some minimum standard of living and associated employment prospects so that the younger segment of the population in particular can be retrained and, how to create conditions that will attract outside people seeking a social life of high quality'. For this reason, the approach to enhancing human resources, particularly in rural areas, must take a broad view that encompasses job conditions and lifestyle considerations for the individual and family unit. The fundamental argument of retaining and attracting suitably qualified personnel to rural areas holds the key to the sustainable development of rural areas.

Consequently, the thrust of rural development policies and programmes toward the creation of new and varied business and employment opportunities in rural areas is rendered void unless people want to live and work in rural areas. Therefore there is a significant need to establish the extent to which labour recruitment and retention difficulties prevail throughout rural areas; the root causes of these difficulties; the implications for all concerned; and the extent to which they are amenable to policy interventions.

What evidence is there of skill shortages?

The context of skill shortages is set against an employment situation in Ireland that in recent years has been characterised by:

- Average annual growth of 5.8% in non-agricultural private sector jobs;
- Substantial growth in full-time jobs;
- Average annual growth of 4.4% in service sector jobs;
- A continuation of the structural decline in the numbers within agriculture;
- Continuing strong flows of young persons into the labour market;

Changing Discourses of Economy, Society and Space 39

- Rapidly rising female participation; and
- A reversal of migration trends from a position of substantial net annual outflows to one of net inward migration (Department of Enterprise, Trade and Employment, 1998).

CSO figures released in 1999 confirm that from a position a few years ago as one of Europe's black spots, Irish unemployment rates have fallen to 6.4%, its lowest since records began. The quarterly national household survey, carried out by the CSO, found that just over 100,000 people (6.4% of the labour force) were out of work at the end of 1998 (compared to 10.4% a year earlier). The figures are much lower than the monthly live register – which has fallen just below 200,000 – but are seen as a more accurate measure of unemployment (O'Sullivan, 1999, p.1). However, against this background of increased participation in the labour market and unemployment figures of less than 6% in Ireland, the question remains as to why there are still skills shortages, and why these skills shortages exist in rural areas (or particular types of rural areas)?

While little empirical evidence exist as yet to support this view, there is a significant amount of anecdotal evidence describing shortages in rural areas throughout the country. These include a lack of farm labourers for harvesting silage in the midlands; hotel staff in Clifden, nurses in Carraroe, or doctors in Roundstone all of which give credence to this argument (McDonagh, 2000). A significant aspect of these skill shortages is that they are experienced across all sectors from farm labourers, manufacturing operatives, services or other professionals (like doctors, teachers, nurses and engineers). The Director of the Small Firms Association (SFA) (*Irish Times*, 1998) suggested that skill shortages not only affected well-publicised areas such as construction, tourism and information technology, but that it was virtually impossible to recruit graduate engineers in Ireland because of intense recruitment drives by global operators who pay better than Irish employers. Likewise there is a problem at a lower skill level (like clerical posts) because young people find these jobs less exciting and with fewer promotional opportunities.

Keeble *et al.* (1992) in their study on rural England found that there were significant shortages of skilled/technical workers and managers/ professionals in many rural firms in comparison to their urban counterparts. Skilled worker shortages were a serious problem for approximately 25% of all remote rural firms with over 33% also having problems recruiting managers and professionals. These shortages resulted in rural firms recruiting their skilled workers from outside the local areas, thereby raising problems like housing availability. In rural Ireland, while employment opportunities may be limited (by accessibility, infrastructure, comparative advantage), the NESC Report (1997) highlighted that there were jobs available in the tourism industry (particularly seasonally), but that these were associated with low pay, long hours and local employees who were either young (15-18-year-olds) or married women. In contrast to this seasonal workforce managerial and specialist staff were generally not recruited locally but were brought in from other areas.

Documentation that further highlights this skill shortage phenomenon is present in a number of other recent reports. For example Ireland's Employment Action Plan (Department of Enterprise, Trade and Employment, 1998) suggests that 'evidence has already emerged of potential labour/skill bottlenecks in particular fields'. In 1998, the Irish government established a partnership to develop national strategies to tackle the issue of skill deficits and future needs for education and training for business. The issue of labour shortages is also acknowledged in the *Green Paper for Adult Education* (Department of Education, 1998). Here it is recognised that a 'persisting problem in unemployment, even in the context of labour shortages, suggests serious mismatches between the available skill pool and the demand'. A 1996 Forfás Study showed that 30% of companies see skill deficiencies as a problem and 60% see a need for increasing skill levels in technology, quality and customer service. The issue of skills shortages features prominently in a 1998 IBEC survey of labour and skills in the services sector. Two-thirds of organisations stated that the main reason they had problems filling vacancies was the shortage of applicants with the right practical skills. Just under half of the participants (47%) stated that they had difficulties retaining existing staff. The *White Paper on Human Resource Development* (Department of Enterprise and Employment, 1997) identified a skills gap in the areas of (i) Job Specific Skills, (ii) Management Skills, and (iii) General Flexibility and Communication Skills. In the CSO figures released in May 1999, not only is a decline in unemployment confirmed, but what O'Suillivan (1999) describes as a 'new and critical problem [of] increasing evidence of labour supply shortages'. The CSO pointed out that 'the potential supply of people to fill jobs had fallen sharply over the last five years, while employment was increasing at a rate of 4-5% per annum. The growth in the numbers of young people coming onto the jobs market is now enough to fill only one of every two job created and there are fewer people with the skills to take up the rest' (ibid.).

In the recently published SFA National Employment Survey (1999) of the 57% of companies recruiting at that time, 97% of those companies indicated recruitment difficulties. These difficulties were cross-sectoral – Services 100%; Manufacturing 94%; Distribution 100% and Retail 88%. Companies also reported that recruitment difficulties were due to one or a combination of the factors below.

Table 2.1 SFA, National Employment Survey, 1999

	1999	1998
Lack of Skills	68%	50%
Attitude to Work	06%	14%
Better off on Social Welfare	26%	36%

While these figures do not contain a spatial breakdown, in comparing the 1999 and 1998 survey results, the 'Lack of Skills' factor seems to be the fastest growing barrier to employers who wish to recruit. In briefly documenting this skill shortage, the most notable issue is that these difficulties appear to exist in all sectors and across a wide range of occupations.

Two further aspects to this debate look beyond this notion of creating jobs. One suggests that there is employment available (evident in the jobs pages of the daily newspapers) but it is not being accessed; and the second focuses on the role played by the informal or 'black economy'. The first situation, that of vacant jobs not being accessed, implies a human resource deficit that is created by a lack of suitably skilled personnel willing to take up vacant positions in rural areas. Teigen (1995) in his paper on creating agglomeration or deglomeration economies suggested that 'the labour force is less mobile than is normally assumed in economic theory [with] greater wage differentials between agglomerations experiencing growth and rural areas with population stagnation or declining population' (p.8). An example of such a situation was the year-long search for a doctor to fill the post of General Practitioner (GP) in Roundstone, Connemara in 1998-99. In this case, finding a suitably qualified candidate was not the problem but convincing the candidate to take up the post proved to be a major obstacle. The demanding nature of such a position in a dispersed rural population area and the difficulty of getting locums to fill in during the GP's time off were the main reasons cited for this reluctance.

The second situation is that of the 'black economy'. Opportunities associated with the informal or 'black' economy appear to exacerbate recruitment difficulties even where people with required skills reside in the rural areas in question. In the SFA 5th National Employment Survey (1999) as many as 41% of prospective employees sought to be paid 'off the books'. The Director of the SFA (cited in the *Irish Times* 1998) suggested that 'the pervasiveness of the 'black economy' is such that employers often find it difficult to match the take-home pay of someone claiming social welfare and doing occasional work at the same time'. However the Irish National Organisation of the Unemployed (INOU) disputed this perspective by suggesting that the myth of unemployed people not wanting to work is dispelled by the fact that 90% of the 72,000 jobs created in 1998 were taken up by the jobless. As such, the INOU argued that employers who were having problems filling vacancies should be investigating what they are doing wrong, rather than what is wrong with the unemployed (O'Sullivan, 1999, p.17).

However valid these arguments, paradoxically, the problem of skill shortages appears to be much more acute in rural areas characterised by higher than average rates of unemployment, continuing net out-migration and long-term decline, rather than in urban centres where unemployment rates are lower. It also appears to be the case that recruitment and retention difficulties are not uniformly spread throughout rural space. The reported incidences of these difficulties lead to the hypothesis that the problem intensifies with increasing distance from major urban centres. The functionality of rural areas therefore appears to be a critical determinant of the incidence of this problem and a factor that varies considerably from one country to another within the EU. As such, this shortage of skills is clearly not confined to a limited number of sectors and occupations. It is a widespread multi-disciplinary and cross-sectoral phenomenon.

What has been done to address this problem?

Generally speaking the problem of a skills deficit in rural areas as 'a cause for concern' has been largely ignored. In rural development policy particularly, the concern to date has been primarily focused on demographic issues, unemployment, under-employment and access to resources. As the 'Celtic Tiger' economy flourishes, the notion that a future lack of skills in Ireland will undermine this buoyant economy has been dismissed as merely a 'storm in a teacup' by most commentators (at least until fairly recently). Recent media coverage of the skill shortage problem being experienced throughout rural Ireland has however slowly brought this impending (and actual) problem further up the policy ladder. This gradual recognition has led to attempts to place more emphasis on the supply of skills to some specific sectors of the economy, as highlighted by developments such as the Forfás Skills Group, the Business Education Partnership Forum and the £250m Education Technology Fund. An example of further strategies being employed is that of Údarás na Gaeltachta. This state agency is specifically targeting Gaeltacht graduates based overseas in an attempt to persuade them to return to positions in the Gaeltacht region (some local communities send their newsletters to former residents to try and entice them back to jobs or as potential investors in their own areas). A major problem in many of the Údarás factories is to find suitably qualified candidates for skilled jobs (in particular

Changing Discourses of Economy, Society and Space   43

managers) who also have a knowledge of the Irish language.

More recently, the Department of Enterprise, Trade and Employment introduced procedures to tackle the growing skill shortage by relaxing the rules that apply to work permits for non-EU nationals. These steps are described as a move designed to ease the mobility and availability of staff who are non-EU nationals but are on assignment from an affiliated foreign company. The move allows multinational companies investing in Ireland to transfer staff from other locations to Ireland with merely a valid confirmation of employment and without a work permit, as previously required. Although the application procedure is quite simple, the length of time (up to 2 months) to receive a permit was causing frustration for potential employers with a number of software companies suggesting that they lost potential recruits to other companies because of the arduous process involved (Lyons, 1999). Also announced on 14 May 1999 was a major new recruitment campaign to be launched by FÁS in Europe and the US in an effort to meet the skills and labour shortages in Ireland. FÁS indicated that they wanted to attract 10,000 workers for vacancies in several sectors and that the initiative was to begin at an employment fair in Cologne in June 1999.

What conclusions can be drawn?

At this stage conclusions can only be tentative. Before outlining some of them, a number of further issues need to be recognised. Such issues cover the fact that people will leave rural areas for reasons other than a lack of a job suitable to their specific skill level; that economic measures are not a panacea in combating this outflow; that the small networks that often exist in remote rural areas are a preventative factor to attracting skilled personnel to rural areas; and finally that, career preference is only one element in people's choice of where they live. In this regard, both the attraction and the retention of human resources to rural areas needs equal attention, that is, acknowledging that people may be attracted to an area if they see opportunities to advance their career, and thereby ultimately leave for a higher position. The brief conclusions that can thus be drawn, are:

- skill shortages are experienced in rural areas and these shortages vary significantly over time and space;

- these shortages are to be found even in areas which produce the necessary skills but from which people with these skills emigrate (the idea, as expressed in the *Green Paper for Adult Education*, of matching skills taught in an area to the demand in that area, as such, may not be a panacea);

- rural areas have certain quality of life limitations that militate against the attraction and retention of trained personnel;

- the skills shortage being experienced has major adverse effects on the success of local development strategies that are being pursued in these areas (local development plans are being encouraged by government and state agencies yet the skills/abilities to implement these plans may be seriously lacking in local communities);

- the limitations relate in part to the restricted variety and size of many local labour markets in rural areas; thus, for example, rendering it difficult for the spouse of an employee to obtain suitable employment in a locality; or, for example, making the area unattractive to a potential recruit because of geographic isolation from people with similar and/or supportive skills;

- 'quality of life' factors which may exert adverse effects on the attraction and retention of skilled labour in rural areas include deficiencies in recreational provision (e.g. multi-channel television, omniplexes, theatre, libraries, restaurants etc.);

- difficulties in accessing various public services (e.g. schools, colleges, universities, health care facilities etc.) also adversely effect recruitment and retention of staff in many rural areas;

- inaccessibility of facilities such as a variety of retail shopping outlets, banking and personal services is another factor that contributes to labour market deficits in rural areas; and

- previous experience of various elements of urban living (relative anonymity, ease of access to educational, social, recreational, commercial services) during periods of (tertiary) education and training militate against the return of young people to their native rural areas or other such areas.

Concluding remarks

Ireland is a place where there is a strong local, yet contested regional identity. It has been suggested in this chapter that this identity is also underpinned by a recognition of cultural distinctiveness. Changes taking place in traditions, the economy, language and culture form a mosaic that reflects the historical and cultural dynamics that are shaping modern Ireland. However, for a country so ill at ease with its own identity (Murphy, 1991; Johnson, 1994), it is hardly surprising that there are several contradictory images of rural Ireland's problems and needs. Economically, there are a number of extremes which have determined the Irish economy, from de Valera's ideal of an Ireland that was rural, frugal and gaelic, to a more international looking market, dominated by a branch-plant economy. Enticed by the generous tax incentives on offer by the Irish government, the branch-plant economy, while providing jobs, only served to undermine indigenous industries and proved to be rather unstable. There is now a shift towards strengthening the indigenous sector and encouraging more Small and Medium Sized Enterprises (SMEs). Emphasis is being placed on developing greater self-reliance, especially on local communities' capacities to create and retain employment from within (Teitz, 1994, cited in Ó Cinnéide, 1995). There is also a move towards developing the 'human capacity to instigate, lead and control development, and to create a culture of development in areas affected by isolation, dependency, emigration, conservatism and cynicism' (Ó Cinnéide, 1996, p.5).

Whatever the image projected, the economic features of rural Ireland are similar to those of other geographically peripheral regions in Europe. These include a dependence on small farms, a lack of local innovation, a lack of influence over major economic forces and decisions, high emigration and a dependency on government-sponsored projects (Commins, 1983). The inherent decline experienced, is manifest in the decline in importance of farming in general; the under-utilisation of resources; the arrival of the 'new rural dweller'; the experiences of social disorder; the different packaging and commodification of rural areas for the tourist. Economically, under-utilisation of resources is a common feature, particularly under-utilisation of labour, natural resources and infrastructure (Cuddy *et al.*, 1990). The arrival of the 'new rural dweller', has brought transformations, with new social values and critical attitudes to development projects that threaten to despoil their new environments (Ó Cinneide, 1992d). Expanding and declining areas of rural Ireland are also experiencing social disorder from congestion and the severing of contact with traditional social and cultural environments, as well as from depopulation, and the attendant problems of imbalance in demographic structure, and a poor social support system. The inevitable decline of agriculture and the growing concern over depopulation in many rural areas, raise questions of what can be done to create a more effective rural economy. The policies of the 1960s and 1970s, of concentrating on attracting foreign investment to the country, although partly successful, are no longer an appropriate model for development. This shift away from inward investment and the focus on the local economy, and its 'abilities to create and retain employment from within is gaining importance.

Significant within this shifting focus is the growing challenge of the human resource deficit being experienced in rural areas. In this light how important a determinant geographical location is, can be questioned. Can it be argued that there is an inevitable link between remote rural areas and their ability to attract key skilled personnel or is there more to positioning in the structure of opportunity (rather than geographical location) (see Mernagh and Commins, 1997)? Whatever the answer, the call for greater participation by local communities in the decision-making process, and a desire to mobilise communities to the extent that they are able to 'help themselves' in creating and maintaining their own local economies, gains currency. As evidenced in later chapters however, while much lip-service is paid to such sentiments (see MacConnell, 1996; MacDubhghaill, 1996; MacDubhghaill and O'Sullivan, 1996; O'Sullivan, 1996g; Rice, 1996) few practical or logistical steps are being put in place to ensure sustained involvement. In fact, it is fair to suggest that part of the problem associated with this failure stems from the cultural traits of the rural Irish and their desire not to be the ones to stand up and 'demand a say' (O'Faolain, 1993a).

It has been the purpose of this chapter to draw together a number of different discourses that illustrate the current situation in rural Ireland. These discourses of geography, culture, history, economics and politics have been used to suggest that the focus on past traditions in Ireland invariably defines the present structures, the culmination of which will mould future paths. These discourses have been shown to be interconnected and create what can be viewed as a number of contested constructions of Ireland. These contestations are in the form of contested mappings, contested constructions of place identity, versions of change and versions of problems and needs. This chapter provides a reinforcing of these contestations, and the important roles played by history and culture in moulding the thoughts and actions of both Irish policy-makers and rural communities alike. It is these changes that play a determining role in the (re)negotiation of rural development in Ireland.

In the next chapter the focus of the debate shifts to exploring the rural discourses which are circulated in Ireland. This chapter deconstructs the changing definitions and approaches to the rural, while linking these changes to the discourses predominantly associated with rural Ireland.

Note

1   This section is based on preliminary work carried out with Micheál Ó Cinnéide, Geography Department at NUI, Galway and Anne Dolan, International Centre for Development Studies, NUI, Galway.

3 Thoughts on Rurality and Rural Ireland

(T)oo often, rural and urban areas have been separately considered ... some would argue that the popular but wholly inaccurate view that rural and urban societies coexist simultaneously but separately represents an outright barrier to the evolution of policies that would address fundamental and escalating problems of societal instability ... rural and urban areas are so inextricably linked that the well-being of rural areas is not just of concern to those who live in them, but also the interest of urban dwellers as well (Ó Cinnéide, 1992b, p.7).

This chapter explores the changing definitions of, and approaches to, the rural, using ideas and debates from Irish and English academic and lay discourses. This investigation redefines the rural as not just a physical space but also as a social construction made up of a whole set of different political, social and cultural meanings. The 'rural' is represented in terms of lived experiences rather than defined spatially or territorially. Emphasis is placed on how the 'rural' has become not only a particular physical landscape but is bound up with socially constructed ideas of communities, kinship and nature. Further, the influence of personal perceptions and background is explored to enhance the thesis that people experience the world at multiple points, times and places (Cook and Crang, 1995) and that their perceptions do not fit conveniently in to neatly structured images of what is rural (Halfacree, 1993). The underlying message is that the 'rural' impinges on almost every aspect of Irish life, socially, economically and in influencing the decision-making process. Examination of the symbolism associated with rurality and how these symbols or myths have become attached to the term rural through everyday social practice, is therefore crucial.

Unravelling the personal point of view

In recent literature much has been made of 'exposing and unravelling the personal point of view' (Cloke, 1995, p.149). This self-reflection, along with an account of my own preconceptions and attitudes towards rural change will form part of the conceptual background to understanding the rural. As I enter the debate on the significance of rurality at a time when there are calls for its abandonment (Hoggart, 1990; Halfacree, 1993), it will be necessary to introduce my own 'lay discourse' of a term which trips so easily off the tongue (Cloke, 1985) into the 'cauldron' of academic theory and the practice of rural studies. My positionality could be described as a rather simplistic view of what it 'means to be rural' (Mormont, 1990) not only in my understanding of the extent to which ideas of the rural are interwoven in Irish culture, but also in understanding the ways in which power 'criss-crosses' the various arenas of the rural (Cloke, 1993). It will be necessary to cross-integrate those perceptions of rural Ireland (for example, Bord Failte's slogan, *Discover Ireland – its part of what you are*) with the type of 'problems' (marginalisation, deprivation, depopulation) related to rural communities *per se*. This endeavour seeks to deconstruct the degree to which Ireland is a 'typical' rurality (or not), and reflect on how this 'rural uniqueness' is being increasingly packaged and commodified for particular 'audiences'. The intent is to explore prevailing constructs of rurality and determine the differing interpretations that influence rural policy and process in Ireland. This reflectivity attempts to acknowledge the 'tangle of background, influences, political perspectives, training [and] situations' (Christian, 1989, cited in Cloke, 1995, p.149) which have helped form and inform my interpretations of rural Ireland.

Predictably, my own background has furnished a series of perspectives linked (consciously or not) to 'typical' rural living. Exposure to poverty, social and cultural isolation, alternative lifestyles and the influx of new rural dwellers, 'disrupting established social hierarchies and provoking new divisions and tension in rural communities' (Lowe *et al.*, 1986, p.23), have all fashioned my reading of the rural landscape. My first stumbling block in this 'self-positioning' was the difficulty in defining 'rural' in terms of a physical space, a social and cultural construction, or as something which is 'manifold and heterogeneous, ... a category that each society takes and reconstructs' (Mormont, 1990, p.41). It is perhaps the instinctive response of 'I come from a rural area' which, despite arguments to the contrary (see Hoggart, 1990; Halfacree, 1993), prevent me from accepting that the 'rural' is no longer a useful category. In fact, paradoxically, this has helped me expand my thinking in terms of viewing 'rural *geographies* rather than a rural geography so as to reflect the unevenness of change brought about in the context of ... political economic trends' (Cloke, 1995, p.160).

Before diving into academic debates on rurality and its effects on Irish identity and rural development, I would like to 'explain' my positionality within this context of rural Ireland. Mine was a typical Irish childhood; I grew up on a small farm in the West of Ireland in the archetypal Irish village with its predominantly white, heterosexual, catholic and nationalist community which revolved around a shop, a church and a pub, and where the dominant activity was farming. These personal experiences and memories of the 'rural' are indelibly stamped on my values and my

Thoughts on Rurality and Rural Ireland   49

personality. At this time, it seemed to me there was little debate about what was understood by rural; rather there seemed to be an unquestioning acceptance of such terms. Generally, Irish society appeared relatively homogenous and predominantly rural in complexion, with rural life seen as in profound continuity with the social patterns and attitudes of the late nineteenth century; a society dominated by social and cultural conservatism. In my own understanding, the rural signifies more that a sense of place, or an identity, or even a closeness to nature, but also a collection of interpretations, experiences, influences, which is manifold and heterogeneous. The rural represents things of great beauty but is also closely bound up with images of hardship and struggle. For me, the rural recalls a number of sights, sounds and emotions (see also Williams, 1973). When I think of my background, I am flooded with images of woods, hills and lakes; of stones, briars and walls; of cows, potato-digging and corn-reaping; a calf being born on a frosty winter night; of working with scythe and horse and cart; of rough and muddy roads, of screeching birds and ploughed land; of the smell of freshly-cut grass in the summer hay season; the multitude of sounds and colours and yet the peacefulness of the bogs and the aching of limbs from harvesting the turf.

With all these wonderful and harsh images, the rural mingles feelings of frustration and isolation, of in some way being unable to participate in the 'wider' world. No one complained about the lateness of buses, as often there was no bus service. In my school days, although transport was often provided to the nearest schools, this often curtailed after-school activities like sports and clubs, while socially, especially for the younger generation, there was the problem of getting to the 'bright lights'. In terms of 'summer jobs', the options were usually few and often some distance away, inaccessible unless you had your own transport, (and in any case family members were usually expected to help on the farm). Although these may be regarded as essentially minor problems, they were meaningful in my experience of rural life and associated with feelings of isolation, deprivation and a particular way of life. Finally, this attempt to understand exactly 'how rural I am', has brought me to reflect on my experiences in a city environment, in Ireland, the USA and Britain, where a different world opens up, and where once inaccessible things, were now within easy reach. Much as I relish the 'convenience', often I sit in a traffic jam (not so convenient), or walk down a street strewn with litter 'tasting' the pollution in the air, or see the homeless begging on the streets, and it strikes me that maybe there are always two 'different' worlds which co-exist, each with its own advantages and disadvantages, each with mutually reinforcing attributes which cannot, and indeed should not, be seen in isolation. It is from these 'experiences' of rurality that the thoughts in this chapter are fashioned.

The complexity of rural Ireland

Rural Ireland has an interesting mix of geography, economy, culture and political attributes. The key themes of 'history', 'change' and 'culture' interconnect to give it a somewhat contradictory character and provide a framework through which to question the complex notions of 'problems' and 'needs', and 'constructions of identity' (see Chapter 2). Few places in Europe are so closely associated with the 'rural' as Ireland. Despite growing industrialisation throughout the country, few places outside the capital, Dublin, are referred to in any other context (for example see Johnson, 1994). Although this fits quite readily into the 1960s notion of rural and urban society occupying two ends of a continuum, a concept now largely dismissed (see Pahl, 1966; Copp, 1972), there is an increasing need to recognise the complex range of activities which give rise to rurality, including agriculture, policy makers, farmers, new rural dwellers and multinational companies (Murdoch and Pratt, 1993). Girvin (1993) suggests that residual elements of the older tradition still retain considerable emotional appeal, as for example does the power of the Church. However, it is now more readily accepted that with transformations in Irish rural society due to social, industrial and culture change, the 'hegemonic nature of the traditional values is gone, with a form of pluralism emerging to replace it' (ibid., p.397). Rural Ireland is therefore marked by different biographies and experiences moulded by a variety of economic, historical and social forces (see Chapter 2). The contemporary social landscape of rural areas is consequently characterised by a complex and often fragmented series of networks, where 'older territorial patterns – of family farms, neighbourhood units, village, church, communities and 'social fields' – are still deeply embedded in rural structures but are now also overlain by new layers of social and economic activities' (Smyth, 1986, p.4). These emerging rural structures, have forced small-scale rural Ireland to come to terms with being projected into a European economic system and exposed in a relatively short period of time to the forces of immigration (the new rural dweller), new consumer practices, commercialisation, population decline, and radical changes in traditional farming practices. Rapid change has been further accelerated by the increased influence of the EU on rural affairs, and the opening up of Ireland to international market exposure, the reverberations of which are only slowly being integrated into Irish economic, political and cultural life. These changes, attributable to national and international influences, have worked their way into rural communities 'through the ongoing everyday life of local inhabitants and their interaction with the wider structures, producing specific societies, landscapes, events and experiences, and thus creating a wide variety of new rural Irelands' (Smyth, 1986, p.7). This creation of 'new rural Irelands' results in a complex mix of social and territorial elements, from family farms, rural tourism and local community enterprises, to calls for regional autonomy and opposition to the constraining state system.

Consequently the complexities involved in developing a theoretical insight into rural development processes should not be understated. That rural discourse cannot be separated from the political and social powers that create them, suggests a need to re-evaluate much of what is taken for granted in terms of the 'rural' in Ireland. This is particularly so when attempting to understand the constructs of rurality which mould Irish rural development policy, process and perception. This arena of debate forms the less than clear zone between the sometimes abstract level of development theory and the more straightforward 'on-the-ground' applications of rural development study and practice. Hoggart et al., (1995, p.4) have suggested that 'socio-economic change in rural areas inevitably covers the whole gamut of societal transformations that nations experience' from depopulation to shared experiences of what residents of a particular area 'call' rural. The theoretical grounding must explore the changing experiences of rural places and people due to changing regulations in production, consumption and the commodification of the countryside. Cloke (1995, p.293) suggests that the rural is now becoming:

> an exclusive place to be lived in; rural communities as a concept to be bought and sold; rural lifestyles which can be colonised; icons of rural culture which can be crafted, packaged and marketed; rural landscapes with a new range of potential from 'pay-as-you-enter' national parks, to sites for the theme park explosion.

In the light of the changing definitions of the 'rural', Ireland's 'unusual amalgam of backwardness and modernity' (Kiberd, 1990), provides a conducive backdrop to debates on rurality and rural idylls and the influence that such an idyll carries in the Irish psyche. The traditional obsession with national identity comes to the fore in the face of the new identities being imposed on rural Ireland. Such identities swing from de Valera's vision of a gaelic, catholic and nationalist Ireland, with frugal homesteads and an industrious countryside, to that of a 'new pluralist, European and technological Ireland, embarrassed at its nationalist past and frantically trying to show our EEC partners that we are as sophisticated as they are' (Kirby, 1988, p.45).

In terms of rural discourse Ireland has tended to equate rural with agricultural (Tovey, 1992), and also to associate the rural with mysticism and conservatism. Rural Ireland is often depicted as a repository for national identity and values. Conceptually, Irish rural discourses have been much more comfortable in dealing with statistics, hard numeric facts and 'policy relevant' information (on farm size, or farm outputs for example) than in any attempt to heighten awareness of the social and cultural marginalisation of rural lifestyles (McInerney, 1995). Nevertheless, there is a slow conceptual shift away from the mechanistic and reductionist view (Sheeran, 1988), with an emerging debate for interpreting different constructs of rurality in Ireland 'by drawing together in different ways, elements of political economic theorisation with elements of the symbolic importance of notions of rural idylls' (Cloke, 1995, p.165) gaining pace. This progressive shift in the debate draws on contemporary literature (albeit describing a largely English experience) to trace the many phases of Irish rural discourse, ranging from de Valera's rustic, idealised Ireland, to the modernisation of a contemporary Ireland which is outward-looking, and vibrant. The debate also takes on board the increasing 'commodification' of Ireland, a scenario in which rural Ireland can be packaged and sold as a playground for tourists from urban areas, Irish or otherwise.

Changing definitions and approaches to the 'rural'

There is a lack of theoretical precision when it comes to dealing with things rural. While the debates on rurality seem continuous, there has been in recent years a new emphasis on the meaning of rural, resulting in the promotion of theoretical paradigms and conceptual tools (see for example Buller and Wright, 1990; Marsden *et al.*, 1990; Shortall, 1994). This increased emphasis on the (de)construction of the rural comes at a time when the issue of rural development is very much central to the political and social arena. In attempting to make some 'sense' of the debate, it is fair to suggest that there have been at least two divergent views of the 'rural' expressed in recent literature. The first is that of the traditionalists, a view which, it could be suggested, has largely dominated the rural development discourses of Ireland up to the 1990s. This traditional view is best represented in the works of Pacione (1985) and Gilg (1985) which have, according to Boylan (1992, p.16) 'eschewed any contamination with theoretical developments in the other social sciences, but have maintained a strong applied component particularly in the area of land use planning'. In contrast, the literature of the late 1980s has sought to encompass developments in other social sciences, including geography, sociology and economics, to name a few, espousing the idea that irrespective of whether urban or rural conceptualisations are used, the same underlying processes and structures are involved. As such, the use of the term rural may be a misleading theoretical concept (Cloke, 1985; Cloke, 1987b & c; Cloke and Goodwin, 1993; Halfacree, 1993).

In other literatures (for example Hoggart and Buller, 1987) the vigour of rural studies has been called into question. Boylan (1992) citing Hoggart and Buller (1987) raises the notion that despite advances to the contrary, there is still the continuing influence of the 'long and lingering adherence, to notions of a rural-urban continuum' (p.15). While recognising Pahl's (1966) critique of this notion, Boylan (1992, p.15) further asserts that for

Thoughts on Rurality and Rural Ireland   53

too long rural studies have 'over-emphasised issues connected with the consumption (or consequences) of socio-economic change' without delving very deeply into the production of the socio-economic or other changes in such rural areas. Despite the recent popularity of studies on rural industries and the importance of service provision (Carey 1995b; McAllister 1995; Cawley, 1999), energy seems mainly directed at the impacts of cuts in these areas with little time given to why such services are curtailed in the first place, and for what reasons. In parallel with the human resource deficit being experienced in rural Ireland (see Chapter 2), there appears to be almost an acceptance of such occurrences, whether they result from market forces, or other economic dictates. A further weakness in Irish rural studies, is the double-edged sword which interchangeably conflates 'agriculture' with 'rural', a trend which spanned a number of decades including the 1990s, whereby the majority of references in literature or policy proposals tend to use these terms interchangeably. This reinforced a one-dimensional approach to development rather than the more integrated and holistic approach now being favoured (see Ó Cinnéide, 1992a; Ó Cinnéide, 1992b; Walsh, 1996). In contrast, there has also arisen a situation of 'an over-insistence on separating agricultural issues from non-agricultural concerns' (Boylan, 1992, p.16), with very few attempts to evaluate how such issues (farm structures, efficiency, innovation) have affected rural areas. The criticism is that in attempting to dispense with the coupling of agriculture with all things rural the other extreme can occur, leaving behind the necessary holistic view.

What of the 'rural'?

For a term that 'trips very easily off the tongue' (Cloke, 1985, p.4), the meaning of 'rural' has proved elusive. Recent literatures (Cloke, 1985; Cloke, 1987a; Cloke (ed.) 1987c; Cloke, 1989a; Cloke, 1989e; Hoggart, 1990; Cloke and Goodwin 1993; Halfacree, 1993) have all sought (with only limited success), to either define the rural, categorise the rural, propose alternative definitions as to its use, or to do away with the term altogether. Cloke (1985, p.5) in his definition sees the 'rural' as:

> areas which are dominated (currently or recently) by extensive land notably agriculture and forestry, [which] contains small, lower-order settlements demonstrating a strong relationship between buildings and surrounding extensive landscape, and which are thought of as rural by most residents, which engenders a way of life characterised by a cohesive identity based on respect for the environment, and behavioural qualities of living as part of an extensive landscape.

In practice, rural areas vary considerably, from those which may still be defined functionally (by land use and geographical location) to those closer to urban centres where 'rural' is more of a socially constructed category. Murdoch and Pratt (1993, p.423) have commented that rather than trying to render one single definition, it would be more beneficial to explore 'the ways in which rurality is constructed and deployed in a variety of contexts'. Lowe et al., (1990, p.40) describe rural as having 'been used in a predominantly pragmatic manner, adjusting to different social, political and economic circumstances as the need arises', and, although it is quite difficult to define what a rural area is, those areas that do not look like 'an overwhelmingly urban environment' must, by default, be of a rural environment.

Halfacree (1993) suggested that the use of either descriptive or socio-cultural terms, have been two rather misguided and conventional approaches to defining the rural. In Ireland, the former definition has predominated. This type of definition describes the rural in relation to its socio-spatial characteristics, concentrating on variables which are observable and measurable, as for example land-use, employment and population. Halfacree (ibid., p.24) described these types of definitions as 'better seen as research tools for the articulation of specific aspects of the rural rather that as ways of defining the rural', and that these were merely attempts to fit a definition to what we already 'intuitively consider to be rural', but did not offer an alternative definition. From a socio-cultural perspective, the emphasis is on the assumption of varying socio-cultural characteristics in relation to the types of environment people live in. That is, a difference between behaviour and attitudes of people who live in small population settlements, like rural areas, and those in large settlements like urban areas. Supporting this perception, many of the common traits of Irish rural communities have stemmed from historical accounts of high degrees of interaction and homogeneity within rural areas. Notions of close-knit communities, where everybody knows and interacts with each other; considerable homogeneity in social traits, language, belief, opinions, mores and patterns of behaviour; family ties, particularly those of the extended family, and the importance of religion (see Bull et al., 1984). While some of these traits can be recognised in rural Ireland, this model of an ideal type of rural (as opposed to urban) society is far too simple and seems to utilize all the positive traits, disregarding the mounting problems and deprivation which faces both rural and urban areas equally (McLaughlin, 1986b; Scott et al., 1991). For the most part, rural communities contain a variety of different social groups and the idea of close-knit, happy and contented communities is no longer (if ever it was) viable. The reality is more likely to include conflict, differentiation-based class division and social status.

The recent tendency to generalise about rural areas to the neglect of their specific problems and state of transition is evidenced by the EU's recognition of three 'standard problem areas' (European Commission,

Thoughts on Rurality and Rural Ireland   55

1988). These are identified as:

- Areas suffering from the pressures of modern life, where conflict between modern agriculture and residential areas have been seen as leading to pollution and environmental damage;
- Areas suffering from rural decline, where out-migration is high, farming is marginal and there is little alternative employment; and
- The very remote areas, which are geographically marginal and where population is sparse and community decline rampant (Cloke and Goodwin, 1992, p.23).

These generalisations indicate that rural areas are in some way homogeneous, and not the complex entities that we think they are. It could easily be argued that within an area of decline there may also be a pocket of growth, and vice versa (for example the rural hinterland of Galway City in the West of Ireland). The problem with an outlook such as the EU's, is that it 'focuses on space, not people, and thereby overlooks the obvious truism that it is people not places who have problems and that different people in the same place can have different problems' (ibid.). It is now generally recognised that people are informed by their everyday experiences, and that their actions will reflect this understanding. Similarly it is only when we understand the various facets of the representations and meanings of rurality that we can begin to examine the relationships between experiences and discourses of the rural. It is becoming increasingly apparent that the 'rural' should not be seen as a merely physical space. A more appropriate model would allow for a multiplicity of social spaces which overlap the same geographical area, with each social space having 'its own logic, its own institutions, as well as its own network of actors – users, administrators – which are specific and not local' (Mormont, 1990, p.34).

The phases of rurality

The idea that rurality is subject to changing perceptions, social constructions and representation is explained by Cloke and Goodwin (1993) as a process which occurs in a number of 'phases'. These phases are not the definitive way to examine changing approaches to the rural, but they do provide a useful guide in analysing the outlooks that have developed. These phases are 'functional', 'pragmatic' and that of rural as a 'social construction'. In terms of traditional definitions (negative, positive and perception-based), the 'functional' phase falls under the negative, with a few specific characteristics of its own, for example:

> tracts left over once the functional city – regions and their hinterlands have been fully delineated from travel-to-work and retailing catchments (Coombes *et al.*, 1982, cited in Cloke and Park, 1985);

Those regions lying beyond the attraction of major urban centres (Greer, 1971).

To what or for whom exactly this 'attraction' is, would seem to remain open to debate. As such the negative approach is often thought of as being 'safe' as it does away with the need to define rural more exactly and transfers the onus of definition to urban researchers. The positive approach identifies different functions which are common in rural space with Clout (1972, p.5) defining the subject area of his rural geography as the 'study of recent social, economic, land-use and spatial changes that have taken place in less densely populated areas which are commonly recognised by virtue of their visual components as countryside'. Other proponents of such positive outlooks include Pacione (1985) who sees the study of rural geography as requiring an appreciation of all 'linkages', both within and outside the immediate rural environment, and Bull *et al.*, (1984) who acknowledges not only the spatial concept of rurality but also its economic, social and land-use aspects. The perception-based notion of rural is seen in the often popular image of the countryside as a place of serenity, harmony and a romantic notion of the good life. Thus the countryside stands for 'all that is important ... it is the expression of the good life away from the stresses and strains of the city' (Cloke and Park, 1985, p.2).

In addition, 'what is rural' can be defined by what people perceive of as rural: '(t)he village can be described as a place where the countryside meets the town and where distinction between rural and urban lies very much in the eye of the beholder' (Moss, 1978, cited in Cloke and Park, 1985). This concept is attractive in some ways, but is rather unconvincing when exposed to deeper questions. The arguments put forward for retaining the category of rural as a pragmatic investigative unit are based on the need for rural studies to counterbalance the predominance of urban studies; the pragmatic requirement for analytically convenient categories such as rural and urban; the need to expose many of the romantic rural myths which have been fostered by a historically anti-urban social science, and the basic belief that rural areas have characteristics distinguishable from those in urban areas (Phillips and Williams, 1984, cited in, Cloke and Goodwin, 1993). Hoggart (1990) in his paper 'Let's Do Away With Rural', is critical of this argument, suggesting that the pragmatic approach is objectionable because it 'groups together places in which social processes of a very different kind are in operation' (p.254). Hoggart's belief is that more progress would be made by focusing on particular social conditions (agency or structure) and evaluating how these 'unfold in particular settings', rather than using 'theoretically derived' criteria which create 'artificial boundaries' separating the rural and the urban. Hoggart's solution is that, instead of dealing with urban or rural areas, researchers should be urged to examine areas 'sectorally'. While stressing that he was not calling for the 'abandonment of the word 'rural' from everyday expression', he was adamant that the 'undifferentiated use of 'rural' in a research context is detrimental to the advancement of social theory' (p.245). Thus, the continually changing nature of the countryside calls for an approach located between functional and pragmatic, that is, looking at the rural as a social construct. Cloke and Goodwin (1992, p.22) suggest that such an approach accepts that 'rural space is neither homogenous nor governed by 'rurality', [and that] entrepreneurs, residents, leisure-seekers etcetera, continue to behave as though 'rural' were real to them, thereby attributing validity to a concept which relies on the social production of meanings'.

Mormont's (1990) article 'Who is Rural? Or How to be Rural?', claims that concepts such as 'rural' remain valid as long as they are built upon a concept used in everyday life by ordinary people in society. Describing rural identity as 'manifold and heterogeneous ... a category that each society takes and reconstructs', Mormont argues for 'distinguishing the rural and the agricultural, and defining the rural in relation to the social and cultural context created by industrial development, now the dominant element of the social system' (ibid., p.22). The emerging relationship between space and society, and the new uses of rural spaces (tourism, parks) have created specialized networks of relationships which include people who live in 'rural' areas (now comprising a diversity of residents as well as visitors) making it almost impossible to define homogeneous economic zones in the countryside.

The technological, economic and social changes taking place in rural areas across Europe are forcing a re-thinking of positions in relation to traditional and new modes of behaviour. The rural is becoming a category which is not so much 'contrasting rural dwellers with others in terms of economic interests, but rather one which defines a world of (primarily moral, but also cultural) values in which rural dwellers participate' (Mormont, 1990, p.30). Rural areas can be seen not only to represent particular landscapes but also to provide a whole set of meanings bound up with socially-constructed ideas of kinship and community. Cloke and Goodwin (1993, p.167), adopting the idea of rurality as a social construct, suggest that such an idea 'allow(s) 'rural' to become an important research category again, because behaviours and decisions will be influenced by the social construct(s) which indicates that a place is rural. The cultural domain thus becomes a crucial research area, and contemporary rural research has become very interested in the way in which meanings of rurality are constructed, negotiated and experienced'. Despite the debate on rurality being increasingly focused on social constructions, perceptions of the rural in Ireland are only slowly changing from being associated predominantly with agriculture to one which is more determined by the new social processes at work in these spaces. This slow rate of change is accounted for by the still large degree of acceptance that 'Ireland's landscape and settlement are still predominantly rural, agricultural and therefore, contrast directly with the urban-industrial cultures of the

European core' (Duffy, 1994, p.80).

Irish rural literature

There have been a number of important contributions (Arensberg and Kimball, 1940; Brody, 1973) to the understanding of Irish rural life. Such was their preoccupation however with 'description rather than prescription ... that an idealised view of rural Ireland was created' (Greer and Murray, 1993, p.3). The pre-conceived notion that 'rural' should be essentially equated with all things 'agricultural', with little evaluation of the wider rural economy, has lead to rural areas being seen 'largely as scenic backdrops to the drama of urban-based investment in infrastructure, industry and services' (ibid., p.4). Greer and Murray (ibid.) suggest that 'rural industrialisation struggles to shed its craft image, rural tourism remains folksy in appeal, while housing and service provision, together with infrastructure, have yet to overcome many of the more abrasive interpretations of the friction of distance' (p.4). The rural-urban dichotomy has been readily applied in the Irish context as it has allowed an ease of division in mapping socio-economic divisions at either end of the dichotomy with a 'relatively clear spatial distinction exist(ing) between urban and rural with two separate 'ways of life' coexisting in their respective spatial domains, with a certain modicum of interaction between them' (Boylan, 1992, p.18). This has undergone change with the emergence of restructured social and economic arrangements and has been replaced with a rural-urban continuum and the movement towards the urbanisation of society.

Although largely dismissed in terms of literature and research, the concept of a rural-urban dichotomy would still seem to play a significant role in the Irish psyche. An important step in Irish rural discourse would therefore be to overcome this idea of two (if not altogether separate) communities, the rural and the urban. This criticism is made because of the tendency by people and policy-makers alike to associate notions of community more readily with rural rather than urban ideology. Wilkinson (1992), recognised this tendency, and suggested that there was a renewed interest, not in the rural-urban dichotomy, but in what he termed the rural-urban variable. Citing Bradley and Lowe (1984), Wilkinson (1992) suggested that this renewed interest had been brought about by the rediscovery of 'locality' and the realisation that 'the restructuring of capital occurs in spatial perspective to no small extent on the local scene [and] thus, critical studies of local planning and decision making have come to focus on rural-urban variations and rural-urban relationships within given localities' (p.27). There has also been a renewed interest in the spatial arrangements of people and a growing awareness of a gap in well-being in the rural-urban dichotomy. It is these lines of inquiry which

Wilkinson suggests demand a 'new appraisal of the meaning of the rural-urban variable and a new look at the contribution of rural life to the well-being of society' (ibid., p.28).

In Irish literature there has been a predisposition to take it for granted that there is such a concept as 'rural' society, and that it is in some way different to 'urban' society. Perhaps the most significant (and debated/disputed) contribution was that of Americans, Arensberg and Kimball (1940) writing on *Family and Community in Ireland*. Focusing on a study of small farming in Co. Clare in the 1930s, this research emphasised the familial nature of the local form of farming as the basis for understanding the rural social system. This was much criticised for its suggestion that 'the rural' in the West of Ireland at that time could be generalised to the whole of Irish rural society (Tovey, 1992). Gibbons (1977) further suggested that 'on every score – the family, the mutual-aid system, the economic and cultural stability of the system, and its politics – their (Arensberg and Kimball) account ranges from the inaccurate to the fictive' (cited in Tovey, 1992). Despite this criticism, Arensberg and Kimball's generalised equation of the rural with farming is typical of Irish rural studies down through the years. Thus, whatever difficulties arise in defining rural today, for much of the previous century, the Irish definition seemed to take for granted that 'rural' meant agricultural, so that for any interpretation of the rural, explorations of farming must come first. The reasoning for this association is debatable, but it could be argued that the primary cause was the fact that most researchers in this area came from an agricultural science background, and furthermore there was a great deal of economic and political importance accorded to agriculture by the Irish State. The 'peasant model' as developed by Arensberg and Kimball dominated analysis of the rural, and the interpretation of rural life was made on the basis of the individual small-farm household organised along lines of gender and generation and the informal institutions of mutual support provided by the local community (Wilson, 1984, cited in Tovey, 1992).

Moving to the 1980s and following Ireland's accession to the EU in 1973, profound changes in all aspects of rural Ireland were evident. No longer was this small island economy shackled by past traditions of self sufficiency and cultural integrity; instead, it had become just a small region in the country called 'Europe'. Those who were still writing about rural affairs in Ireland now became preoccupied with 'documenting and analysing state development policy and structural trends in agriculture' (Tovey, 1992, p.101). Despite such preoccupation, a new agenda in terms of rural development discourses began to emerge. This new agenda attempted to reinterpret the fundamental concepts of community, rurality and development which Irish society had, prior to this, accepted almost unquestioningly. These fundamental changes have been in the declining overall importance of agriculture in rural areas and, in the areas where agriculture still plays a dominant role, its recognition more as a business rather than a 'way of life'. This change is an anathema to the previously-held traditional and historical notions of rural Ireland and its association with rural-based community and kinship (see Bull *et al.*, 1984). While statistics (see Commins and Keane, 1994) have shown that farmers are now in a minority amongst rural communities in most parts of Ireland in the 1990s, the notion of the declining economic and political power wielded by the farmers is probably misleading. Nevertheless, with such change in rural structures modifying the exclusive focus on farming, there is now more of a need in the 1990s to look at 'the rural' as a construction made up of a whole set of meanings, political and socio-cultural, a vision of rurality more accurately seen as a lived experience rather than a physical space.

This movement away from physical space to the notion of the rural as something of a lived experience is dwelt on in the next section. Drawing on literature relating to rural idylls and the experiences of living in an Irish rural space and culture, the argument is, that while there are common characteristics, the Irish 'rural' idyll is different (harsher) than its English counterpart and plays perhaps a greater role in the Irish psyche.

The rural idyll

Cloke and Milbourne (1992) suggest that at this stage 'the idea of a rural idyll is at best speculative' and that in current debates 'much more needs to be known about the degree to which it is important in representations of the rural; the varying nature of idyll [and] the relative significance of 'pro-rural' factors as opposed to 'anti-urban' factors' (p.359). The emergent academic interest in this area (Mingay (ed.), 1989; Short, 1991; Cloke and Milbourne, 1992; Cloke, 1995a) increasingly deals with the notion of diverse rural idylls being experienced differently. It is generally accepted that rural areas are not homogeneous and that the perceived idylls of rural lifestyles in one nation will not necessarily be replicated elsewhere (Cloke, 1995a). There is the conception that rural idylls are seen in a static, natural or sanitised way, which recreates past landscapes and objects rather than social relations. Jackson (1989) suggests that the rural is a cultural and landscape image, 'an ideological domain where meanings are contested, negotiated and experienced' (cited in Cloke, 1993, p.55). Cloke (1995a) argues that it is 'far too simplistic to attempt to understand the nature of rural life in a particular village in terms of one composite and commonly held construct of rural idyll' and that surely the 'everyday processes of in-migration, and of the 'sedimenting' in of different rounds of colonisers into a particular place mean that different versions of idyll are continually being brought to that place, and ageing with the experience of living there' (p.176).

Within this concept of in-migration (but more importantly in Ireland emigration), it is not only the experience (as Cloke suggests) of 'living there', but, in the case of Ireland, of living elsewhere, that fashions the perception and the realities which abound of rural Ireland. While popular images of the countryside often portray rural areas as a superior environment to that of towns and cities, there are other sides to Irish rurality, from exploitation in the sale of goods to attempts at manipulation of the psyche (see also Derounian, 1993).

Contrasting 'pictures'

The true 'picture' of the Irish countryside is far from the traditional view of the rustic idyll or a romanticised unchanging area: the terms in which its English counterpart is often depicted. While the English rural idyll depicts a kind of romantic beauty, pervaded by nostalgic traces of a rustic past, images of tranquillity and rose-covered cottages, the Irish depiction is often much harsher. Here too, there are images of thatched cottages, green fields, scenic beauty, friendliness and harmony, but there are also images of uncompromising and unfertile lands, wave-lashed coastlines, remote expanses of bog, signs of struggle, of famine, and of poverty. This depiction carries connotations of wildness, isolation and hardship sharply in contrast to the safeness and shelter of the more fertile village England. These images of contentment and isolation have permeated Irish rural discourses not only influencing policy makers but also being expressed, and in many cases vindicated, in literature and popular rural imagery. Implicit in idealised literary portraits of Irish rural life in the earlier years of this century was the assumption that 'a traditional culture still intact, inherited from a rich past, would surely compensate the Irish countryman for any discomforts he might be forced to endure in his humble but heroic condition' (Brown, 1985, p.67). In some ways many of the negative images of rural Ireland have been painted over by a more conservative, sanitised and rustic version. The much loved and frequently used depictions of whitewashed thatched cottages signifying the heart of Irish rurality, with its 'permanently burning turf fire as [an] image of its primeval vitality', tried but scarcely managed to mask the hardly idyllic experience of families raised in such houses where conditions were poor and overcrowding was commonplace (Healy, 1968). The social reality of rural Ireland was more dynamic and hardly as bucolic as has often been depicted.

People not place

Deprivation affects people not places and policies should be devised accordingly (Scott *et al.*, 1991). The power of popular rural imagery must be overcome if the level of poverty and deprivation in rural areas is to be recognised. Cloke and Milbourne (1992, p.359) suggested that the 'notion of problems may itself be undermined if particular representations of what rural life is like and should be like are dominant in the minds of relevant politicians, professionals and rural dwellers'. Cloke (1985) identified rural poverty in many under-developed areas as defying 'all current attempts at amelioration', suggesting that its concurrent environmental problems are only now receiving 'the emphasis achieved in developed areas'. McLaughlin (1986a, p.89) argued that the biggest obstacle facing rural policy makers in the latter half of the twentieth century is that of successfully challenging the 'popular images of rurality' and also of unravelling those images which have become 'woven into the fabric of the policies currently being advanced to solve the problems of rural deprivation which those very same images have helped to create'. Cloke and Milbourne (1992, p.359) suggested that the 'representation of 'problems' for rural residents have tended to emphasise political and economic questions relating to the distribution of income and of opportunities connected with houses and services [but this] does not explain how and why a particular set of structured opportunities may be experienced differently by different individuals and households'.

It is not just policy makers who do not 'see' deprivation in rural areas. In many instances rural dwellers may not see themselves as deprived and may 'prefer' their isolation. Cloke and Milbourne (1992, p.359) recognised that the ideas of deprivation or disadvantage can become a contradiction in terms 'both for those who do experience hardship (but will perhaps see this as an acceptable trade-off for the benefit of rural living, or will seek some reason to conceal or underplay the stigmatic acknowledgement of hardship) and for those who do not (and perhaps are anxious to reproduce the culture of an idyll by playing down any hardship that comes to their attention)'. McLaughlin (1986a, p.81) also recognised hidden deprivation, suggesting that those who were unable to manage in rural areas could only blame the 'inevitability of the geography of rural space whose solution would probably destroy the very qualities of the rural environment which all rural inhabitants currently enjoy and which, to some extent, must be considered as some compensation for whatever social or economic stress may exist'. This view was also referred to in the study conducted by McDonagh (1997) where the preference for 'living in a deprived part of the West of Ireland rather than in a deprived part of Dublin city', indicated how deprivation in the countryside can in some ways (and by some people) be seen as 'not all that bad' in comparison to deprivation in the city or urban environs.

In the remaining sections this vision of rural life and the differing notions of rurality which exist in Ireland are also bound up with notions of rurality that are circulated at various stratum from local, regional,

Thoughts on Rurality and Rural Ireland 63

national and international perspectives. It is these notions of rurality that continue to play a significant role in the Irish psyche and consequently influence the process, policy and practice of rural development in Ireland.

An Irish rural 'heritage'

Up to now this chapter has focused on rurality and rural idylls, here I will suggest that there is no Irish rural idyll. My argument is that the 'rural idyll' is largely an English construct and its Irish counterpart, with its unique cultural background, shares only superficial traits. It is my belief that these differing cultural experiences give rise to contrasting outlooks on rurality and rural life in general. For this reason, rather than an Irish rural 'idyll', this section will look at an Irish rural 'heritage'. Heritage may be an over-used term (as much in Irish vocabulary as in any other), but it is used here as it best covers the range of interpretations of rurality which exist at international, national, regional and local levels. The desire is not to find 'the rural' or 'the heritage' but to explore existing representations of rural Ireland, and the notions of rural heritage being circulated and reproduced. The dominant representation of an Irish rural heritage as a strong close-knit community with a healthy and carefree environment is examined, and the link between rurality and national identity explored, as suggested in rural areas like the West of Ireland being seen a 'repository of national identity and values' (Anon, 1994a, p.10).

The increasing fascination with heritage (see Hewison, 1987; Phillips and Tubridy, 1994) in Ireland (and in Europe) is described by Crouch (1994, p.93) as '(t)he allure of authenticity – something that is demonstrably grounded in history and is celebrated as such – (co-existing) with a desire for the non-authentic – something obviously 'plastic', that is enjoyed for its own sake'. This is supplemented by an increasing desire to discover one's roots, a factor which is very prominent in the Irish-American tourist industry and which undoubtedly is a useful tool in promoting Irish tourism. Crouch (ibid.) describes heritage as 'paradoxically [having] become effective both as historically rooted heritage, and as 'manufactured' heritage'. There is a search to experience a different 'other'; in some ways trying to be part of a spectacle or image, yet also sitting on the outside looking in: 'A traveller in search of the <u>real</u> Ireland ... craic agus ceol, the Connemara that the camera can never capture .... the silence of Carrauntoohill at dawn' (Cara, 1995, p.27, emphasis added).

Irish rural heritage can be approached from a number of vantage points. Although the 'Irishness' of today is largely fashioned by experiences over the last seventy years or so of independence, much of its identity and its heritage have been moulded by a British influence ('however unpalatable this may be to doctrinaire Irish-Irelanders' (Murphy, 1991, p.79)). These vantage points, which inevitably form the nucleus of most aspects of Irish life, are those of nationalism, language and religion. The popular nationalism of the last century sought a prosperous and independent nation and also established an iconography and symbolism (shamrocks, harps and Celtic crosses) which have become associated with patriotic feelings and sentiments. Literary figures and artists have, also promulgated the image of Ireland as a rural, almost pastoral nation. The vision of rustic dignity and rural virtue has been popularized in poems, paintings and on stage. Brown (1985, p.65) commented on how in the writings of 'Yeats and Synge, rural figures have been employed as images of wildness, pagan exuberance, earthy intuitive knowledge of deep-rooted things', celebrating what he describes as, 'a version of Irish pastoral, where rural life was a condition of virtue in as much as it remained an expression of an ancient civilisation, uncontaminated by commercialism in a belief that rural life constituted an essential element of an unchanging Irish identity'. The emotional thrust of Irish nationalism has been 'anti-urban, [and] inclined to see the real Ireland as exclusively rural and peopled by a peasantry who in essence were not only Gaelic-speaking but Catholic as well' (Lincoln, 1993, p.205). In this, the case of rural Ireland was even more important in its relations to Irish nationalistic ideals. For O'Connor and Cronin (1993, p.5) using the West of Ireland as representative of rurality suggest that '(t)he West was the wild, vigorous, anarchic opposite to the trim, organised, verdant richness of the Home counties. For Nationalist thinkers the West stood in opposition to urban industrial materialism and provided access to the Real Ireland (a notion still consecrated in postcards)'.

A second aspect intrinsic to Irish life was highlighted by the revolutionary generations of the 1960s who sought to restore the Irish language to its former place of dominance in an Ireland that was not only 'free but gaelic as well'. A commonplace belief in Irish culture was that 'Ireland without the Irish language was spiritually deficient, even impoverished' (Brown, 1985, p.62). With the Irish language surviving mainly in the Gaeltacht areas of western Ireland, attempts were being made to market the area for its 'unique character and culture'. In accessing the Irish past through language and culture, the Gaeltacht area is seen to be offering itself as a representation of true 'Irishness' with 'holidays to the Gaeltacht [being] developed and based on language, song, dance, folklore etc., to highlight the unique character of the area' (Ní Fhlatharta, 1994, p.1). Keane et al., (1993, p.407) also recognised this impending shift in emphasis from language/identity to language/economic asset, and suggested that local Gaeltacht communities were becoming more aware of the potential value of their linguistic and cultural assets and that 'many of the communities in the region see economic opportunities in the development of cultural tourism products [and] through this new awareness to build a better identity within the region which in turn can provide important support for the language'.

The third concept, perhaps the most prevalent 'outside' perception of Ireland, is that of a strongly dominated Catholic country, where religious beliefs and practice are intense. In Ireland the concept of religion is not simply a form of belief; more importantly it forms a dominant force within the social and political processes of the country. In fact it would have been quite acceptable to speak of 'Catholic' and 'Irish' in an interchangeable way, somewhat similar to the Irish perception of 'Protestant' and 'English'. In support of this view Murphy (1988, p.133) quotes Fr. Tom Burke (a noted Dominican preacher) who in 1872 made the following comment:

> (t)ake an Irishman – I don't care where you find him and you will find that the very first principle in his mind is 'I am not an Englishman because I am a Catholic!' Take an Irishman wherever he is found all over the earth, and any casual observer will at once come to the conclusion, 'oh, he is an Irishman, he is Catholic'. The two go together.

This affiliation of Catholicism with identity has been echoed throughout the nineteenth and twentieth century, as has been the correlation of Catholicism with nationalism: 'The man who is a good Catholic is a good Nationalist and the best Nationalists are to my knowledge the best Catholics too' (John Dillion, 1890, cited in Murphy, 1988, p.134).

In the Ireland of the 1990s, these former cornerstones of Irish identity have somewhat lessened in their influence. The process of an independent nation, although largely achieved, has been swallowed up in a 'Europe of the Regions'. The efforts to revive the Irish language have waned largely due to emigration and increased anglicising pressures and public apathy. The launch of Telifís na Gaeilge (now TG4) in October 1996 may represent a rung on the ladder to recovery or at least to the stabilisation of the Irish language, but because of its embryonic stage little conclusion can be drawn at this stage. The former dominance of Catholicism, although still high by European standards (approximately 96% of the population are Roman Catholic), has been replaced by an 'à-la-carte Catholicism (as opposed to) the former take-it-or-leave-it doctrinal menu' (Murphy, 1991, p.80). Despite these valid observations, the influence of these 'forces' in Irish rural life cannot be underestimated, and their significant leverage merits consideration throughout this book.

Scales of heritage

Rural areas in Ireland have formed a central component of the national identity (O'Connor, 1993) and the role of Ireland's rural heritage has been pivotal in its evolution. Looking at the different scales of circulation of

Irish rural heritage, the following evaluation (drawing on the works of Cloke and Milbourne (1992) and O'Connor (1993)), examines a number of different cultural influences that play a role in the changing lifestyles of people in rural areas. Cloke and Milbourne (1992) commented that not only were different meanings associated with the rural circulated and negotiated on a national scale, but they are also experienced on regional, local and individual scales. They concluded that within any particular rural space (residence, work, recreation), 'there will exist cultural constructs of rurality which combine different scales of received and circulated meanings and this diversity of constructs can be linked to different scales of circulation' (ibid., p.361). The issue of scale therefore is 'a useful starting point for interpreting variations of idyll and for recognising different levels of power relations associated with cultures of rurality' (Cloke, 1995a, p.176).

Internationally

In contrast to Wales, Scotland or England, it is at an international level that the scale of circulation of rural Ireland is more often than not expressed. It can be suggested that the images of Ireland have for the most part 'emanated from outside the country, or have been produced at home with an eye on the foreign (or tourist) market' (Gibbons, 1986, cited in O'Connor, 1993, p.69). The use of certain aspects of Irish culture, the Irish people, its landscape and history, has been constructed in a manner which offers people an 'escape from the pressures of modernity to the simplicity and authenticity of the pre-modern', a construction of 'Ireland and the Irish people as 'other' to the modern industrial metropolitan centres of Europe and the US' (ibid., p.76). The easiness with which the international scale fits into Irish rural discourses perhaps provides a yardstick for the one constant characteristic which dominates Irish history, that of emigration. The image conjured up by emigration is that of a haemorrhage of Irish rural youth, the rural 'brain drain' referred to by Walsh (1992a). Images of the Irish emigrant have changed over the years, from the days of the young Irishman 'leaving at the age of seventeen with no qualifications, a couple of pounds in his pocket, no addresses except for a vague notion that some of the lads have a room in Earls Court, wherever that is' (Coogan, 1975, p.148), to those young people of the 1990s who go abroad either for the 'craic' (enjoyment) or to gain some work experience, or those who just wish to escape the restrictions of their own communities (see Ní Laoire, 1995). The volume of emigrants leaving Ireland leads to the creation of various perceptions, by those most recent; those who are second and third generation emigrants (brought up on stories of 'what life was like in the old country', the main targets of 'roots' tourism); to those who buy holiday homes in Ireland in order to become 'real' participants in Irish culture, yet do not wish to live there permanently.

Recent emigrants, whether by choice or necessity, are only too aware of the social and economic problems they have left behind, and are under no illusions as to why they have left or had to leave (see Donovan, 1996). These emigrants differ to those of previous generations in their educational qualifications, social background and geographical origins. One of the most salient features of recent emigrants is their high level of educational qualifications. Walsh (1992a, p.31) suggested that there is a 'significant relationship between social mobility, education and migration which indicates that the propensity to emigrate among the upwardly mobile middle classes (41%) is twice as high as it is for those classified as downwardly mobile'. With higher education levels, there is also a desire for more rewarding employment and 'the most sophisticated and rewarding types of employment tend to be heavily concentrated in the major cities of the core economies' (ibid., p.31). The second or third generation Irish emigrants have different perceptions of what rural Ireland is like. They are usually a group who have been brought up on stories of leprechauns and shamrocks, on tales of struggle against the 'auld enemy', on stories of working with horse and cart. It is from such expectations that the concept of heritage management and policy has emerged as key growth areas in Ireland, with the creation of various heritage centres and theme parks, giving 'the visitor the impression of an immediate confrontation with the past – as if you were there' (O'Connor and Cronin, 1993, p.8). Surveys indicate that contemporary tourists expect to see Connemara (in the West of Ireland) maintained as a 'locale of romantic 'authenticity', as a place of unspoilt scenery and way of life [and] that locals will be tempted to adapt to visitors expectations'. The main danger is 'that Irish people will become spectators of their own history, existing for the entertainment of others rather than their own enlightenment' (ibid., 1993, p.8).

People who buy or build a holiday home in order to experience the 'real' Ireland and become part of the Irish culture (on a temporary basis) comprise the third category. This group is important because of their increasing numbers and their effect on rural Ireland. Examples of vibrant summer influxes and derelict winter villages in rural areas from Donegal to Kerry tell their own story. This frequently-occurring phenomenon can have a debilitating effect on local inhabitants who remain in such areas, and raise tension between the 'newcomers', the locals and the planning authorities. Such tension was highlighted in an article in one local newspaper dealing with planning permission, when it was suggested that 'Holiday Home Owners are Top Planning Objectors' (Anon, 1995a). Reinforcing this argument, the same issue was again raised at a regional meeting of the Irish Rural Link group (1994) when it was suggested that, 'in scenic areas local people cannot afford to buy houses because the cost is prohibitive. Foreigners can come in and buy up sites and houses pushing up prices and

68 Renegotiating Rural Development in Ireland

squeezing out the local people. There need to be more incentives to people building in rural areas to stay and live there' (Brady and NíChúinn, 1995, p.2). In this way, new rural dwellers can become not only a focus for tension within a community, but also an obstacle for further development as they often prevent any encroachment in to 'their' environment.

Nationally

At a national level there are a number of different representations of the rural. These range from the extremes of seeing the 'rural' as a problem-free, world of peace, tranquillity, with a close-knit community living in harmony with nature, to alternative images of poverty, low wages and unemployment. In Ireland the circulation of rural heritage is often firmly rooted in the importance of agricultural life. The farmer is seen as close to nature and as providing 'an alternative to the sins and pollution of urbanism' (Cloke and Milbourne, 1992, p.361). The rural is often seen as a 'refuge from modernity', with some rural areas being described as 'place(s) of unspoilt scenery and way of life' (O'Connor and Cronin, 1993, p.8). Crouch (1994, p.94) suggested that rural Ireland is promoted in the sense of 'home' but is seen also to offer an almost perfect 'other' for the tourist (Robert Flaherty's famous film of 1934, *Man of Arran* being symbolic of the wider process). This association between national identity, landscape and a sense of place has been located to the forefront of Ireland's attempts to revitalise and revivify the nation (Smith, cited in Nash, 1993). The notion of an Irish identity provides a number of diverse concepts, giving way to not just one identity, but a number of different representations of Irishness. For some this is based on the re-emergence of the Irish language, but for others there are a number of wider issues. Certain elements in Irish culture render it distinct from others, as for example the huge revival of traditional music, (note its association with internationally recognised groups such as U2), and the unprecedented interest in Irish dancing, (the Irish dance extravaganza entitled *Riverdance* received worldwide acclaim). Other distinctive areas include the continued popularity of gaelic football and the ancient sport of hurling, and despite the rival attractions of other sporting codes, its governing body, the Gaelic Athletic Association (GAA), has achieved unbridled success over the last century and today is perhaps one of the most influential organisations in rural and urban Ireland.

These images suggest the revival of past traditions, stem from a need for authenticity, and a desire to reconstruct past countryside images. Cloke and Milbourne (1992, p.362) have suggested that '(r)ural landscapes ... both material and imagined, continue to be landscapes of power', and that not only is rural heritage 'associated with the construction of particular ways of life', but it also can be bought and controlled. With this in mind,

Thoughts on Rurality and Rural Ireland   69

it is fair to suggest that wealth and power underlie the ideology of the heritage (idyll), and in a somewhat similar way the cultural notion of rural heritage can itself be powerful in that it can be used to promote or sell anything from houses, to cars or furniture. To confirm the significance of rural imagery at a national level, there were recommendations in 1928 regarding the design of the Irish coinage, with images of Irish animals and wildlife replacing the old traditional symbols of round towers and shamrocks. Although there were objections that such depictions were insufficiently 'christian' for the Irish nation (again highlighting the importance of religion), those in doubt were firmly 'persuaded that the images selected bore intimately on the rural nature of Irish life' (Brown, 1985, p.75). Ireland's coinage was subsequently issued in 1928 depicting its agricultural, rural and sporting life with images of a woodcock, a chicken, a pig with piglets, a hare, a wolfhound, a bull, a hunter, and a salmon. Past countryside images circulated at this level, are 'produced and reproduced in art, literature, television and radio programmes, commercial advertising, newspapers/magazines and academic texts' (ibid.), as well as 'being promulgated through 'country' organisations, the designers of homes, home furnishings, clothes and other products in which idyll can be commodified as taste or style' (Cloke, 1995, p.177).

Regionally and locally

The constructs of heritage which are circulated at regional and local scales are also important in understanding how rural areas and rural lifestyles are changed and structured. Gilbert's (1988) review of the new geographies of regions discussed three conceptualisations of regional specificity (cited in Cloke and Milbourne, 1992), namely:

- The region as a local response to capitalist processes;
- The region as a focus of identity, where specific sets of cultural relationships occur between groups of people or particular places; and
- The region as a medium for social interaction, where certain relationships occur which link individuals and groups together in society and which concern all aspects of life including the economic and the cultural.

The latter two concepts are important in understanding regional cultural constructs of the rural and can be relatively easily recognised. For the most part, rural regions have been widely examined in terms of contrast with the urban-industrial nature of other regions. Cloke (1995, p.178) suggests that even though:

Rural regions may well represent the spatial organisation of particular social processes associated with the mode of production, social divisions of labour and networks of accumulation and political domination, ... it is important to temper any potential reductionism here with a recognition that it will be the *interconnections* between identity, interaction and political economy which will characterise regional ruralities (original emphasis).

The prominent regional traits for rural Ireland (or at least those most frequently circulated) are suggestive of remote, self-contained worlds, with secluded villages where the inhabitants are mostly families who have lived in the area for generations, and who are often Irish-speaking. Rural areas are frequently depicted as 'place(s) of fundamental natural forces, of human figures set passively or heroically against landscapes of stone, rock and sea' (Brown, 1985, p.73). Today, many of these features would seem to have disappeared due to greater mobility and technology, but there is evidence of such images being circulated for different reasons, particularly where the 'traditional regional constructs of rural places are ... being reproduced, reintroduced and reinforced ... with particular regions ... becoming foci for political and cultural struggles' (Cloke and Milbourne 1992, p.363). In any event traditional regional constructs of rural places are changing especially in areas which have become increasingly associated with commodification for tourism and leisure purposes, and the creation of what Kiberd (1990) suggests is a lifestyle modelled on a 'Western leisure class'. Examples of such leisure promotions are often seen in the regionalisation of such features as literary figures, producing 'commodified regions', (for example, Bronte country, or Wordsworth country, in England). Similarly in Ireland there has been a huge increase in the popularity and 'marketing' of such places associated with literary and historical figures, such as 'Joyce's Dublin', and 'Yeats' Sligo', as well as the 'selling' of sights such as 'Pearse's Cottage' or 'Lynch's Castle'. This is just one type of commercial commodification, which helps to sustain a regional cultural consciousness in many areas perceived as rural. Such commodification however, can have adverse effects because attempts 'to promote a specific regional construction of the rural (or 'a country') may well involve attempts either to undermine dominant national constructs, or to compete with alternative regional constructs in the various discursive contexts over rurality' (Cloke 1995, p.179). Such dangers and their threat to national constructs were echoed by Kiberd (1990) when he put forward an Australian poet's description of some of the counties in Ireland as becoming: 'playgrounds for the wealthy which the mere Irish strive to keep up to scratch [resulting in] the cultural life of the nation seem(ing) less often geared to meet the people's needs and more often addressed to the whims of foreigners. The native elite even learn how to act like foreigners in their own country. Some advertisements (*Discover Ireland, its part of what you are – Bord Fáilte*) which might once have been beamed at transplanted exiles in America are now directed at the natives' (p.10). These types of regional constructions are intrinsically linked and further, are all powerful agents of political and cultural struggle and in the undermining of national constructs.

There is a further interpretation circulated at local level. Here, the individuals' response to localised constructions of heritage can stem from both their experiences of what they see as the meaning of country life, as well as from the different strategies – influenced by such things as class, gender, ethnicity – adopted for living in or enjoying rural places. In rural Ireland the local constructions of heritage are coloured by landscapes of picturesque villages surrounded by mountains, green fields and lakes. The social environment is characterised by overwhelming traits of friendliness, closeknit communities, and close family ties. Increasingly, in the last decade or so, there has been a concern with the apparent loss of community resulting from a drop in farm employment. In the absence of alternative sources of work, there has been an exodus from rural areas by 'traditional' dwellers, followed by a huge influx of city-dwellers. Many see these newcomers as attempting to impose their lifestyles on their respective areas. Such conflicts can lead to notions of who is welcome or who belongs in a rural community, 'thereby reproducing and reinforcing processes of socio-cultural marginalisation' (Cloke, 1995, p.180). This reinforcing of divisions within rural communities was highlighted in the tensions and disputes which have arisen between new rural dwellers and those native to their rural communities, particularly in regard to development and issues such as planning permission for houses (see for example Anon, 1995a; Brady and NíChuinn, 1995).

Conclusion

In drawing together these discourses there have been attempts in recent literature to align current themes in post-modern and post-structural thinking with that of rurality as a social construct (Cloke and Goodwin, 1993; Halfacree, 1993). This seeks to deconstruct the 'rural' and in so doing analyse different discourses and representations of rurality. Halfacree (1993), examining the contrasting ways of dealing with objects in the world suggested that rather than a singular academic discourse, discourses on rurality should be routed through lay discourses with a greater input being allowed by everyday people in efforts to influence academic and policy debates. Falk and Pinhey (1978) suggested that rural social scientists should take as much blame as any other, in neglecting the ordinary person's view of the world, 'leading to theoretical-empirical myopia' while Halfacree (1993, p.32) argued that, '(l)ay discourses are ... not to be regarded as rooted in a probable myth but should be seen as interpretative repertoires derived from a disembodied but none-the-less real social representation of the rural'. Suggesting that, if the rural is to be accepted as a social representation, then it is all the more essential that ideals be routed through lay discourses, Halfacree intimated that even by doing this, there would be no expectation that people's ideas on rurality would fit nicely together or that they would have a clear, or well-structured image of 'the rural'. He concludes that the main problem of current literature on the rural is a failure to distinguish between the rural as a distinctive type of locality and the rural as a social representation – 'the rural as space and the rural as representing space' (ibid., p.34).

A number of questions arise from the changing constructs of rurality, from the survival of 'former' rural areas as they are being increasingly looked at in new socio-economic functional ways, to the new political-economic interpretations which may be seen as inimical to the survival of the category 'rural'. In dealing with rural as a social construct, there is an attempt to state the importance of rurality, but as a social rather than a geographical construct. One can empathise with Dewey (1960) when he suggests that the only definition that seems to be agreed upon by writers on rural or urban topics are that in some vague way the terms rural and urban are related to country and city, to community variations in size and density of population; yet even at this level what is meant by country, city or size is very much open for debate. The most alarming facts are that rural areas in most parts of the world face a very uncertain future (Cuddy and Ó Cinnéide, 1990; Ó Cinnéide, 1992a; Ó Cinnéide, 1992b). There does not seem to be in any country (least of all in Ireland), a broad vision of the future for rural areas. Rural areas are suffering from depopulation, increasing counter-urbanisation and human resource deficits, yet there are few strategies to plan a future direction, either socio-economically or environmentally. Two mutually exclusive visions of the countryside, one as the green and pleasant land that people visit and fantasise about, and the other as a place where people live and work, should not be allowed to develop. Rural areas can not be viewed in isolation, but must be seen as the concern of rural and urban dweller alike.

Such debates highlight the importance of a cultural dimension in the conceptualisation of the rural and in the symbolic importance of rurality. Rural areas are seen to have multiple meanings and can not be characterised in a homogeneous way. Rural communities can no longer be seen as isolated, self contained or bounded units, and the rural is not merely a physical space but a socially and culturally constructed discourse inflected by various kinds of individual and collective thought and action. What is also apparent is that the conceptuality of the 'rural' plays an important role in the Irish psyche. Indeed, much of the social and cultural conservatism prominent in Irish rural discourses is due to the significant weight attached to nationalism, language and religion in Irish society. Rural Ireland has been characterised not only as a 'fund of moral and social values – a potential model of harmony, compared with the conflicts that were tearing society apart' (Mormont, 1990, p.23) but also is seen as a 'badge of national identity [and] a mark of national distinctiveness'. Consequently while the academic debate on rurality in England seems firmly entrenched in social constructions, the debate in Ireland is still somewhat in the grip of the traditionalists and still encourages in many ways, the equating of rural with agriculture. Many of the debates on rural areas and rural development seem more likely to be marshalled by the CAP and price support systems, rather than cited in discourses of isolation, marginalisation and hidden rural poverty. It is however the moulding of these issues, through conflict between the maintenance of a 'traditional' Ireland and the increasing pressures of modernisation, which are leading to a redefining of the rural in Ireland.

4 Deconstructing Development – Irish Style!

The dream of Development is dead for many people across the world – whether Rwanda, Mexico or the West of Ireland. We have just completed three development decades – 60s, 70s, 80s. All people were to be rescued from poverty and marginalisation during these decades. This did not happen but instead the development myth robbed the poor and weak of their skilled subsistence living and left them either destitute or slaves to the economy. Broken individuals, families and communities are leading more and more people to turn their backs on the economic systems that have dominated them and are beginning to create their own local economies (Bohan, 1994, p.2).

Recent literature (Harriss, 1982; Buller and Wright, 1990; Boylan, 1992; Cuddy, 1992; Commins and Keane, 1994; Crush, 1995; Escobar, 1995; Munck and Fagan, 1995) has highlighted the important conceptual framework that development provides for understanding and evaluating rural change. In the previous chapter, attempts to deconstruct the rural have shown a continuous and difficult debate. This chapter moves further into the debates that feed into, and compound, the difficulties associated with the formulation of rural development in Ireland and examines the extent to which rural development 'process' and 'practice' have evolved in terms of the changing relations between the state and the private sector. The context is set by the opening quote from Fr. Harry Bohan, which links Third World development discourses (for example Crush, 1995, Escobar, 1995) with First World development discourses (for example Buller and Wright, 1990; Hoggart, 1990; Commins and Keane, 1994; Hoggart *et al.*, 1995). It is important to draw from these literatures (at least in some small way) which up to now have been largely kept apart, to understand the fundamental issues that concern rural development in Ireland. A number of questions will be raised including: what rural development means in an Irish context; whether current policies do enough to further development goals; where local communities fit into the development process, and whether there is a 'new' approach to rural development emerging. There will be an examination of development both as a 'process' (that is essentially being judged in terms of difference between developed and underdeveloped regions or countries), as specifically targeted policies and, how development is increasingly being seen as 'spectacle'. This chapter helps break down the traditionally sectoral ways of evaluating rural development practices, so that important connections between community development and other sectors of rural development can be realised.

Defining development

> Development has captured the centre stage of history. This ambiguous process is often depicted as the crucible though which all societies must pass and if successful, emerge purified: modern, affluent, and efficient (Goulet, 1971, p.13).

Development as a concept is impossible to define. For the most part, development has become part of everyday language where the use of the term is taken for granted, a somewhat unconscious acceptance of a particular point of view which leads to almost generalised universal usage (almost all of us know what development is until we are asked to explain it!). Recent literatures (Buller and Wright; 1990; Kearney *et al.*, 1994; Lee, 1994; Munck and Fagan, 1995) have all put forward the idea that development is more than just economic growth but is instead a multi-dimensional process. Development does suffer from being associated with the ideological fickleness of words such as 'progress' and 'revolution', yet Buller and Wright (1990) argue for using development as a term to describe specific processes of betterment and positive change. Munck and Fagan (1995, p.110) suggest that while development holds a central place in many debates, it is seldom deconstructed 'it is a discourse made up of a web of key concepts which are simply taken for granted in both its conservative and radical guises. Development is an amoeba-like concept – denoting everything and nothing'.

The debate on what exactly constitutes 'development' thus continues. From Welch's (1984) suggestion of it being a 'catch-all term' to Perroux's (1983, p.1) paradox of 'the desire for progress and mistrust of its consequences', a definition remains elusive. Writers such as Bury (1955), Redfield (1970) and Wallman (1977) describe development philosophically, as something which implies evolution towards some ultimate good (all these notions being specific to particular times and places), while Goulet (1971, p.19) indicates the important relationship between development and the concept of power, suggesting that development implies '(i)mages of the good society, prescriptions for obtaining it and symbols for generating enthusiastic allegiance to it [but] above all ... it deals with power'.

The power-development relationship is reiterated in Escobar's (1995, p.213) reflection on development as 'an apparatus that links forms of knowledge ... with the deployment of forms of power and intervention, resulting in the mapping and production of ... societies'. Perroux (1983, p.13) argues for <u>new</u> development which is 'global', 'integrated' and 'endogenous', a concept which has to do with 'man as subject and agent'. Goulet (1971, p.13) suggests that development is something which 'covers the entire gamut of changes' by which a social system operates in its movement from a 'condition of life widely perceived as unsatisfactory in some way towards some condition regarded as 'humanly' better'. Geertz (1963) in his writings on Indonesia tried to determine the conditions of such a move from an 'unsatisfactory' way of life, and referred to patterns generally associated with a developed economy, including '(a)lterations in the system of social stratification, in world view and in ethos, in political and economic organisations, in education, and ... in family structure ... the commercialisation of agriculture, the formation of non-familial business concerns, the heightened prestige of technical skills *vis-à-vis* religious and aesthetic ones, and industrialisation [have] become ... the primary political goals of the nation as a whole'.

In the 1940s and early 1950s, development was perceived as an effort to replicate the West (First World countries). As interpreted by Third World countries, this involved a transition from a predominantly traditional, to a more 'modernised' and technologically advanced society. Bruton (1985) argued that this concept had an adverse effect on the growth of development theory and '(w)ith only limited exceptions, in both the literature and in practice, development has come to mean a replication of the West [and] the equalisation of development with westernisation [has] impeded the construction of an authentic development theory'.

Escobar (1995, p.211), reflecting on the high degree of development and the elegant discourses of the 1960s when development was chiefly a 'matter of capital, technology and education, and the appropriate policy and planning mechanisms to combine these elements successfully', suggests that while many consider development to be dead, or to have failed miserably, 'few viable alternative conceptualisations and designs for social change are offered in its place'. The spectre of development continues to be regarded on the one hand as an aspect of modernisation and a movement towards 'economic and social modes of existence characterised by relatively high levels of material living and rational control over [the] environment' (Goulet, 1971, p.14), and on the other hand, being described as historical, diverse, complex, contradictory and a central feature of all human conditions, a 'process of becoming and a potential state of being [which] would enable people in societies to make their own histories and geographies under conditions of their own choosing' (Lee, 1994, p.128).

Agazzi (1988, p.13) equated the concept of progress with development in that they both indicate a change in a forward direction, 'a change that is not the expression of a single modification in time, but rather of a modification in the positive sense, of an improvement'. He acknowledged the misleading nature of forward movement suggesting that there is 'an unwillingness to admit that, once begun, the path of progress can sometimes take a reverse turn' (ibid.). This idea reinforces the notion that the development process (especially in the area of economic growth) in many instances may benefit some more than it does others. Further, it can lead to increased economic and social disparity within and between different groupings of people who are involved in, or indeed left out of, the same process. Thus, development can be seen as an expression of a process of accumulation and growth with no real pre-established direction.

Our intuitive way of looking at development as change and progress, its economic definition of a means of increasing GNP, coupled with the either conscious or unconscious way we equate development with Westernisation, has made it difficult to formulate or achieve a genuine model of development. Lee (1994) rounding on such intuitions, raises several objections against the conventional meanings given to development, especially those which define it in terms of a number of outputs without actually specifying the way in which such outputs are produced, or clarifying the social relationships between them. Lee's targets include such indices as the HDI (Human Development Index) and GNP per capita figures (it is worth noting that the USA has the worst HDI of the industrialised countries). Lee finds a further difficulty with the conventional meaning of development in that it is interpreted in a non-dialectical and ahistorical manner and that an '*a priori* definition of development is made from a very narrow base and is then imposed upon the diversity of the situations and conditions of change of human existence' (ibid.). This concept of development, with its contradictory, often perverse courses of change, is therefore far from easy to define. While it would be unfair not to credit Western society with the wide range of authentic values, such as equality, liberty, justice, democracy, respect for human dignity, dissemination of education which it has tried to generate (Agazzi, 1988), Hettne (1990, p.2) warns that '(t)here can be no fixed and final definition of development, only suggestions of what development implies in particular contexts'.

The process of development

In the light of recent literature (Hoggart and Buller, 1987; Buller and Wright, 1990) the main difficulties of interpreting development as a 'process' can be seen to include: determining the length or final stage of the process; exploring whether the notion of betterment is a necessary part of a process; outlining the specific targets of development (for example, what they are, their organisation, and their conflicts); and evaluating development as a means to some end. Development is often judged in terms of the differences between so called 'under-developed' and 'developed' countries. Ball (1974) suggests that development is a *gestalt* process, consisting of a number of interactive elements which, on their own, may not constitute development (cited in Buller and Wright, 1990). These elements are essentially the means by which the process operates, and may not be of any great consequence individually. Hoggart and Buller (1987, p.26) suggest that development must be a sustainable process which changes not simply people's physical conditions but also their control over such conditions, whereby 'outside aid can certainly help in this process, but if, on the withdrawal of such aid, people are incapable of sustaining the improvements that have happened then what occurred was not development but a short-term improvement in living conditions'. This appraisal raises the idea that the development process is a learning one, and that in order for 'true' development to take place there must be changes in both the mental and material conditions that reinforce these ideals.

The equation of development with some form of 'betterment' can very often be misleading. Many so-called 'developments' although bringing short-term gains can often, in the long-term, be disadvantageous (for example, there was heated debate on the siting of an Interpretative Centre in an environmentally sensitive, yet employment-hungry area of Co. Clare). The association of development with 'betterment' does not necessarily bring positive results; as Brookfield (1975, p.xi) suggests, '(d)evelopment of the poorer countries of the world may even make their people poorer, but it is still development'. This contradiction confirms that development is very often dependent on one's viewpoint and ideological standing. Buller and Wright (1990, p.4), acknowledging this, suggest that there are however common threads, which run through the development process. These they identify as being improvements in people's well-being, gains in people's access to the means to sustain that improvement and improvements in self-determination. A possible result of this process might be that, having gained a say in their future, people might then reject any further progress, while others may actually become anti-developmental. For example, new rural residents may object to others 'moving in' on the grounds that it will spoil their view or the surrounding environment (see, Brady and NíChúinn, 1995; NíFhlatharta, 1995).

In terms of the targets of development, it has been argued that 'as a process of social and economic improvement, development must act upon defined groups or classes of people, rather than either single individuals or 'things' (Buller and Wright 1990, p.4). Copp (1972, p.519) suggests that the 'ultimate target of rural development is people. It is not infrastructure, it is not factories, it is not better education, or housing or even communities'. These are only means, and without a 'people impact' they are not sufficient. A number of points are raised in such an approach, in particular the need for the correct identification of so-called marginalised groups. All to often a village or a parish is mistakenly seen as a close-knit or homogeneous community with shared characteristics and interests. This is rarely the case, and false assumptions of community can confuse, and undermine, the developmental process (see Murdoch and Day, 1995). Another issue lies in the correct identification of marginal or disadvantaged groups, and the realisation that 'improvements in the well-being and self-determination of one group may directly or indirectly hinder similar improvements in another' (Buller and Wright, 1990, p.4). This dispels the ideal that development should be judged by the degree to which it entails some form of achievement, as this would imply the necessity of identifying the end-state of a developmental process, as well as attaining the particular means to such an end. Buller and Wright (1990, p.5) suggest that such an accomplishment would be both 'personally and ideologically value-laden'. Ward and McNicholas (1998) also urge caution particularly with regard to how the notion of rural or community is constructed by state agencies. These authors question whether 'particular constructions of 'rural communities' in specific localities involve not only different representations of rurality but also particular ideas about who counts as part of 'the rural community' and what counts as the community interest' (ibid., p. 38).

In considering the concept of development, there is therefore a need to adopt a multidimensional perspective that takes into account the role of cultural values in establishing priorities. Further, a belief is emerging that it is 'constructive to view rural development as a broad notion, encompassing all important issues pertinent to the individual and collective vitality of rural people and places' (OECD, 1990, cited in Kearney *et al.*, 1994, p.16). Such an encompassing ideal involves education, environment, public services, and capacity for leadership, governance and cultural heritage. This viewpoint dispels the common assumption, too often associated with Irish rural development, that development is merely the adoption of some project, with the objective of obtaining some gain, usually in economic terms – in essence a development 'spectacle'. Political-speak increasingly focuses on participation, inclusion and empowerment but from the entrenched paternalistic nature of Irish government, there may be a tendency to involve only key actors (rural professionals) in the governance of rural areas (see Chapter 6). Kearney *et al.*, (1994, p.16) expanding on this idea, suggest that development is a process 'by which is meant the creation of social products such as upgraded local leadership, a culture of enterprise and innovative action, or the enhanced capacity of people to act in concert, purposefully and effectively so as to cope with the threats and opportunities they face'. This process cuts across various sectors, operates at different levels and begins from a number of starting points. Starting with local conditions (as it is out of these conditions that change will occur), Keane (1996, p.5) suggests that the particular emphasis on actors will depend on '(a) where the area is at in terms of factors like the strength and diversity of the local economy, its level of social infrastructure, its institutional capacity and the degree of social cohesion present in the area, and (b) the goals and objectives that are set as part of the proposed development actions'. While this hierarchy of goals (quality of life; social infrastructure; institutional capacity and social coherence) is seen as important in the context of creating a development process, rural development discourse does often appear to suggest that people can invent their own path to development. Thus, while area-based approaches are currently in favour, 'there is little evidence that the approach to problem analysis and policy design has been adequately worked out' (ibid., p.4).

Why rural development?

> What after all is rural development? Is it a field of study and research? Is it a form of state intervention to promote the well-being of rural people, or is it something which is happening anyway no matter what the academics or the bureaucrats do? (Best, 1983, p.27).

There seems to be an unconscious acceptance within Ireland that rural development belongs in the realm of government agencies and policy makers. Victim of an over-association with agricultural development, (like its UK counterpart), as a research focus it has '(s)uffered from a narrow scale of analysis, a lack of sufficient generalisation and an over concentration on the effects rather than the causes of social and economic change' (Buller and Wright, 1990, p.1). In recent years there has been however a shift from looking at rural development as an adjunct of agricultural policy to seeing it as an area of policy concern in its own right (see Shortall, 1994). The challenge lies in breaking down the traditionally sectoral ways of looking at rural development processes and as Buller and Wright (1990, p.2) suggest, making the 'explicit connection between different sectors of rural change, notably agriculture, rural community development and other implicitly rural development policies'. There is no fixed definition of what rural development is, only interpretations of what it can or must do what it excludes and includes. Jasma *et al.* (1981) define rural development as 'an overall improvement in the economic and social well-being of rural residents and in the institutional and physical environment in which they live' (cited in Shortall, 1994, p.235). Buller and Wright (1990) recognising rural development as a key concept in contemporary rural studies suggest that while it may suffer from ideological fickleness or be seen as 'a lazy thinker's catch-all term' (Welch, 1984) there is a need for what they term a tentative definition. This tentative definition professes that 'development is an ongoing and essentially interventionist process of qualitative, quantitative and/or distributional change leading to some degree of betterment for groups of people' (Buller and Wright, 1990, p.3).

As a concept, rural development has a long history and is generally seen as a continuous process (no country can say that it has achieved rural development) which must adapt to changes in both circumstances and aspirations in policy, practice and research. Entering an era where it has become more fashionable than ever for political leaders to talk of rural development, the credibility of earlier development strategies is now being questioned. Some of the main objectives of rural development have been to reduce inequalities in income and employment, improve quality of life and access to public goods and services, and alleviate poverty. Harriss (1982, p.15) has suggested that the term rural development refers to a 'distinct approach to interventions by the state in the economies of underdeveloped countries [and developed ones] and one which is at once broader and more specific than agricultural development [and] it may also be used ... to refer to processes of change in rural societies not all of which involve action by governments'. Rural development has also been described as a process of endless variety, having as its main aim 'the overall balanced and proportionate well-being of rural people' (Poostchi 1986, p.1). Factors of influence include economic, social and educational levels, as well as communication levels between institutions and people involved.

The rise in popularity of rural development is described by Lea and Chaudhri (1983) as 'mainly symptomatic of the failure of technocratic and growth strategies pursued by most developing countries in the 1950s and 60s'. The economic growth of the period 1950–60 did not, as perceived, 'trickle-down' to the poorest sections of the community. Most development policies were found to be benefiting the rich and local elite, with a steady increase in poverty and inequalities in income. The late 1970s warranted a move away from the pre-1970s belief that development implied urbanisation and industrialisation. No longer would it be sufficient, for example, for Irish governments to build factories or industrial parks in areas of Connemara or along the coast of Mayo, and then claim that these areas were being successfully developed. Rural development could no longer be limited to increasing production, raising productivity, increasing employment and mobilising what land, labour and capital were available (ibid., 1983). Poverty and inequality had also to be reduced, and quality of life issues and active participation in decisions were imperative to successful rural development. Rural economies were seen as not merely part of the regional or national sector but as an important element in the international arena. City and countryside have become inextricably linked in functional and financial terms. Despite the fact that there is no great consensus (even amongst EU members) as to what can be described as rural (see Chapter 3), the challenge facing rural development policies is one of trying to improve the social and economic activities of rural areas, while trying to safeguard their natural resources and heritage.

Why intervene in rural areas?

While there is no common strategy, the broad rural development goals of

EU Member States are described as being both economic and societal with 'the development and/or protection of key national elements of the built and natural environment in rural areas' (OECD, 1993, p.16). As indicated earlier, when a rural development approach is conceived in Ireland it is regarded mainly as an interventionist process, with efforts mostly in the context of public policy to moderate market-led changes. The question therefore arises: why intervene? How will an increasingly dominating urban society benefit from helping to alleviate rural problems? Should not all areas of society be left to their own economic devices and why, as many would argue, should public monies be used to subsidise rural communities? In order to answer some of these questions it might first be prudent to suggest that it is a misconception that rural and urban societies exist independently of each other; it is necessary to recognise that rural and urban societies must be viewed holistically (see Ó Cinnéide, 1992b; Boylan, 1992; Wilkinson, 1992). Nevertheless, while this may appear quite rational, it could prove much more difficult in practice.

Many commentators (Cuddy, 1991; Wilkinson, 1992; Commins and Keane, 1994) suggest that despite many arguments against rural development, there are valid reasons for undertaking it. As Wilkinson (1992, p.25) argues, 'rural development is everybody's business, not simply the business of the world's small, weak cadre of rural advocates' and it would be naïve at best for any policy intervention to emphasise *the rural* or *the urban*. Wilkinson (ibid., p.26), consulting the works of Deavers (1990) in his writings on the United States, suggests that there are three valid reasons for rural development:

- Economic efficiency, where it can be realistically assumed that not taking advantage of rural resources and the opportunities for profit-making in the countryside would be widely seen as a form of negligence;

- Equity, as in all pursuits in society there are inequalities in distribution from which Wilkinson suggests the 'tension between rising expectations and lagging fortunes can undermine societal integration' (ibid., p.26); and

- The need to care for the environment in which we live. Here, Deavers suggests the argument is based on society's interest in being certain that rural land and resources are properly maintained and used wisely and that all members of society have a stake in the stewardship of rural areas (a current attempt would be the REPS introduced in Ireland).

Taking these arguments on board, the need for rural intervention appears justified. This justification should be carefully balanced with measures that are practical and economically defensible. As Wilkinson (ibid., p.26) suggests, 'there are equally valid [and perhaps] stronger reasons for not having a rural development policy'. He argues that there is a school of thought that 'modern governments, being committed above all else to exploitation of resources for profit, conspire with investors to keep rural communities in a dependant and underdeveloped state' (ibid., p.27). From this point of view, the challenge for rural development is ever more demanding. Assuming we accept that there is sufficient justification for rural development, it then becomes necessary to examine the ways in which rural development is thrust on a waiting society. In this context, the role of development agencies and the notion of development as specifically targeted policies will be explored in the next two sections.

The development milieu

Deconstructing the representations of Ireland (see Chapter 2), Crush's (1995, p.14) suggestion that 'the primary element in development narrative is a setting of the geographical stage' is reflected in Munck and Fagan's (1995) observations concerning Ireland's developmental position, and their sense that Ireland is ill-defined by its peripherality. They suggest that such ill-definition is an exercise in tautology whereby 'Ireland is excluded from the development process because it is peripheral, and Ireland is peripheral because it is excluded from the development process' (ibid. p.111). Escobar (1995) and Crush's (1995) argument that the representations of development as 'never the disease only the cure ... with a remarkable capacity for forgiving its own mistakes and reinventing itself as the remedy for the ills it causes' (Crush, 1995, p.16), allied to its ability to create abnormalities ('the poor', 'the illiterate', 'the landless') before treating or reforming them, present many parallels with Irish development discourses. The most obvious is in the representation of many rural areas in terms of remoteness, isolation and deprivation, and in the state's attempts to rectify such disparities through various rural development programmes and strategies (for example, LEADER – see Chapter 6). Consequently, Munck and Fagan (1995) have suggested that the development model in Ireland is extremely weak and in need of reconstruction and is allied to the promotion of democratic involvement. Munck and Fagan (ibid.) further dismiss the current application of Mjoset's (1992) ideas of a 'vicious circle' of underdevelopment as merely the application of Third World development perspectives to the Irish case (cited in Breathnach, 1995). While this seems somewhat rash, their argument that 'it is indicative of the parochialism of much of the development debate in Ireland that there is little reference to the long-standing international discussion on the relationship between development and democracy' (ibid., p.113) is significant. It is this relationship, encompassing political preconditions and the concept of genuine self-sustaining development, that is important and the necessary (but missing) element of development discourse in rural Ireland.

The transformation of development into outcomes requires a planning system to overcome what Keane (1996, p.1) describes as the 'large gap that typically exists between the language of theory (with its precision, boundaries and objectivity) and that of practice (with its fluidity, instability and subjectivity)'. Such a system involves changes from centralisation to decentralisation, from top-down to bottom-up. While there are no guaranteed systems, Friedmann (1987) identified four different concepts of planning: policy analysis; social mobilisation; social learning and social reform (cited in Kearney *et al.*, 1994). Policy analysis, promoted in the 1950s-60s, relied on centralised top-down strategies; its opposite, social mobilisation (1970s) concentrated on participation and negotiation, while social learning and social reform are sandwiched between both, essentially learning through participation, with only gradual change over time. Veggeland (1991) has suggested a circular motion of transition from rationalist, centralised planning to negotiational, local planning, leading to what Amdam (1992) suggests would be a planning system influenced by delegation, decentralisation and deregulation (cited in Kearney *et al.*, 1994).

Uphoff (1993, p.607), describing the attributes of the last three decades, suggested that while the 1960s and to a lesser extent the 1970s were dubbed the 'development decades', and the 1980s the 'decade of debt and disillusionment', the 1990s will be written about as the 'decade of deregulation, democratisation, and decentralisation', or possibly, 'the decade of disorder, disinvestment and decline'. In order to avoid the latter scenario, Uphoff suggests the need to create a 'positive synergy among the state, the market and civil institutions, [and a] need to understand how these alternative channels for raising economic, social and political productivity can be made to function better, respectively and collectively' (p.607). The widening gap between the state and the private sector has in recent years led to greater enthusiasm for the creation of voluntary organisations, non-governmental organisations and grassroots organisations. References to grassroots organisations however are more rhetorical than rigorous and are generally associated with 'bottom-up' development rather than with the 'top-down' approach characteristic of decision-making in Ireland. Uphoff and Esman (1974, cited in Uphoff, 1993) argued that to suggest grassroots organisations and non-governmental organisations can make important contributions to rural development in the 1990s and beyond, does not mean that they are inherently or invariably superior to state or market alternatives. The 'populist' fallacy, they argue, is equally as mistaken as the 'paternalist' fallacy when it comes to assessing the virtues of grassroots or non-governmental organisations. These organisations, while being limited (in terms of resources etc.) or even flawed channels for promoting development, do however deserve more attention that they have received. Citing examples from Malawi, Haiti, Pakistan, Kenya, Peru and elsewhere,

Uphoff (1988) suggests that there is growing evidence that 'working with and through collective action organisations at local levels can produce improvements in productivity and well-being more far-reaching than the stereotype that local efforts benefit only a few communities or a few families'. Essentially this would be part of a movement toward a system of governance where the government within the system acts more in a role of 'catalytic agent' (see Stoker, 1998) or 'facilitator/co-ordinator' (this will be explored more fully in Chapter 6).

Parallel to the growth of grassroots organisations, the role of rural development agencies has also long been at the heart of rural development policy in both Ireland and Britain. Predominantly, such agencies are founded on policies of 'financial intervention and infrastructural provision as the means of overcoming the social and economic ills of marginalisation' (Buller and Wright, 1990, p.7). In today's rural world the efficacy and objectives of such agencies are continually being questioned, as broad-based community input, into the planning and implementation process and a greater focus on change from within the rural community become more common (see Bryant, 1992). While there is general acceptance that societies do not benefit equally in terms of social and economic change, and that rural society, particularly those on the periphery of the capitalist economy, have been 'left behind' (see Buller and Wright, 1990), there is equal recognition of the need for governments and state agencies to tackle such disparities. In this sense many development initiatives in rural areas imply policies or programmes defined by financial incentives or interventions; they are part of a development 'spectacle'. Just how successful these programmes are is open to debate, as indeed is the whole concept of what determines 'success'.

The writings of Buller and Wright (1990) provide a brief evaluation of some of the British development agencies that highlight some similarities with Ireland. Perhaps their most notable suggestion is that the illogicality of state investment in rural areas is often outweighed by the fact that, in the majority of cases, private sector capital is not overtly threatened and any potentially disruptive public response from such areas is overcome with little direct capital involvement. Williams (1985) suggested that the establishment of the Highlands and Islands Development Board (HIDB) was exactly such an attempt to defuse growing devolutionist pressures (cited in Buller and Wright, 1990). British development policy has been directed mainly through three rural development agencies; the Rural Development Commission (RDC), the Development Board for Rural Wales (now Mid-Wales Development) and the HIDB (now Highlands and Islands Enterprise or HIE). Such agencies were built on the assumption that underdevelopment was solvable, being merely a matter of structural and resource disadvantage, and that the 'knock-on' effect of development policies would lead to growth in these areas (Buller and Wright, 1990).

The process of factory growth and job creation, like its Irish counterpart, while 'doing something' rarely had a sufficient knock-on effect to halt rural service decline. The role of these Boards is changing however, not only in response to government prompting, but also due to intimations of resource-cutting and possible terminations. The emphasis is now shifting away from 'grant-aid' to 'marketing-aid'.

Further changes in policy directions have also been made within rural communities, with a movement towards what Bryant (1992) labels 'sustainable community development'. Cloke and Laycock (1981) suggested there was a movement away from large macro-planning initiatives to development policy being put in the hands of small-scale, community-wide organisations operating closely with the voluntary sector (cited in Buller and Wright, 1990). This, as Varley (1991a, p.84) suggests, may be an attempt by governments to push responsibility for 'local development and employment onto localities themselves'. Nevertheless it seems to point towards a new phase or focus of development where changes are not only required within rural communities, but also in long-term planning. The culmination of this is likely to be a more decentralised approach and more effective partnerships between government and community sectors.

Development discourse therefore, despite enormous continuity over time, changes its language, strategies and practices. This change is due in no small part to development's reciprocal relationship with shifts in 'who holds power and who dominates whom' (Crush, 1995, p.7). Further, it is the suggestion here that development in Ireland is travelling on two paths. The first path lies in the possibility of a shift from a paternalistic Ireland to one where new social movements and grassroots groups search for alternative ways of organising societies and economies. This signifies a situation whereby development in Ireland (and elsewhere) is entering a different domain in which 'the 'natural' need to develop is suspended and in which communities can experiment with different ways of organising societies and economies' (Escobar, 1995, p.215). Colcough and Manor (1993) acknowledge this shift by suggesting that while the state has traditionally been seen as the main conductor and conduit of development, more recently there have been changes which suggest that the state is perceived and presented as the main obstacle to development (cited in Munck and Fagan, 1995). As such, a call for the rejection of the entire paradigm becomes increasingly evident, accompanied by a search for 'alternatives to development', manifest in innovative grassroots movements and experiments where there are 'links between development and the marginalisation of people's life and knowledge' (Escobar, 1995, p.216). The second path being pursued is the development discourse currently favoured in Ireland, which views development as 'spectacle'. Here, as in Debord's (1983) society of the spectacle, development becomes a series of spectacles designed to pacify the new grassroots/social movements that are beginning to activate. Somewhat mirroring Escobar's (1995) suggestion that development colonises reality and becomes reality, development discourses in Ireland seem to be embodied in endless programmes and strategies all of which share the belief that 'development is about paving the way for the achievement of those conditions that characterise rich societies: industrialisation, agricultural modernisation and urbanisation'. This view of development is dominant in contemporary Irish development discourse, with successive governments designing development plans and programmes along such lines, from the 'enticing' of foreign investors in the name of development, to the supposedly more integrated partnership approach to rural development which is currently popular. This scenario is in keeping with the school of thought which sees development as something imposed on a landscape and as such requiring management and intervention (Crush, 1995). In essence this is the policy of 'being seen to be doing something' (McDonagh, 1998, p.53).

The narrative of Irish rural development policies

There are many literatures outlining the history of rural development in Ireland (Breathnach, 1984; Breathnach and Cawley, 1986; Ó Cinnéide and Cuddy, 1992; Ó Cinnéide and Grimes, 1992; Murray and Greer, 1993; Commins and Keane, 1994; NESC, 1994). Development as a specific policy is particularly pertinent in Irish development discourse. Despite the best of intentions, not all areas benefit to the same degree from specific social or economic changes and often the areas on the periphery are hardest hit. Such peripheral areas are consistently either left behind by development processes occurring elsewhere or may actually suffer as a result of them (Ó Cinnéide and Keane, 1990), thereby increasing the necessity for governments to introduce specific policies to alleviate disadvantage. The interpretation of rural development in Ireland adheres strictly to this type of development 'spectacle' which is based on policy and programmes. The recognition of divisions within Ireland, for example, in terms of the 'leaving behind' of the West by the more urbanised East, has encouraged successive governments to attempt to alleviate such disparity through intervention in the form of growth centres, industrial dispersion and special regional packages (the Western Package in the 1980s for example). The policies and programmes pursued by different governments, many of which have been successful for their duration, have often left little in the way of long-term benefit (for example it could be suggested that programmes such as LEADER, did not leave the lasting impression that was hoped for). The initiation of development policy often brings its own problems by causing conflicts between different groups, like land-use planners and agricultural developers. There can also be contradictory aspects within the same policy. For example, the increased modernisation of farming activities to improve the welfare of rural farmers and families often leads to rural depopulation and decline. As a result, rural development defined in terms of policy objectives, results in a largely political debate. The question is, whether such policies are the way to advance in terms of rural development, or whether they are merely papering over the cracks.

The 1960s are an appropriate place to begin Ireland's rural development narrative. The similarities of rural development problems and strategies between that decade and today are striking. During the 1960s rural was still very much equated with agricultural. There was however a leaning towards rural development issues, and the thinking of the day suggested that an 'integrated approach' to rural problems presented the solution to the ills of the countryside. The issue of rural and regional development came to the fore during the agricultural crisis faced by Irish farmers during the 1960s. The government of the time conceded that some measure of price support was needed but also pointed out that the capacity of the Irish exchequer to support domestic farm prices was not comparable with other European countries. As a result, state expenditure was concentrated on measures designed to improve agricultural productivity and competitiveness. In 1961, the Irish government set up an informal inter-departmental committee (the Inter-Departmental Committee on the Problems of Small Western Farms) to examine measures which could further aid the special problems Irish agriculture was experiencing. Agricultural development alone was not enough to halt migration from rural areas, and it was proposed that rural industries, tourism and tourist attractions be developed in areas at risk from depopulation (Commins and O'Hara, 1991). Other recommendations included the need to bring about closer co-ordination between various government departments (leading to the foundation of the County Development Teams in 1963). Furthermore, to build up the failing sense of community initiative, each area was to have a group of representatives to discuss ideas with public service staff working locally, for the development of their areas. In addition, in 1963, An Foras Taluntais recommended a programme of local community development where local initiatives could provide mechanisms for channelling resources and aid to local communities (An Foras Taluntais, 1963). The *Second Programme for Economic Expansion* (1964) and *Third Programme – Economic and Social Development* (1969–1972) both used these recommendations but in the intervening period between these publications there was a shift in the approach to rural development issues. The second programme discussed rural development solely in the agricultural context rather than devote a chapter exclusively to it. Significantly, however the third programme linked rural development to regional development and in particular, western development (Commins and O'Hara, 1991). Although several measures were introduced during the 1960s to achieve greater equality between farmers in rural areas (including the setting up of pilot area development programmes in each of the twelve western counties which combined advisory services with organised action by the farmers themselves), the second and third programmes for economic development also emphasised the importance of non-farm economic activities. These included agri-tourism and activity holidays (Commins and O'Hara, 1991). The growth of small industrial estates was also planned, providing employment to rural dwellers, although then, as now, strong debates took place about the merits of concentrating industry in growth centres or encouraging its dispersal.

During the 1960s the Irish government's policy for rural development was designed predominantly to ensure more intensive use of land, retention of people in agriculture, the creation of viable farming units and the provision of adequate employment opportunities for those who leave agriculture (O'Hara and Commins, 1991). These aims highlighted a recurring trend in Irish rural development history, the perception that rural development was a problem facing farming populations, with policies directed accordingly. During this period, the Local Government (Planning and Development) Act of 1963 gave local authorities more responsibility with regard to planning, with an emphasis on physical planning. Rural development policy consequently began to move towards regionalism, with nine regions designated, based on elements of physical planning, and regional boards established for Health and Tourism. Regional Development Organisations, with no executive authority, were established to provide a co-ordination forum for groups of local authorities and other agencies (Commins and Keane, 1994). In 1968, Buchanan's study of regional planning suggested a number of growth centres throughout the country. Although the proposals were not implemented in their entirety, two centres (Galway and Waterford) were chosen for the location of industrial estates, with the added statement that industrial activities should be dispersed where feasible, because of social and demographic considerations (Government Statement on Regional Policy, 1965, cited in O'Hara and Commins, 1991) (interestingly, there are similarities here with the current proposals of the NDP 2000–2006 and its recognition of the importance and development of 'gateways'). However the link between industrialisation and regional and local development was all but severed in the early 1980s when increasing job losses in Dublin and the viability of some high-tech industries took precedence over any spatial dispersal of employment (see Commins and Keane, 1994).

In 1973, the most significant event to affect rural Ireland since Independence in 1922 occurred with Ireland's accession to the European Economic Community (EEC) (now the European Union (EU)). It is difficult to predict what would have happened had Ireland not joined, but on joining, its policies for agriculture and rural development were in effect passed over to the EU with the 'implicit expectation that they would be solved through a sectoral policy, *viz.*, price supports in the CAP' (Commins and Keane, 1994, p.103). Within the EU, Ireland as a whole was targeted for funding from the European Regional Fund. The reasoning behind this decision was that Ireland as one region stood to gain more from the Fund, and not, as many suggested at the time (and it could be argued are still suggesting), a 'preoccupation with centralised control of EC funds by the Dublin administration' (O'Hara and Commins, 1991, p.21). The main foundation on which Ireland's entry into the EU was built was that of the CAP and the Regional Fund. Although CAP raised farmers' incomes and channelled money into rural areas, these policies also caused rural development (despite its limited capacity in the 1960s) to lose its focus between 1973 and the mid-1980s, with O'Hara and Commins (1991) arguing that '(t)here was an implicit belief that the largesse expected from EC policies, especially from the CAP and Regional Fund, would take care of the country's rural problems. Secondly, the IDA reduced Irish regional policy mainly to the implementation of regional industrial plans. The third factor was that the emphasis in public policy shifted to national fiscal management as the country's economic condition deteriorated over the 1970s' (p.18).

The main rural development policy strategy of the late 1970s and early 1980s appears to have been defined by its absence, apart from that suggested by Lee (1989) of making the greatest short-term gains in the fastest way possible. The emphasis on top-down development was exposed in terms of its limitations, with its weakness manifest in its 'over-dependence on externally controlled investment, the consequent vulnerability to international forces, the limited development of local linkages, the low skill content of much of the employment and weak development of indigenous sectors ... and the limited participation of local interests' (Commins and Keane, 1994, p.210). The CAP replaced existing agricultural policies with its price supports and its agenda of increasing farming productions and incomes, and according to Cuddy (1991, p.30–31) had 'a direct positive impact on all rural areas through raising product prices to farmers and thus raising their incomes'. The CAP's original goal was to reduce European dependence on imported food by increasing productivity. The increased use of agri-chemicals and more intense farming methods resulted in produce surpluses. The now famous butter and beef mountains and wine lakes continued to grow as the demand for different products expanded. The rise in output and the simultaneous decline in demand forced the Community to expand its exports, triggering trade wars (European Commission, 1996). Despite this, by its very nature, the CAP's price policy shielded farmers from the realities of market pressures. At the same time it was not improving conditions in LFAs which continued to experience declining populations. Far from the notion of all boats being lifted by the rising tide, Kelleher and O'Mahoney, (1984) suggested that the impact of the CAP price policy was to widen the prosperity gap between the larger and smaller producers, due mainly to the fact that the price support was in direct proportion to output and therefore those with the greater output received greater support. Despite this consequence, Cuddy (1991, p.31) still argued that the 'income support provided by the CAP played an important role, both directly and indirectly, in sustaining the economy of rural Ireland'. As a result CAP went through a period of reform between 1992 and 1995. Reform was achieved through encouraging greater care of the environment, bringing down prices, supporting woodland development and the development of additional sources of income. Surpluses were reduced and the 'set-aside' of farming land was encouraged. The reform of CAP coincided with a radical shake-up in the way rural development was viewed at European level. It was no longer seen as purely an agricultural problem but a regional one. The argument however remained that the disparities within Ireland had not vanished, and that while Ireland had a 'regional' status within the EU, regional recognition was not evident within the country itself (see Euradvice, 1994).

There are three possible reasons why rural development was placed on the back burner for over a decade in Irish politics. Firstly it was thought that CAP and the EC Regional Fund would cure any domestic rural problems. Secondly, the IDA became the main flag bearer of Irish regional policy, which in effect reduced it to regional *industrial* policy. Finally, as the country's economic condition deteriorated public policy shifted to national fiscal management (Commins and O'Hara, 1991). The Irish government itself, while successfully negotiating large amounts of funding through CAP had no long-term plan on which to base it. As CAP was predominantly a farm price support policy, the end result was to increase polarisation between small farmers and large farmers, the rural poor and the rural rich. The bias towards the larger farm holders was partially offset by area-specific measures designed to support small farmers in LFAs who received headage payments. The early 1980s disbanded the Land Commission and land acquisition became a function of the free market leading to a growing emphasis on part-time farming as a solution for small farmers. Furthermore, as all of Ireland was recognised as a single region by the government and consequently by the EU, regional policies fell into disfavour and, as such, the Regional Fund was used to help finance the public capital programme. It is possible that this decision reflected the obsession with keeping the funds centralised in Dublin (Commins and O'Hara, 1991). Over this time the economic climate continued to deteriorate and regional and rural development continued to be eclipsed by more urgent economic considerations, leaving the EU to provide what support it could to rural regions through CAP.

From the mid-1980s there developed a new-found interest in rural development, particularly in response to the added recognition given to rural areas by the EU. The growing realisation that CAP was not reducing regional disparities and that many communities were experiencing a crisis brought about by conventional top-down development thinking led to the publication of *The Future of Rural Society* by the European Commission (1988). This seminal document marked a clear shift in EU policy from a top-down approach to the recognition of the need for a grassroots movement with respect to rural development. The report stressed the need for an integrated approach to resource development, the need to diversify and the importance of a bottom-up movement with control of local resources left in local hands (European Commission, 1988). Ireland's response to rural development issues largely reflected the thinking in Brussels, and policies were implemented as a direct result of Commission requirements (see Commins and Keane, 1994). Cuddy (1991) identified a number of events including the changing economic and political conditions, the changes and reforms to the CAP, the General Agreement on Trade and Tariffs (GATT) negotiations, the Single European Market (SEM) and the proposed enlargement of the community and developments in Eastern Europe, which were creating a new context for rural development in Ireland. As a result, the concepts of Integrated Rural Development and 'bottom-up' development, echoing the debates of two decades previous, became common parlance in 1990s policy rhetoric (see O'Hara and Commins, 1991).

The main policies associated with rural development in Ireland of the 1990s have been channelled through the National Development Plans (NDPs), the recent publication of the government White Paper on rural development (Department of Agriculture and Food, 1999) and the current designing of the National Spatial Strategy (NSS). In the next section these policies are critically assessed to determine the government's current stance on rural development issues in Ireland.

Ensuring the Future – A Strategy for Rural Development in Ireland

Both at national and EU level, rural development has continued to emerge as a prominent theme of public policy. Nevertheless, coherent sets of policy responses have not been formulated. Historically the Irish government also admits that there has been 'no generally agreed or universally understood definition of the nature and scope of public policy for rural development' (Department of Agriculture and Food, 1999, p.19). In 1999, the publication of *Ensuring the Future – A Strategy for Rural Development in Ireland* (Department of Agriculture and Food, 1999) (hereafter referred to as the White Paper) sought to address this situation by establishing a coherent plan that would inform future government policies, and governmental response to the issues of concern in rural Ireland. The White Paper contains what the Irish government refers to as the 'overarching strategy' for rural development in Ireland. Through a series of government commitments, this policy formulates a so-called 'coherent strategy for rural development [that] identifies the policy responses at national, regional and local levels which will most effectively address the issues of economic and social underdevelopment in rural areas' (ibid., p.1). The stated objectives of this document are a commitment to 'ensuring the economic and social well-being of rural communities' (ibid.). This rural development policy agenda is defined as all policies which 'are directed towards improving the physical, economic and social conditions of people living in the open countryside, in coastal areas, towns and villages and in smaller urban centres outside of the five major urban areas' (ibid, 1999, p. vi). In addition, policies are to facilitate balanced and sustainable regional development while tackling the issues of poverty and social inclusion. The commitments in the White Paper are to be financed by monies made available through the NDP 2000–2006. The 'rural proofing' of proposed national policies to assess their probable impact on rural communities represents the critical element of this current approach by the Irish government toward rural development. In highlighting the 'seriousness' of its approach, the Department of Agriculture and Food are to provide the ongoing policy focus for rural development and, to reinforce its new role, have added the term Rural Development to their title. In this light it is notable that rural development has once again been inextricably linked with agriculture in government policy circles.

The main objective of the White Paper is to identify and implement a strategy that will:

- Increase employment opportunities in rural areas to compensate for the decline in employment opportunities in the agricultural sector;
- Counter migration and depopulation; and
- Meet the needs for public service delivery in terms of access to the range of services which are required to sustain rural communities.

The future vision of the rural development policy agenda is somewhat lightweight in content with a government commitment to implementing 'a comprehensive, coherent and sustainable strategy to provide the conditions and environment in which rural communities can prosper' (Department of Agriculture and Food, 1999, p.19). It further commits to:

- Ensuring the economic and social well-being of rural communities;
- Providing the conditions for a meaningful and fulfilling life for all people living in rural areas, and
- Striving to achieve a rural Ireland in which there will be 'vibrant sustainable communities', sufficient employment and income to allow individuals and families to live with dignity, a respect for the rural environment and the cultural identity of rural communities will be valued and retained.

The basic principles on which this strategy is founded are:
- An inclusive approach to sustainable development;
- An integrated multi-dimensional approach to policies for economic and social development and co-ordination of top-down and bottom-up approaches;
- A perception of rural development which takes account of regional and local variations; and
- The establishment of participative institutional arrangements at local, regional and national levels to guide policy formation and implementation.

The government has identified six main elements of importance in the strategy for rural development.

- The first emphasises an increased focus on rural development through institutional mechanisms to ensure the government commitments of the White Paper will be achieved. Along with the lead Department (of Agriculture, Food and Rural Development), a Cabinet Sub-Committee is to ensure policy co-ordination at the highest level as it is recognised that in practice, government policies tend to remain largely vertical and sectoral in their application and implementation (Department of Agriculture and Food, 1999). A national Rural Development Forum has been established to debate current issues and review existing programmes. The government is also to establish a Rural Development Fund that will finance policy orientated and rural research, pilot actions and evaluation. The Department of Agriculture, Food and Rural Development will also administer the fund.

- The second main element is the achievement of balanced regional development through a spatial development strategy. The government is to implement this regional approach through the NDP 2000–2006, Regional Assemblies, Regional Authorities, County Development Boards, State Agencies and investment incentives (see Chapter 6).

- The third main element of the strategy for rural development is the provision of services and infrastructure. Acknowledging that rural areas pose problems in service delivery due to diseconomies of scale, the government commits to 'providing essential public services in rural areas [to] support dispersed, viable rural communities' (ibid., p.30). In order to achieve this, emphasis on competition policy, the removal of regulatory burdens and the enhancement of the skills base are advocated. There is also a strong emphasis on the dispersal of Information and Communications Technology (ICT) which theoretically can reduce the disadvantages that isolated rural areas suffer due to their peripherality. Although the advantages of connecting rural areas to the fibre-optic network are discussed, no concrete plans for the roll-out of broadband services are mentioned.

Also recognised is the role a good public transport system has to play in reducing marginalisation. However, other than a mention of various pilot programmes operating under the aegis of Area Development Management (ADM), there is practically no discussion on how to design or implement an adequate public transport system that will be beneficial to rural areas.

- The fourth area of concern concentrates on the holy grail of sustainable economic development based on indigenous potential and inward investment. The Irish government suggests that the most effective way of achieving this ideal is through a carefully managed public finance system based on sound macro-economic policies. In other words, responsibility for job creation in the regions would appear to rest first and foremost with the government, as opposed to within the regions themselves. The White Paper identifies five policy areas as being of particular importance in 'creating new opportunities and in assisting rural communities to prosper' (ibid., p. 37). These are: agriculture; food; marine and natural resources; enterprise; and tourism. Within the agricultural sector there is strong emphasis on environmental protection, alongside a similarly strong emphasis on competitiveness and increased capital investment. Both aspirations would appear to conflict. Off-farm employment is advocated as one of the solutions to the population decline in rural areas. The food sector is closely allied with agriculture and recommendations are made that these links should be strengthened. The increase of land under forestry to 1.2 million hectares, with the proviso that forestry development is compatible with the protection of the environment is the only natural resource examined in the section on marine and natural resources. Once again under the marine section, the protection of the environment is lauded as one of the main elements of the government's strategy and furthermore promises to develop new fisheries (ibid., p.41). Regional development is one of the pillars of the sector on enterprise and it is felt that balanced regional development will rely to a large extent on investment secured by the IDA. There is also a strong role envisaged for indigenous SMEs who will be supported by the County Development Boards, County Enterprise Boards, LEADER, Area Partnerships and ADM Community Groups. While reiterating that rural tourism plays an increasingly important role in the economy of rural areas, the White Paper admits that the rural tourism sector lacks a cohesive strategy and identifies the need for a coherent policy at national level.

- The fifth element of the national strategy for rural development concentrates on rural development. It recognises that 'development of the human resource base in rural areas is critical to the maintenance of vibrant communities' (ibid., p. 47). The government believes that it can achieve this through education, training and community development.

- The sixth and final element is social inclusion. The government believes that the creation of dynamic rural economies provides the best chance to reduce disadvantage in rural areas but they will not in themselves address the problem of poverty and social exclusion. The strategy for reducing marginalisation seems to rely entirely on the National Anti-Poverty Strategy established by the government and the 'poverty proofing' of all policies to assess their impact on the poor. However, no concrete examples of policies designed to tackle poverty in rural areas are evident in the Paper.

The government plans to promote this vision of rural Ireland by setting up County Development Boards which will consist of a partnership between local government, local development bodies, social partners from the voluntary and community sector and representatives of relevant state agencies at local level. The identification of suitable policy responses to rural problems and a review of existing programmes will be undertaken by the newly established Rural Development Forum. The first National Rural Development Forum was held in Nenagh, Co. Tipperary on 2 May 2000. It was established to debate current issues in rural development, to review existing programmes and to identify suitable policy responses to rural problems (submissions came from ADM, Bord na Mona, Council for the West, Comhar LEADER na hÉireann, Combat Poverty Agency, Comhaltas Ceoltóirí Éireannn, the Equality Authority, Irish National Organisation of the Unemployed, Irish Creamery Milk Suppliers Association, Irish Congress of Trade Unions, Irish Rural Link, Keep Ireland Open, Macra na Feirme, Mid-West Regional Authority, PLANET, Rural Resettlement Ireland and the Western Development Commission). Along with the creation of the Rural Development Fund, the Area-based Partnership approach to addressing disadvantage at local level will be continued as will the LEADER programme and the Local Authority Area Committees (Department of Agriculture & Food, 1999).

The continued role of a bottom-up approach is confirmed by the ongoing support for the Area-based Partnership initiative which addresses disadvantage at local levels; the LEADER programme and the Local Authority Area Committees. The setting up of the County Development Boards indicates a shift toward a more territorial approach to development and a move toward new forms of rural governance (see Chapter 6). This Government White Paper describes a commitment to providing rural development policies that are 'formulated with a sustainable development framework, thereby ensuring that the environment is protected and the natural resources are exploited in a sustainable manner' (ibid, p. 55). As part of this policy the government suggests that this commitment to the environment is bound up in the realm of sustainable development. Within this objective, the location of jobs in close proximity to settlement is seen as paramount, with the protection of the landscape requiring a 'co-ordinated approach and the integration of environmental concerns into all rural development policies and programmes' (ibid.).

Within this aspirational strategy several areas of potential conflict are obvious. For example, there would appear to be friction between the differing government policies of 'rural proofing' and 'eco-auditing'. The emphasis on environmental protection rivals the emphasis on increasing industry in rural areas. There is also a clash of interest between environmental protection and the emphasis on increasing competitiveness in agriculture, increasing and intensifying the number of inland fisheries and increasing the area of ground under conifer plantation. There are moreover very few concrete policies discussed to bring about social inclusion and stabilise rural populations. These conflicts between 'rural-proofing', 'eco-auditing' and 'poverty-proofing' exist because by their very nature, they strive for very different, and contrasting results.

A number of further conflicts arise within this government policy despite the commitment to either introducing new policies for rural areas or ensuring that there is 'a rural dimension, where necessary or appropriate, to existing policies to meet rural conditions' (ibid., p. 22). This so-called co-ordinated approach is questionable in light of the conflicting policies emerging from government departments. In particular it is interesting to note the differences between some government policies and strategies that have directly opposing impacts. For example, issues of marginalisation, exclusion and the need to provide services for those in remoter rural areas are very much discriminated against by policies that implement tax rises, Vehicle Registration Tax (VRT) increases, motor tax increases, fuel price increases, and the non-exemption or subsidisation of the National Car Test (NCT). Within the White Paper, other commitments that can be called into question in light of the afore-mentioned policy instruments include the recognition by the White Paper that economic development is dependent on modern infrastructure and service provision in order to enable rural areas to be competitive and sustainable. The provision of infrastructure is critical to ensuring that rural areas are attractive places in which to live and work (ibid., p.22). Furthermore, there is a Government commitment to 'providing essential public services in rural areas to ensure a proper environment for economic development, promote social inclusion and support viable rural communities' (ibid., p.2). Yet there is no substantial proposal on how this is to be achieved. If anything there is huge potential for possible conflict between the 'eco auditing' and 'rural proofing' strategies advocated. The inherent contradiction in policy is further highlighted by the White Paper's recognition that the 'problems of isolation and unequal opportunity are compounded by distance from services and amenities [and] the provision of transport is a major priority for those living in rural areas especially in the context of a tendency towards service concentration in larger areas' (ibid., p.7), which sits uneasily with its recommendation that the 'distribution of a network of urban centres [as] an essential component of an effective rural development strategy' (ibid., p.27), with its associated increase in the concentration of services etc.

Ostensibly, the rural environment is to be respected and development in rural areas is to take place in a sustainable manner. Yet there is a strong push by the government toward building more roads and town and village by-passes, which will have a direct impact on the rural environment. Interestingly, balanced regional development is allegedly the underlying basis of the White Paper. Yet the capital state grant rate has been reduced from 50% to 35% in the BMW region (the 'Objective 1' region in Ireland), and the feasibility study grant rate has been reduced from 75% to 60% also in the BMW area. Rather than reduce the grants on offer, there is an argument that they should be increased. Further, the White Paper suggests the predominate flow of public funds to rural areas should follow a sectoral rather than an area-based route. This raises a number of questions on the whole issue of balanced regional development and what is understood by this aspiration. Administrative procedures for 'rural proofing' are to be introduced for application by all departments to ensure that policy makers are aware of the likely impact of proposals on rural communities yet numerous conflicts exist between policies and within the policies themselves (e.g. between the NDP and the White Paper).

The White Paper suggests that 'if rural areas are to compete successfully for inward investment and remain competitive for indigenous industry it is essential that they have a modern infrastructure (ibid., p.30). The White Paper nevertheless advocates that the rural environment be protected in the same breath as the NDP promotes the building of more roads and by-passes. However, these conflicting policies have little to say on the provision of public transportation as an alternative. Contradictions deepen as the White Paper suggests that the government is committed to providing, within a strategic framework, a range of modern infrastructure in rural areas, which will promote sustainable economic growth, and the maintenance of the rural population. Again however there are no strategies for the provision of public transportation in rural areas, particularly those not being served by the limited services currently available. The only attempt to address this is through the rather obvious and unhelpful suggestion that the absence of an adequate public transport service in all areas means that transport is a major contributing factor in marginalisation and that 'innovative approaches to transport provision in rural areas is required' (ibid., p.32). These policies seem even more poorly formulated given the recognition that the 'difficulties experienced by vulnerable groups such as the elderly and disabled are compounded by physical isolation' (ibid., p.51).

If the policy framework described in the White Paper is to be successfully applied, co-ordination between the different levels of government, hitherto absent, will be important. The White Paper implies a status quo in the current vertical and sectoral policy structures despite the overall strategy of the paper for the creation of a multi-sectoral, integrated and well co-ordinated policy framework which addresses public policy issues which do not fall within the remit of any one particular department (Department of Agriculture and Food, 1999). Despite the government's description of the White Paper as being a 'comprehensive and cohesive approach' for rural Ireland and the White Paper's many noteworthy strategies, the lack of concerted proposals make it extremely lightweight in terms of its likely impact on rural Ireland. Reactions to this 'likely impact' were foremost in the Dáil and Oireachtais discussion on the White Paper. Criticisms included those of Deputy Connaughton (2000) who described the White Paper as 'like most documents on the future of rural Ireland published down through the years in that it is detailed but it contains many woolly conclusions'. Deputy Hayes (2000) also pointed out that the White Paper would be a 'waste of time and effort unless it leads to the implementation of new and effective policies that lead to real rural development'. In fact, along with the many questions raised in this section, it was Senator Caffrey (2000) who perhaps best summed up some of the failings of the White Paper when he suggested that it was 'in total conflict with the situation on the ground' and that the contents of the White Paper were nothing but 'aspirational codswallop'.

The National Development Plans

Up to 1993, the National Development Plans introduced various efforts at local area-based approaches to rural problems. The most prominent of these was the Integrated Rural Development Plan (1988–1990), and the Programme for Economic and Social Progress (1991) which were 'committed to establish(ing) a national programme for integrated rural development which would draw upon the experience of pilot programmes and other initiatives' (Commins and Keane, 1994, p. 116). While the sentiment was applauded, very little was carried out on the ground. In fact, Commins and Keane suggest that the major drawback of the National Development Plans to 1993, was their over identification of rural development with agricultural issues (rural development was referred to under the sub-headings of agriculture, horticulture, forestry and such like). The NDP, 1994–1999 (Department of Finance, 1993) contained no specific section on rural development either. Despite this, Commins and Keane (ibid., p. 117) suggested that this plan 'show(ed) a considerable advance on previous official thinking in that it recognised a distribution between *sectoral* strategies (for industry, natural resources, tourism) and *area-based* initiatives' (authors' italics). Some of the important conclusions of this Plan was the government's recognition of:

> the importance of a local dimension to enterprise and employment creation and the importance of developing the capabilities of local communities to contribute to tackling unemployment and pursuing

100   Renegotiating Rural Development in Ireland

local development ... the general role which local initiatives can play as a catalyst for local economic development [and that] the development of infrastructure at local level to promote growth in both enterprise and broader community-led initiatives is therefore a key task. It involves empowering communities to sponsor innovative projects for training, enterprise and local developments as well as enabling them to focus mainstream programmes for the unemployed in a better way in their local areas (Department of Finance, 1993, p.69).

The limitations of these NDP proposals lie in the emphasis on enterprise being uni-dimensional rather than multi-dimensional, and the focus on areas characterised by a high concentration of long-term unemployment and environmental deprivation which appears to be biased towards urban centres (ibid.). In the 1994 Programme for Competitiveness and Work (PCW, 1994), more attention was given to rural development than in the NDP (1994–1999), with its main objectives being to 'maximise the number of viable farms and farm households in rural Ireland, at sustainable living standards in line with those in other sectors of the economy' (PCW, 1994, p.39). What this brief excerpt indicates (for a more detailed account see Commins and Keane, 1994, CWC, 1992) is that while numerous elements relevant to an integrated rural development policy have been circulated in Irish development discourse, no clear-cut policy framework or set of long-term objectives have been put in place.

The National Development Plan 2000 to 2006

The NDP 2000–2006 (Department of Finance, 1999) emerges from a very different economic environment to that of its predecessor. The previous background of budget deficits, widespread unemployment with its social and economic implications, and poorly balanced regional development, is in stark contrast to the prosperous economy of today. Despite this success there are still a number of problems evident in Ireland, problems of exclusion, marginalisation, a growing gap between the affluent and the poor and the lack of equality in terms of regional development (in fact the NDP declares one of its main objectives as balanced regional development and this inequality and the new structures of regional and rural governance that are emerging will be explored more fully in Chapter 6).

The basis of the NDP 2000–2006 is formed by three inter-regional Operational Programmes; Economic and Social Infrastructure, Employment and Human Resources, and the Productive Sector; two regional Operational Programmes, the BMW Operational Programme and the South and East (S&E) Operational Programme; and a separate Operational Programme for the PEACE Programme which operates in the border counties and in Northern Ireland. Although the Regional Operational Programmes will have the most immediate and visible effect on rural Ireland, the Inter-regional Operational Programmes also contain elements that will be of great importance to rural areas. Under the Operational Programme for Economic and Social Infrastructure, £IR17.6 billion will be invested in infrastructure countrywide. Almost three times more will be invested in the S&E region than in the BMW region, although a large proportion of this will be invested in the Greater Dublin Area. There will also be investment in primary and secondary roads and in regional public transport. Investment in water and waste water infrastructure is also provided under this Operational Programme, however three out of the five headings under which funds will be invested in water and waste water, have an urban bias. It is claimed that the investment in physical infrastructure will have a positive effect on rural areas by making it more attractive for industry to locate away from larger urban areas. It is also alleged that improved public transport services will make it easier for rural people to commute (ibid., p. 201).

Table 4.1 Economic and social infrastructure investment by region

	£billion	Per capita
S&E Region	12.9	4.7
BMW Region	17.6	4,855
State	4,861	4,856

Table 4.2 Economic and social infrastructure investment by sector

Category	Total allocation for 2000–2006 period (£million)
National Roads	4,700
Public Transport	2,234
Water and Waste Water	2,495
Coastal Protection	35
Energy	146
Social and Affordable Housing	6,000
Health Capital	2,000
Total	17,610

A total provision of just under £10 billion is proposed for investment in the Employment and Human Resources Operational Programme (see Table 4.3). The employability sub-programme places a strong emphasis on social inclusion measures in the education sector and labour market integration. Measures include early education, school completion, early literacy, third level access programmes, traveller education and career guidance. In the labour market sector provisions are made for the long-term unemployed and socially excluded; also included are action programmes for the unemployed; early school leavers progression to employment, and skills and sectoral training for the unemployed and redundant workers. These measures provide back-up for the ideas and commitments produced in the White Paper on Rural Development (Department of Agriculture & Food, 1999). A provision of £1.62 billion is being made for educational and training infrastructure in facilities, particularly in Research and Development and the technology sector, and it is hoped that this will be an important element in assisting the regional development strategy.

Table 4.3 Employment and human resources investment by region

	£billion	Per capita (£)
S&E Region	7.1	2.8
BMW Region	9.9	2,651
State	2,936	2,729

Table 4.4 Employment and human resources investment by sector

Pillar	Total allocation for 2000–2006 (£ million)
Employability	4,631
Entrepreneurship	413
Adaptability	4,647
Equality	202
Total	9,893

The third inter-regional programme covers the productive sector, including agriculture and fisheries. This programme will have a strong impact on rural development in the regions as one of the main aspects will be to support Foreign Direct Investment (FDI) in the BMW Region. The IDA is committed to ensuring that at least 50% of all new jobs from greenfield projects will be in that region. A separate programme will be implemented for CAP rural development accompanying measures. A total of £3.4 billion will be spent on the:

- Rural Environment Protection Scheme;
- Early Retirement Scheme;
- Compensatory Allowances; and
- Forestry Measures.

Table 4.5 Productive sector investment by region

	£billion	Per capita (£)
S&E Region	2.8	1.7
BMW Region	4.5	1,073
State	1,713	1,243

Table 4.6 Productive sector investment by sector

Category	Total allocation for 2000–2006 (£ million)
RTDI	1,946
Industry	1,903
Marketing	337
Agricultural Development	278
Fisheries	45
Total	4,509

One of the main chapters within the NDP (2000–2006) concerns rural development. Overall investment under the NDP which will directly impact rural areas amounts to £6.7billion. Although the instruments used to promote rural development will be the same in both regions (Table 4.7) a disproportionate amount will be spent in the BMW region. The S&E region is far more urbanised than the BMW region and the funding reflects this distribution. Under the inter-regional programmes indirect investment will take place on a nationwide scale, while at a regional level direct investment will take place.

Table 4.7 Productive sector investment by category and region

Category	National £million	BMW Region £million	S&E Region £million
Agriculture and Fisheries Development	410	203	207
CAP Rural Development Accompanying Measures	4,324	2,474	1,850
Rural Enterprises (includes agriculture, forestry, fisheries)	495	285	210
Training in Agriculture, Food, Forestry and Fisheries	152	72	80
Rural Infrastructure	2,694	1,303	1,391
Capital investment in Food & Fisheries, marketing and R&D for Agriculture, Food and Fisheries	479	200	279
Total	8,554	4,537	4,017

One of the central components of the strategy for rural development lies in the commitment by the government to a 'rural proofing' policy. This 'rural proofing' is to be introduced by all Departments 'to ensure that policy makers are aware of the likely impact of all proposals on rural communities' and thereby 'contribute significantly to integrating the strategy for the economic and social development of rural areas with the objectives and principles of other policy initiatives' (Department of Finance, 1999, p. 207). Further outlined within this chapter are strategies for regional development; agriculture, forestry and fishing, and rural infrastructure. The minimalist and traditional treatment of rural infrastructure raises a number of questions regarding the commitment and understanding of the government to balanced regional development and maintaining viable rural populations. The section dealing with rural infrastructure deals specifically with issues of good quality drinking water and the quality of the built environment in rural towns and villages in terms of their attractiveness as places to live, work and to appeal to industry. The issue of transportation and communication infrastructure is less well addressed. The NDP does recognise that the rural economy is dependent on 'an adequate transport infrastructure' and that 'given the dispersed nature of rural population, roads are the most critical component of transport infrastructure as far as rural dwellers are concerned' (p.206). In response to this the NDP is allocating £1.6 million (2,031.6 million Euros) toward improvement and maintenance of regional and local roads and because of the importance of non-national roads in the more peripheral areas (particularly in the West region), 44% of this money will be allocated to the BMW region.

This emphasis on road-building as a panacea for regional mobility and accessibility seems somewhat misguided. The notion that building more roads will in some way lead to a more balanced regional development and relieve the current congestion problems as experienced in many towns across the country seems short-sighted, particularly with the NSS yet to be completed. Investment in major road infrastructure at this stage would almost certainly determine the NSS as there would be pressure to make associated investment decisions. In fact Breathnach (2000) suggests that the road investment programme as envisaged by the NDP may be misplaced. He argues that while growing road congestion is problematic, there is little evidence that this is effecting new productive investment. In fact, Breathnach further suggests that the main problems for regional locations are to do with 'access to adequate supplies of skilled labour and support services [and] where over one half of new annual inward investment is in services activities which mainly rely on telecommunications, one may question the fact that the NDP proposes to spend £8.6bn on road building and just £120m on telecommunications' (ibid., p.5). Consequently, those issues that need the greater commitment, such as the human resource deficit in rural areas (see Chapter 2) or the development of the telecommunications network, are the most neglected while funding flows towards more tangible development which fulfils the criteria of the development 'spectacle' by giving rural communities something to look at!

Further, there still remains a large gulf between policy aspirations and practical implementations in the identification by the NDP of the important role of gateways in the development of rural areas. The main urban centres are considered to be the most successful gateways that are experiencing sustained economic performance, however the majority of these, with the exception of Galway, are located in the South and East of the country. One of the key components of the government's Regional Development Policy is the expansion/promotion of the existing gateways and the targeting of a limited number of strategically placed centres which display potential. The selection of these gateways will be determined by their potential ability to stimulate economic growth in the towns and villages in their hinterland. As such, only a limited number of gateways are required and the government suggests that the location of possible gateway towns be identified by the forthcoming NSS. This in theory will help to achieve balanced regional development throughout rural Ireland. The fact that these gateways will be identified only *after* the monies from the NDP have been allocated (as with infrastructural development) indicates a certain lack of co-ordinated planning and basically puts the 'cart before the horse' (see next section).

This lightweight background policy frames the allegedly longer-term strategy for rural Ireland outlined in the White Paper on Rural Development. As described previously this White Paper sets out the Irish government's vision for ensuring the social and economic well-being of the rural communities of Ireland. The NDP 2000–2006 is seen as the 'vehicle for delivering the commitments in the White Paper' (Davern, 2000) through funding the operational programmes which will underpin the aspirations and commitments contained therein. However, the conflictual nature of the White Paper along with its lack of strategic thinking form a fragile basis on which to build the future of rural Ireland.

The National Spatial Strategy (NSS)

The NSS is described as being a broad framework for the entire country, identifying development patterns for certain areas and setting down policies for the location of different types of development in the future (Department of Environment and Local Government, 2000). Having a NSS is certainly desirable and should benefit those parts of the country in need of targeted policy responses. The reality however is that the tardy arrival of the NSS, after the NDP, combined with the nature of its programme of spending smacks once again of the 'spectacle' of development. Effectively it can be viewed as purely optical development, complying with directives without necessarily believing in their need. Undoubtedly there may be a lot of important foci arising from the NSS but essentially it seems more a case of developing a strategy after decisions have been made. If the government has already committed to providing millions of pounds in funding for a certain infrastructural development, the NSS is unlikely to be able to alter this, and indeed it is more likely to accommodate the decision. This likely scenario undermines any radical or even conventional strategy that the NSS might seek to achieve.

The remit of the NSS is to be conducted in four stages, namely: the preparation of the report on the scope and delivery of the NSS; providing a description and analysis of the spatial structure and functioning of Ireland, including trend scenarios; developing opportunities and choices in patterns of development and a final stage of definition and choice of strategies, priorities and implementation mechanisms. In particular the NSS is to 'identify general spatial patterns for areas and set down indicative policies in relation to the location of industrial development, residential development, services, rural development, tourism and heritage; and develop and present a dynamic conception of the Irish urban system together with its links to rural areas, which recognises and utilises their economic and social interdependence' (Department of Environment and Local Government, 2000).

The NSS is allegedly designed to form the most important part of government policy to achieve more balanced regional development. It is to provide a broad framework in which policies in areas such as tourism, services, enterprise development and agriculture can be reviewed, and it is also expected to provide a framework for future investment in infrastructure. The entire NSS is to be finished by December 2001.

That the government is not waiting for the final NSS report to be published does raise some significant questions. One of the key areas in the NSS will be to identify strategic infrastructure to facilitate the development of 'gateways' (Department of Environment and Local Government, 2000). It appears that the Irish government's strategy is guided by the notion that the greater the investment in infrastructure, the greater the economic growth, and the reduction in isolation and peripherality: 'even more infrastructure investment is needed if economic growth and social development are to continue. We have no choice therefore but to accelerate investment in infrastructure' (ibid., 2000). A significant question nevertheless is whether there is potential conflict between the NSS and the NDP. For example, if the NSS recommends investing in the infrastructure of regions other than those identified in the NDP, what will be the outcome? If as is likely, this is the case, then what will become of the investment programme already underway? Moreover, the current efforts by the Irish government at decentralisation of administrative units (that is, dispersing various departmental offices throughout the country with the decision-making power retained in Dublin) would also lend itself to a presumption of the NSS findings. The Irish government's plans to move almost 10,000 public servants from government departments to various regional locations have obvious implications for the chosen areas. Issues of residential development like transport, services and education all become essential considerations with the indicative strategies of the NSS becoming redundant prior to their development. A NSS would surely be the optimum opportunity to decide on such targeted growth rather than the *ad hoc* manner in which it is now conducted with its political point scoring and protecting of constituencies. The fact that such relocations may in fact be contrary to the NSS suggests a predetermined government path and a lack of real commitment by the government toward their professed desire for balanced regional development.

Conclusion

The debate on what constitutes development continues. Nevertheless, attempting to understand development provides an important conceptual framework for evaluating rural change. Development eludes easy definition; one such tentative attempt by Buller and Wright (1990, p.3) is deliberately open-ended and flexible, professing that 'development is an ongoing and essentially interventionist process of qualitative, quantitative and/or distributional change leading to some degree of betterment for groups of people'. In many cases development can also be self-contradictory, where so-called developments, while bringing short-term gains, can also lead to longer-term disadvantage. One significant aspect therefore, is that in order for development to take place it must be a sustainable process that goes beyond improving people's conditions to improving their control over such conditions. Consequently, the concept of development needs to adopt a multi-dimensional perspective that takes into account the role of cultural values in establishing priorities. A situation whereby it is 'constructive to view rural development as a broad notion, encompassing all important issues pertinent to the individual and collective vitality of rural people and places' (OECD, 1990; cited in Kearney *et al.*, 1994, p.16).

It is interesting to explore how the EU (as an umbrella organisation) recommends various policies and strategies to its members, who invariably interpret and apply these in different ways. While some countries have a pre-EU developmental history (for example the Highlands and Islands Development Board (HIDB) in Scotland), which has drawn on other political or economic responses, others seem to be merely responding to EU policies to obtain financial assistance (for more detailed accounts see Nicholls, 1976; Clout, 1987; Lloyd, 1988; Rodriguez, 1990; Williams, 1991; Clout, 1993; Cole and Cole, 1993; Syrett, 1995). Ireland, in terms of its approach, has pursued endless programmes, strategies and projects all seemingly focused on the same goal, namely that development is about paving the way for the achievement of those conditions that characterise rich societies; industrialisation, agricultural modernisation and urbanisation. However, rural development needs to be recognised as a multi-dimensional process rather than merely economic growth. Consequently, the Irish government's understanding of rural development as the pursuance of a series of 'spectacles' designed to pacify emerging grassroots and social movements who are demanding an input in to the decision-making process, is increasingly being challenged.

For this reason there is a growing dissatisfaction with top-down approaches and greater calls for local community involvement. For such involvement to be successful, the necessity for appropriate structures of governance and the development of suitable regional institutions is paramount. Hume (1997) noted that outside Ireland, there has been considerable progress towards new forms of rural governance and the regionalisation of political power structures. Citing population figures to dispel claims by some governments that their national populations are too small to regionalise, Hume outlined some of the successes of decentralised government:

- Spain, with seventeen regions ranging in population from 260,000 in Rioja to 6,500,000 in Andalusia;
- Italy, with twenty regions and two autonomous provinces with populations from 113,000 in Valle d'Aosta to 8,900,000 in Lombardy;
- Germany, with its explicitly federal structure of fifteen Lander (from East and West) and Berlin ranging in population from 659,000 in Bremen to 17,000,000 in Nordrhein Wesphalen;
- Belgium is also moving to a federal system composed of Flanders, Wallonia and the Brussels region (ibid., p.36).

While the type of devolution differs from country to country, they nevertheless have common traits. For example these regional bodies are elected, have revenue raising powers and responsibilities for education, social services, regional planning and are free to inter-link with other regions. France, with twenty-six elected regional councils, has tended to lessen its regional powers in recent years, while Greece and Holland have decentralised regional administrations but lack regional strategic economic powers. The regional policy element of the most recent NDP 2000–2006 in Ireland and the current development of a NSS are welcome objectives in the Irish regime. However, as argued in this chapter, the level of commitment of the Irish government to balanced regional development can be questioned. Not only are there discrepancies in the sequencing of the NSS being developed after the NDP but also, as highlighted by Breathnach (2000), in the view implicit in the NDP statement that regional development is separate from national development: 'the central regional policy objective in the Plan is to achieve balanced regional development [a] prerequisite for implementation of the policy is the achievement of the macro-economic objectives on which the Plan is based so that the necessary resources for investment can be made available. The first steps towards the implementation of the policy can be undertaken before the completion of the NSS ... from the outset of the NDP, investment within and between the regions will take full account of regional development policy' (Department of Finance, 1999, p.46). This implication is further criticised by Breathnach (2000) not only because it reflects what he describes as the 'old-fashioned view that regional development is an equity issue whereas national development is an efficiency issue ' (p.2), but more so because despite the regional effect linked to NDP spending, the absence of a clear regional strategy (until presumably the NSS) could lead to 'such expenditure actively working against the basic objective of balanced regional development' (p.3). Supporting this view the argument put forward by the CSF Evaluation Unit (1999, p.52) is that 'given the central importance of the regional gateways to the NDP's regional development policy and the importance of the NSS to investment decisions ...

serious consideration should be given to expediting preparation of the NSS'.

Up to the latter part of the 1990s, Ireland's regional administration has been largely tokenistic. There is however a growing move, however small, towards greater decentralisation and regionalisation. The most significant occurrence in recent years along this path has been the consideration by Britain during 1997 (albeit in terms on a national scale), of Scottish and Welsh devolution proposals. This dismantling of centralisation in Britain may lead to a similar devolution of power (on a regional scale) being sought in Ireland. This very real possibility promotes the recognition of regions as powerful political and economic actors rather than convenient administrative units. It is also because of this possibility that top-down development strategies, like those explored in this chapter, will be challenged by a more regionalised and bottom-up approach, where the 'local' becomes a determinant in future development discourse. As a continuation of this emerging debate, Chapter 5 traces the narrative of Irish rural development into the arena of local development. In this chapter the need for greater participation, the emergence of new forms of rural governance and the increasingly promoted roles of regional structures and administration are explored. Chapter 5 also investigates the changes taking place in the rural sphere, and the broader changes in state structures and processes of government which are combining to force a shift from government to governance (see Marsden and Murdoch, 1998). How significant this shift is within Ireland will be teased out by exploring the growing emphasis on local development and the partnership approach, and on new structures to administer rural development programmes.

5 Retrospect and Prospect – the Role of Church, State and Community in Rural Ireland

Recent literature (for example, Commins and Keane, 1994) has shown rural Ireland to be in a process of extensive structural upheaval that will leave the country greatly transformed and far from the rural idyll evoked in images in the past. There is an emerging concern about the way rural communities function (see Sorensen and Epps, 1996), how classes, interest groups and personalities, holding varying degrees of power, combine to influence community affairs and contribute to the regeneration of their own areas (see Keane, 1990; O'Cearbhaill, 1992a&b; Asby and Midmore, 1993; Kearney *et al.*, 1994; Murray and Dunn, 1995; Lorendahl, 1996, among others). This chapter adds to the understanding of this reconfiguration of rural Ireland and deepens awareness of Irish development issues in particular. Contextually, this chapter sets in motion a debate on issues of governance and the concepts of partnership and participation. The emergence of new forms of rural governance; the changing relationship between citizen and state and, the promotion of community and voluntary effort to instigate economic and social development in rural areas are all gaining pace. The transition from rationalist centralised planning to negotiational local planning (a system influenced by delegation, decentralisation and deregulation) (Kearney *et al.*, 1994), will require alternative channels between state and community to raise economic, social and political productivity (Uphoff, 1993). The declared change from 'investment in physical capital to investment in developing the knowledge, the skills and the entrepreneurial abilities of the local population' (Keane 1990, p.292) seems as yet however, unfulfilled. This chapter explores the role of community in Irish rural development and particularly attempts to assess the frustrations experienced by bottom-up development initiatives. The Developing the West Together group, formed in 1991, will be used as a vehicle to structure these "frustrations" and provide a useful insight to the barriers experienced by community development groups in rural Ireland.

Empowering rural communities

The role of the state is increasingly being reconsidered throughout rural Europe. Many debates are unfolding around the delivery and relevance of government policies and programmes and the consequent balance between the requirements of the state and how these requirements affect local communities (for example, the restructuring of services in rural areas). The current process of rapid rural change is therefore an opportune time to explore the Irish government's commitment to rural development at a time when increasing significance is placed on partnerships between the state (national and European) and the local community. Irish rural development policy has invariably been an appendage to agricultural policy and, to a lesser extent, regional policy (Commins and Keane, 1994); and no clearly formulated or consistent set of policies have emerged (see Chapter 4). There has been a tendency to conflate rural not only with agriculture (in government publications, for example), safeness, friendliness, community and family – but also with backwardness, isolation, poverty and a pre-modern society. However a redefining of the rural is taking place. This redefining has been brought about by the combined forces of modernisation, pressure from market forces, increased mobility, spatial diversity, new uses of the countryside and new rural dwellers.

Since the late 1980s, there has been considerable change in the Irish state's approach to rural development policy. The initial belief in the 'trickle-down' effects of macro-scale planning has waned, and there is now a greater concentration on small-scale development, or what is more generally known as the bottom-up approach. Commins and Keane (1994, p.13) argue that the recent trend 'to question top-down policies, though not in itself an adequate response to the problem, has come about because it is now realised, by many, that these policies were rarely developmental [and] ... (w)hen governments felt that by creating jobs in large factories [this would be true especially in the Gaeltacht areas] they had successfully "developed" a region, what they were actually doing was papering over with subsidies the fundamental factors which cause under-development in the first place'. In fact, Irish development discourses show an obvious lack of complementarity between policy making and policy implementation. In many cases a degree of contradiction exists, as for example in policies which promote the need to centralise facilities (schools, Garda stations, post offices) on cost efficiency grounds and the desire of local communities to retain these services in their rural areas where possible. Rural development as a policy issue would therefore seem to require a broader and more strategic framework than has been the case to date.

Consequently, policy statements by the Irish government have placed increasing emphasis on the significant role partnerships can play in terms of rural development. Such trends are also in evidence on the EU stage where the promotion of local and regional actors play a key role in the reconfiguration of rural development not only in terms of policy, but also in relation to the administration of these policies. The complexity of the emerging forms of rural governance cannot be over-stated nor can the fact that they are gaining currency in Ireland. The increased role for private, community and voluntary groups in developing and maintaining their own local economies does however demand institutional and organisation changes and a level of governance devolved to the regions within Ireland.

Empowering communities to have greater influence on their own development is based on a number of processes of social 'animation', 'partnership', 'participation' and 'capacity building'. Development in this regard is seen not only as an economic concept, but also as one that recognises the whole human condition and accepts numerous possible conceptions and paths for realising development objectives (Keane, 1990). Hoggart and Buller's (1987) suggestion that development must be a sustainable process, which changes not simply people's physical conditions but also their control over such conditions, is also important. Specifically, the use of intervention measures or subsidies is of no use if, on their withdrawal, the improvements are not sustained. Where this happens (as for example in the plethora of pilot programmes that come and go) there has been merely a short-term improvement in the living conditions of certain groups of people. There is however a growing shift away from the 'natural' need to develop, to one where communities can experiment with different ways of organising societies and economies (Escobar, 1995). Consequently, the development process is a learning one, and in order for 'true' development to take place there must be a change in both mental and material conditions (Rogers, 1987; Healy and Reynolds, 1991; Varley, 1991a; Varley, 1991b; Wilkinson, 1992; Frazer, 1994; Kearney *et al.*, 1994; Shortall, 1994).

What of the community and voluntary input to rural development in Ireland?

As rural Ireland continues to mould its future by combining traditional and modern forces in a search for its own model of modernity, a recurring problem in Irish development policy lies in the interpretation and boundaries of community development. Despite numerous arguments (Bradley and Lowe, 1984; Hoggart and Buller, 1987; Buller and Wright, 1990), for its replacement with 'locality', and the false assumptions of harmony and homogeneity that the term community conjures up, the word 'community' continues to loom large in the vocabulary of Irish rural development. Buller and Wright (1990, p.12) suggest, that in development policy 'community' combines three notions: a locational, a cultural and a functional notion dealing respectively with: where the development programme is placed spatially or administratively; the people on whom 'a sense of community identity can sometimes be fostered but more often foisted by outsiders'; and the 'assumed socio-economic unity within which development policies can be integrated and sustained'. Buller and Wright (ibid., p.6) further argue that for all the interpretations of development as 'positive' change, specific state-led policies play a crucial defining role, and that 'broad assumptions of rural community homogeneity, and therefore common needs and experiences, have been the hallmark of British [and even more so Irish] development policy'.

Many debates have unfolded around the delivery and relevance of government policies and programmes and the consequent balance between the requirements of the state and the effects on local communities. The issues of economic efficiency, equity and balanced regional development are prominent in development discourse. Conflict between market-led development and social concerns increasingly promote divergent paths to be pursued by policy makers and individuals. Between these outposts the community and voluntary sector (a mix of individuals, groups and organisations) does its work, disseminating information, attempting to influence government policies through pressure groups and processes of bargaining, discussion or persuasion. In fact community-led development is assuming a considerably raised profile. Increased dissatisfaction, along with a growing tendency towards self-reliance, has forced the bottom-up approach to be accepted as a necessary ingredient for development in the majority of rural communities (Ó Cinnéide, 1986; O'Cearbhaill, 1992a&b; Murray and Dunn, 1995). Furthermore, there is the perception in community development that effective organisation can make a significant contribution in the mobilisation of physical, human and financial resources.

The manner in which local communities can be motivated and mobilised to actively participate in their own development also raises a number of important issues. Varley (1991a, p.84) suggested that the less enthusiastic observer may see the use of communities as a 'rhetorical device that serves to legitimate an array of new state measures or .... as a rather desperate response, in the wake of the failure of market forces and state stimulation to halt rural decline, to push responsibility for local development and employment generation onto localities themselves'. Shortall (1994) also expressed some reservations about the role communities play in Ireland, particularly in relation to the centralist Irish regime. She suggested that 'doubts have been expressed about the extent to which community empowerment or community development is possible without a reorganisation and decentralisation of systems of governance and power' (p.247). Whatever the reasoning, whilst accepting the need for the formulation of policies at national or EU level, one sees a growing need

Retrospect and Prospect 115

for mechanisms whereby the people directly affected by specific development initiatives have an opportunity to express their needs. It is therefore desirable that, in the context of their local situation, people should have an input into the dialogue which leads to the choice of the macro strategy (Conway, 1991).

Development policy in Ireland can also be criticised for its over-dependence on the notion that rural communities are bound up in homogeneous groups supported by familial ties and a desire to work constructively. The reality is one of various cliques or groups of people working independently of each other, often dominated by an elite who become adept at creating an 'illusion of consensus' (Eipper, 1986; O'Cearbhaill and Varley, 1993). It has been suggested that communities in Ireland possess various powers not only to create jobs and economic growth, but also to deliver a wide range of social services (McAllister 1995; Carey 1995a). The NDP 1989–1993, for example suggested that priorities will be set by the communities themselves, who will be responsible for ensuring that local potential will be realised. The NDP 2000–2006 also promotes a greater role for communities in developing the rural economy, while the government White Paper on rural development (Department of Agriculture & Food, 1999) suggests that there is 'considerable community and voluntary effort which can be mobilised to promote economic and social development in rural areas'. Conway (1991, p.75) however argued that all emphasis on bottom-up planning 'would require a corresponding commitment to decentralisation in public decision-making and increased citizen participation. Otherwise local rural areas would get increased responsibility for economic development of their area without corresponding powers for public action, which would amount to abdication of responsibility by central authorities'. In all, communities are being given added responsibility to create their own local economies (see Varley 1991a; Bohan, 1994). This move toward new forms of rural governance (albeit without increased resources), while welcome and indeed almost inevitable, can also lead to the 'blurring of responsibilities' with a 'stepping back of the state [and a pushing of] responsibility onto private and voluntary sectors and, more broadly, the citizen' (Stoker, 1998, p.21).

Community, development and avoiding the pitfalls

Voluntarism and community groups in rural Ireland continue to be very much entrenched within the rural development policy of the country. Historically, community enterprise has been the hallmark of the Irish countryside from the mutual aid given by neighbouring farmers (the 'meitheal' system of the nineteenth century) to the present day multi-purpose community co-operatives combining economic, social and cultural goals (see Ó Cinnéide, 1986). An example of the growth of community action and self-reliance occurred in the Gaeltacht areas in the 1960s where general discontent with government policies became fused with local cultural identity, leading to an unprecedented growth in local and community development co-operatives (Breathnach, 1986). In more recent times these organisations are described as reputedly offering solidarity with the people, knowledge of local conditions and a greater reaction to local needs. Such claims support the common assumption that rural society is somehow more caring and responsive than its urban counterpart. Rogers (1987) suggests that whether this is true or not is unimportant, since the real significance is that people *believe* in the rural archetypal 'caring community', and indeed go so far as justifying apparent deprivation by arguing its unimportance 'either because material things are judged less significant in the countryside, or because there exists a sense of responsibility and of charitable service in the higher echelons of rural society which ameliorates material disadvantage' (p.356) (see also McLaughlin, 1986b).

Dillion (1989) listed several reasons for the involvement of local communities in the development of their own areas. His argument was based on:

- the communities' right to make decisions about their environment and living conditions;
- the need for local democracy so that planning is not something removed from people on the ground;
- the idea that the use of community organisations may have a better chance of securing commitment from statutory bodies or politicians; and in many cases,
- the belief that community involvement will lead to more co-ordinated and integrated development at the local level.

There are however a number of potential obstacles to the successful inclusion of communities, namely: hostility of local elites to the promotion of innovative strategies; the danger of 'cosy' relationships developing between a few voluntary/community sector power brokers and statutory representatives (see Frazer 1994), and the possibility of intra-community rivalry and competition. Frazer (ibid.) also expressed some concern about community animation and its role in rural development. He suggested that there were a number of important issues that were barriers to empowerment at a community level, in particular:

- Issues of representation. Those that are most socially excluded must be targeted for inclusion;
- Issues of time. Frazer, recognising that participation takes time, presents a strong case for a preparatory phase to develop capacity building within communities;

- The danger of tokenism. That is, involving people who are genuinely disadvantaged without giving them the support and resources they require to make an effective contribution;
- Unequal power relations. The advocating of partnerships as opposed to donor-recipient relationships; and
- Representation versus participation. That is, the community sector engaging in a more structured way with the political system.

However, if it is accepted that participation at local level leads to increased resources, greater commitment, a people-centred approach to planning and more integrated development, then communities will obviously benefit. Nevertheless, the present balance of power in the state-community relationship depicts a different picture. This was clearly illustrated in the submission of reports in preparation for the National Development Plan (1989-1993). While seven newly-created regions and working groups were set up for the purpose of "consultation" and making contributions to the proposals for the NDP, these were 'dominated by civil servants from Dublin ... with the chairpersons of county councils thrown in to give a veneer of democracy' (McDonald, 1989, p.36). The tokenism of such a gesture was underlined when it transpired that none of the proposals were submitted to the EU, except those which corresponded with what already had been decided by the Department of Finance and the Department of the Taoiseach (ibid., p.37). As such, the government made no serious attempt to consult local people on development issues in their own areas; and where such attempts were made, these were minimal and in many cases mere patronising gestures (O'Donohue, 1989). In fact, the response of the Irish state has been ambivalent and noncommittal, despite the relative success of some community groups and co-operatives. Breathnach (1986, p.79) suggested that this was due in part 'to the fear of these local initiatives as a potential threat to existing power structures [or] a more likely explanation is a sceptical and disparaging attitude on the part of professional technocrats regarding what are seen as the enthusiastic but inevitably incompetent efforts of local amateurs'.

Lowe and Buller (1985) have also argued that rural voluntary organisations are 'marginal to the major social issues confronting rural areas and remote from the vast majority of rural residents ... and are likely to remain poorly equipped to act as very forceful pressure groups on behalf of the rural poor and deprived' (cited in Rogers, 1987). Rogers (1987) recognised the validity of this comment, and put forward three elements attributable to any rural voluntary organisation, namely: that resources are invariably inadequate to match the substantial problems facing rural areas; that funding is precarious, that is, while voluntary bodies act as mediator or advocate, their protests may be modified due to their relationship with funding agencies, and that 'the system in advocating locally-responsive voluntary action to 'fill in' the gaps, in particular in rural services, left by inadequate statutory activity, effectively side-steps the real nature of rural problems which, it is argued, lie in the established political and social structure of rural areas' (ibid., p.358). From this perspective, not only is the role of the voluntary and community sector in the decision-making process questionable, but the promotion of partnership and participation as advocated in rural development policy in Ireland, seems of a superficial and unconvincing nature.

Participation and animation – rhetoric or necessity?

Considerable weight has been given to the contribution that communities can make to the regeneration of their own areas (see Keane, 1990; O'Cearbhaill, 1992a; Asby and Midmore, 1993; Kearney et al., 1994; Murray and Dunn, 1995; Lorendahl, 1996, among others). In 1990s development discourse it is a commonplace that 'the most important element in the rural development process is the population that the policies are designed to serve' (Asby and Midmore, 1993, p.1). While social and economic policies for rural areas have tended to concentrate on exploitation of natural resources, it is only in recent years that there have been efforts to invest in human resources and in generating development from within local communities. In fact participation has never enjoyed as much official legitimacy as today (Stiefel and Wolfe, 1994). The concept of partnership (explored in Chapter 6) and participation by people in the institutions and systems that govern their lives was described by the Food and Agriculture Organisation (FAO) (1981) as a 'basic human right'. It has become increasingly clear that there is a necessity for realignment of political power in favour of disadvantaged groups for social and economic development and, a recognition that 'rural development strategies can realise their full potential only through the motivation, active involvement and organisation at the grassroots level of rural people' (Burkey, 1993, p.56). As with the rather vague use of the term community, the use of 'partnership' and 'participation' in relation to development is currently very fashionable in Irish development discourses. The emergence of such concepts however, is not new to Irish rural policies, and seems to be a (re)introduction of the alternative development proposed in the late 1960s and early 1970s where 'slogans such as participation, democracy and self-reliance are prominent in official statements and resolutions of all international organisations and agencies, including the World Bank, and plans of action call for the involvement of NGOs and grassroots organisations' (Stiefel and Wolfe, 1994, p.220). Nevertheless, despite this new-found legitimacy, there would seem to be a gap in understanding when these terms are used in the public and voluntary domains.

In general terms, popular participation has been equated with the empowerment of the powerless (Collins, 1992). However, this equation needs to be broken down into the specific questions of why people want to participate, what can be gained, and what are the main stumbling blocks? Although the language of participation is central to the post-modern vocabulary, it is not as new as its recent popularity suggests (Third World countries have long advocated its merits) (ibid.). Participation can not be seen only as a development strategy but more importantly as a development objective. Participation is generally defined as the taking part in activities in a way designed to influence events in a positive manner, whether in the areas of policy formation, implementation, or evaluation. The growing demand for active participation in recent years is perhaps due to a combination of factors, including higher levels of education, greater access to information via the media and the realisation that government activities have a greater impact on the quality of life than ever before (de Buitléir, 1992).

Exploring the concept of participation, (see O'Cearbhaill, 1982; Commins, 1983; Breathnach, 1986; Ó Cinnéide, 1986; Rodgers, 1987; Farrington *et al.*, 1993; Hewison, 1993; Uphoff, 1993), a number of problems can be recognised. An issue that often arises, is the question of who controls the group. Critical to the success of participation is whether voluntary/local groups come to be seen as the voice of the local communities at government level, or the eyes and ears of the government at local level. The complexity of the issue is further compounded by the selective participation of groups (see Shortall, 1994), where those already operating in positions of power are more often than not accepted as the most appropriate leaders (for example the role of the priest in rural Ireland). This situation reinforces the patron-client relationship, rather than changing it to any great degree. Furthermore, it has been suggested (Kearney *et al.*, 1994) that it is more often than not the better off community groups, that is, those with more knowledge, connections, ability and resources to attract funding, which create the most attractive package for development projects (for example, LEADER), rather than the less well-off groups who, paradoxically, are most in need.

The concept of participatory development also involves a lot of good intentions, but very little 'real' participation, in the sense of having a genuine say in policy formation at the level where it can be put into practice, and the right to make a real contribution to society and self development (Fay, 1989). Burkey (1993) makes the argument that participation is an essential part of human growth, a process whereby people learn to take charge of their own lives and solve their own problems. In the debate on the meaning of participation, Burkey asks whether 'participation is a *means* used to achieve development or an *end* in itself, that is, by establishing a process of genuine participation, development will occur as a direct result' (ibid., p.58, original emphasis). While Burkey does not indicate how such genuine participation is to be achieved, or what constitutes such a process, there is the view that participation is one of more 'learning by doing', praxis as distinguished from theory. Oakley and Marsden (1984) give examples of two main vehicles for participation, that is, the use of community development programmes which are designed to prepare rural populations to collaborate with government development plans, and the establishment of formal organisations which provide some structure through which rural people can have a voice in development programmes. While the former model would seem too radical and challenging a concept for Irish civil servants and politicians (see Fay, 1989), the latter model would seem to reflect, more closely, the structures under which current rural development is pursued. The crucial factor, however, is the ease with which such organisations can 'become centres of formal power dominated by the few' (Burkey, 1993, p.60), and consequently lead to a further disempowering of those they are designed to empower (see later section on the frustration of bottom-up initiatives).

The use of participation can therefore serve as a 'catch word', an "in" reference which has to be used when talking about or encouraging development and empowerment of local communities (see Burkey, 1993). Its use often implies a coming together of people and ideas in common pursuit of a particular goal, the development of self-confidence, initiative, responsibility and co-operation. All too often however participation comes to represent the many being dominated by the few. Other difficulties stem from the general lack of resources which community organisations usually experience. This situation causes a compromise with the elite to ensure survival, and results in many organisations being absorbed by the formal agencies, ultimately becoming the institutionalised agents of state policies (see later section). It is for these reasons, particularly the fear of losing their autonomy and selling out to the state (see Collins, 1992), that community groups are often wary of partnerships with the state. Whether these misgivings can be overcome however, is debatable. As a step in this direction, Dillion (1989, p.42) suggests that there are a number of principles that should inform participation, that is, accountability, additionality, and active involvement. The last of these is perhaps the most important, in that groups 'should not confuse consultation with participation and should be careful to propose structures which ensure the local involvement on joint committees etc. is more than a token involvement' (ibid., p.42). The recent outcomes of the Programme for Economic and Social Progress (PESP) 1991 also indicated a strong reluctance to change. While many, viewed PESP as ideal for local participation, with its inclusion of employers, unions and some community groups, in reality it excluded large sections of Irish society. Similarly, the NDPs, which theoretically encourage participation, are shown to be hastily drawn up with little local input and little bearing on submissions to the EU.[1]

It is therefore becoming clear that policies become ineffective without sufficient involvement and debate by local people (Keane, 1990;

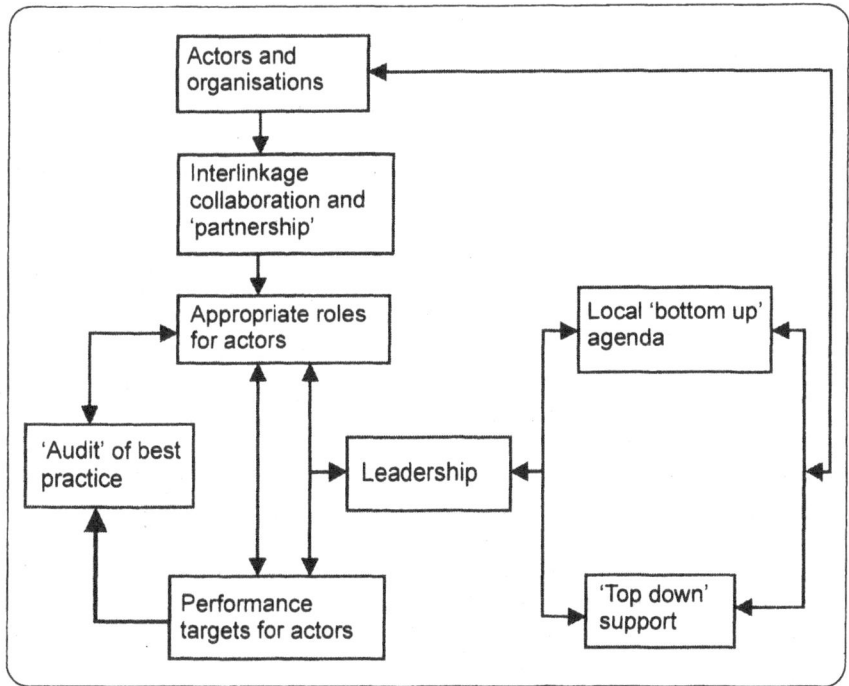

Figure 5.1 The animation of local development (Bennett, 1989)

O'Cearbhaill, 1992a; Ó Cinnéide, 1993a). The main pre-requisite to ensure greater participation is granting a greater time span for the discussion and implementation of rural policies, and a resistance to the 'too often quick results demanded by those who hold the purse strings' (ibid., p.48). The fundamental success of any participatory developmental programme is an integrated approach to the treatment of rural and urban development, since changes in either have implications for both. A more evenly distributed funding mechanism, absent since the designation of Ireland as a region within the EU, is also important. Ultimately, the central issue of participation is wrapped up in the distribution of power, power which is 'exercised by some people over other people and by some classes over other classes ... and any serious advocacy of increased participation implies a redistribution of power in favour of those hitherto powerless' (Stiefel and Wolfe 1994, p.4).

What of animation?

Significant to this redistribution of power is the development of animation capacities. The fundamental role of animation is to 'improve the effectiveness of the human resource factor in local development' (Kearney *et al.*, 1994, p.22). This means, essentially, getting people involved, allowing people to have their say and make their contribution to whatever development objectives are under consideration. The recognition of human resource development as an integral part of the strategic planning for rural areas, is suggested by Mackay (1989) as requiring active involvement at local and regional levels, because '(c)entralised control is remote and ill informed. It creates an environment which is unlikely to reflect the imperatives and desires of the population ... no sustained economic development is possible without human development' (cited in Asby and Midmore, 1993, p.8). The strategy of involving local communities is a slow process, particularly the building of co-operation and confidence at local level. Bennett (1989) described this process as one of obtaining the most appropriate match between actors and roles, all of which are interlinked (Figure 5.1) and of determining the effect and success of local development (cited in Kearney *et al.*, 1994).

A perceptible shift is therefore apparent in the move from top-down sectoral policy to a more bottom-up partnership arrangement. This shift, however, still gives rural communities in Ireland only limited opportunities to influence the development process. Ó Cinnéide (1992b, p.12) has suggested nevertheless, that, whether from the top-down or bottom-up perspective, it is becoming increasingly apparent that 'the most effective path to rural development involves the integration of the top-down functional approach with the bottom-up territorial approach'. While this is a compelling prospect, to create an egalitarian institutional framework that could facilitate such integration provides the real challenge. There has, in the last decade, been a greater enthusiasm for the creation of voluntary organisations, non-governmental organisations and grassroots organisations but, if local development in Ireland is to succeed it must be able to harness all elements of the rural base; the private sector, local co-operatives, community interests, local authorities, state agencies and the farming community (Keane, 1990; Kearney *et al.*, 1994). The success of local development is however hampered by the complex structures through which local governance proceeds (County Enterprise Boards, LEADER, Area-Based Partnerships) (see Chapter 6). However, the desire by local communities to 'have a say' not only gains pace internally, but is encouraged externally (by the EU) through the development and promotion of alternative delivery channels between state, community and citizen to raise economic, social and political productivity.

The role of the Church in Irish rural development

> The hierarchy, needless to say, is the strongest pressure group in the country, and the everyday influence of the clergy is so great that it is easy to appreciate why the Irish have so often been described as priest ridden (Coogan, 1987, p.162).

The reconfiguration of the affinity between state, community and citizen forms a complex relationship between different actors and networks. In Ireland, the Church also plays an important part in this relationship. Overall, while there has been a lack of any coherent strategy, the role of the Church in development, and specifically, the role of key individuals, has been significant. In the remainder of this chapter the deconstruction of the key debates in Irish rural discourse are traced through the rise and fall of the 'Developing The West Together' group (DTWT) formed in the West of Ireland in 1991. This group, consisting of Church, state and community actors, is used as a vehicle to explore the representations and strategic partnerships being forged in the renegotiation, representation, reproduction and repackaging of ideas and alternatives for rural renewal in Ireland.

There is evidence of a strong tie between Church and state in Irish society. Keogh (1988, p.154) argued that the Church 'has an independently powerful manipulative capacity in the area of politics – a lobby that is unstoppable once it has set out to oppose a political or social manoeuvre by any government since the foundation of the State'. Tobin (1984, p.38) in fact equated the ecclesiastical structures in Ireland with the political structures, and described the Church's make-up as being closely aligned to that of the main political party, Fianna Fáil. They were both, he suggested 'organisation(s) that reached to the most remote parts of the country; sensitive to the demands made on [them], and efficient in satisfying them; receiving the unswerving loyalty of [their] partisans; brutally impatient with dissidents; and for all the intimacy of [their] local units, subject to strong and authoritative direction from the centre'.

Peillion (1984) pointed to the existence of a striking congruity between the dominant ideological mood and the views of the Catholic Church, and pointed to 'the Church's ability to influence and shape the general ideological setting' (cited in Szuchewycz, no date, p.46). The manner in which the Church has been able to achieve such an influential position in Irish society has also been explored by Inglis (1987, p.6) who viewed it as a major power-bloc operating primarily in the social and moral spheres of life and whose influence, from this base, extends into the spheres of economics and politics. The ecclesiastical 'commanding of respect' also has a spatial distinction, with a strong bias toward rural areas. This greater 'presence' of the Church in rural areas has its roots both in the conservatism of rural Ireland and in Irish colonial history, 'where loyalty to the Church was synonymous with loyalty to the country' (Hussey, 1993, p.384). The relationship between Church and rural may also have its roots in the perception of rural areas being in some ways less progressive than their urban counterparts. Overall, in terms of community structures and organisation, the churches and religion have a more organic role to play in rural Ireland than they have in large urban centres. Consequently the Church's immediate contact with thousands of communities and parishes, make it an ideal advocate. Its credibility however is determined by 'how effectively [the Church] engages itself at grassroots community development level' (Connolly, 1995, p.2).

Leadership and local development

The linkage between the Church and development in Ireland has been very much initiated by innovation and leadership provided by key individuals. Sorensen and Epps (1996) suggest that there are two types of leaders, legitimizers (prominent citizens with prestige) and effectors (professionals or technicians), and that there is an important connection between effective community leadership and local development. In their study of four Central Queensland towns in Australia, they make a strong case for 'a direct link between the quality of more general community leadership and the pace and form of local development' (ibid, p.113). Lorendahl (1996, p.149) also highlighted the importance of what he termed "key persons", that is, activators or change agents who act as community entrepreneurs and encourage other members. In fact it is suggested that in order to promote local development, 'it could be a wise step for governments at different levels to allocate resources, time and money, to such key persons to develop the collective entrepreneurship' (ibid.,), necessary for local development.

In an Irish context the tasks of animation, capacity building and local leadership have been very much left in the hands of local enthusiasts. These 'legitimizers' are usually spurred into action by a particular cause (be it as diverse as an airport or co-operative) and are rarely able to maintain a long-term development process. These dynamic personalities or "burning souls" as suggested by Amdam (1996) are in many cases returned emigrants, academics, or particularly in Ireland, members of the clergy. The type of local development pursued by these 'legitimizers' is often shown to have a significant leaning toward tangible accomplishments rather than consultative roles. In the case of rural Ireland, there are many examples of the role played by prominent clergymen in stimulating local development, particularly in the work of people like Monsignor James Horan, Canon John Hayes and Father James McDyer (see Figures 5.2; 5.3 and 5.4). These brief extracts illustrate the part of "key" actors, particularly from the Church, in stimulating local development in Ireland. They also reflect the influence of the clergy in the development arena. While this has been the case, Kearney *et al.*, (1994, p.25) suggest that the current emphasis on stimulation, assistance and facilitation contrast with the 'role of initiators and leaders that were usually the characteristics of the dominant personality in previous attempts at local development'. However, the degree to which dominant personalities can be pushed to the sidelines, and replaced by animators, is open to debate particularly in

Monsignor J. Horan and Knock Airport

To take a literally very concrete example of the Church's influence, one cannot underestimate the physical existence of the much criticised Knock Airport' (Coogan, 1987, p.78). The name of Monsignor Horan is synonymous with development in the West of Ireland. Mostly for religious reasons, and the desire to make Knock a major international pilgrimage site, Monsignor Horan was inspired to pursue the development of an airport in the region. Apart from the religious implications, Monsignor Horan was also aware of the emigration from the region and the desire for more employment opportunities. In 1979, a group came together consisting of business people, county managers, county development officers, and the Irish Tourist Board among others. This group established a committee and elected Monsignor Horan as its chairperson. Dismissed by many, (especially the Dublin-based media), as an 'Irish white elephant', with jibes as to 'what do we want with an airport on the top of a mountain in the middle of a bog', Monsignor Horan pursued relentlessly the concept of an airport 'up in Knock'. The attacks on the airport proposal were directed against the idea of building - and at greater cost, maintaining - an airport with runways capable of accommodating passenger jets out in the remote fogs and bogs of Mayo (Coogan, 1987). Proponents of the airport pointed to the socio-economic impact of the project on the region as a whole, as more important than the merely fiscal point of view. Following strong political lobbying and the considerable influence of the Monsignor, a decision to approve the airport was made. Despite having been temporarily shelved during a change in government, the airport was finally built thanks to the persistence of Monsignor Horan. His achievements, despite considerable opposition, are perhaps best placed in the 'resource development category which is part of the harmonious/consensual model of development, as his work involved an emphasis on the achievement of concrete development tasks enhancing the communities' economic resource structures (Connolly, 1995, p.51).

Figure 5.2 Monsignor J. Horan and Knock Airport

Canon J. Hayes and Muintir na Tíre

Muintir na Tíre [is based] on a belief that effective community development requires that area-based self-help groups should be representative of their localities, take on a challenging programme of work and continue to retain the confidence and support of the local population' (Varley, 1991a, p.85-86). In 1931 a Tipperary priest, John Hayes, founded 'Muintir na Tíre', a rural organisation based on the parish structures, and designed to carry out practical projects and was generally 'not sectoral but embraced all the people of the parish' (Connolly, 1995). Despite the non-political involvement pursued by Canon Hayes, in 1948 Muintir na Tíre submitted a Parish Plan to the Minister for Agriculture which strongly underlined the notion of parish co-operation and self-help. This was a step that Kennedy (1981) suggested created a whole new scenario between statutory and voluntary bodies. Muintir na Tíre's initial fear of the interventionist state gave rise to its call for subsidiarity, and its right to organise area-based groups working between the people and the state. Varley (1991a, p.84) suggested that whatever the initial apprehension of Canon Hayes about state involvement in self-help activity, 'lobbying the state soon came to figure prominently in the programmes of individual parish councils'. Rapid urbanisation, and a decline in membership, forced Muintir na Tíre to reorganise into community councils in the early 1970s. Its philosophy was now that the main pre-requisite for effective community development was a partnership between state and local community groups. Despite the state's unwillingness to recognise Muintir na Tíre as a 'partner' in any real sense, the organisation continued with its desire to create partnership-type relationships. Conceding that community councils had generated 'social returns' in the form of amenity provision and group water schemes, Varley (ibid., p.87) suggested that 'the verdict of some State officials [was], nonetheless, that area-based self-help groups can make only negligible contributions to job creation and the delivery of social services'. Muintir na Tíre, continuing their campaign for the devolving of decision making and reform of local government, were rewarded with the 1971 White Paper on Local Government reform which promoted the involvement of voluntary councils. These proposals, however, inspired fears on the part of the politicians of an alternative power base appearing in Irish society and as such, were not implemented (Roche, 1982, cited in Varley, 1991a, p.88). Other problems for Muintir na Tíre included: its historical concentration within Munster and southern Leinster to the detriment of those community councils in Connacht; its 'limited funding and resources; the inability of the organisation to halt the downward spiral in the annual State allocation of funding; the dominant role of priests and teachers which posed a threat to, and were biased by, civil servants; the lack of leadership roles for the wider community' (Connolly, 1995, p.44). In 1994, recognising the need to develop new strategies for creating sustainable employment, Muintir na Tíre commissioned studies of four communities in North and South Tipperary, which came to the ultimate conclusion that a partnership arrangement between statutory, social partners and the voluntary sector was the way forward.

Figure 5.3 Canon J. Hayes and Muintir na Tíre

Father J. McDyer and Glencolumbkille

The young who remained at home inherit a farm, but today they inherit more isolation than land. The Inishkillane community is intensely demoralised. The present structure of the population shows a spiral of decline which has not been checked' (Brody, 1973, p.13). Fr. James McDyer, assigned to the parish of Glencolumbkille, was faced with a community without electricity, poor roads and an ageing population. Spurred into action, Fr. McDyer, addressing a conference in 1964, outlined four vital pre-requisites for the salvation of small farm households: co-operation, education, capital and a spirit of enterprise (Tobin, 1984). McDyer dismissed comparisons between the West of Ireland and other developing countries insisting that, Ireland had modern utilities and infrastructure, and was hampered more by its farming techniques, low output, low marriage rate, and a reluctance by older farmers to pass on their land to their younger sons. Although his proposal for joint ownership of lands to maximise potential was dismissed by community and state alike, McDyer was very aware of the need for an industrial base to secure the future of his community. He suggested in his autobiography that 'it was all very well to have the infrastructure laid on in roads, electricity and eventually water supply, but I knew we must have industry if we were to trap migration at its source' (McDyer, 1982, p.71). Fr. McDyer subsequently initiated the 'Save the West' campaign, a slogan which became a national catch-cry, for his message of self-help. Opposition to McDyer's campaign came from the government and civil servants, but agreement was reached and pilot programmes for development were set up in the more neglected districts. However, these were so widely scattered that they had little impact (Connolly, 1995). (Such concessions from the state mirror Buller and Wright's (1990) theory that the motivation behind state interventions is largely driven by a desire to defuse devolutionist pressures). McDyer's main philosophy centred on encouraging ordinary people to take power into their own hands and to realise the value of the collective effort. He attributed his failings to, 'misinterpretation and misunderstanding of what he said was their proposal; loss of interest in the annual general meetings; [and] bureaucracy as the main stumbling block that caused apathy and inertia' (ibid., p.47). Some of the weaknesses of McDyer's work were suggested by Regan and Breathnach (1981) as: his concentration on a select group of individuals rather than involving the community at large in many of his activities, thus providing very little 'real participation' (attributable to either his dominant personality or the powerful position priests held in rural society of the time). Other contributory factors included: an over eagerness to get quick results without first reaching a consensus; his suspicion that there was constant opposition to his endeavours; poor management, which displayed his inability to assess the economic viability of a project (the centralised control which he exercised adding further vulnerability); and a style of going 'straight to the top' (see Connolly, 1995). Regan and Breathnach (1981) further suggested that despite their popular image, Fr. McDyer's operations had very little real co-operation or popular input, relying almost entirely on grants or loans for capital. Ultimately, McDyer' 'Save the West' campaign showed a poor understanding of the concept of participation. Such participation does not occur overnight and entails patience, education, organisation and democratic power, as well as the need to design projects on a sound economic basis.

Figure 5.4 Father J. McDyer and Glencolumbkille

the context of Irish culture where there is a reluctance to become 'involved'.

The frustration of bottom-up development

> Something has been going on west of the Shannon. You might see it in a cold hall, at night in Loughrea, where small farmers from the district are trying to express their sense of their own economic and cultural plight in a new language. They are in a "core group", and they are trying to "identify and prioritise the functions" of a core group so as to "participate in a process" which – they desperately hope – might arrest the decay of the world they know. Or at least draw attention to it' (O'Faolain, 1993a, p.11).

Since the late 1980s there have been significant changes in the structure of Irish communities; changes in attitudes and the way people view themselves, their environs, their community, history and future. This section explores claims that locally initiated development organisations allow rural communities to mobilise themselves to oppose national policies, and create alternative models for development in their own region. In the early 1990s a unique combination of Church, state and community united (albeit loosely) to promote an alternative model of rural development in Ireland. The coming together of this 'partnership', called Developing the West Together (DTWT), provides an interesting insight into the frustration experienced by community groups in rural Ireland and to the combination of circumstances; political, social and cultural, that led to the eventual paralysis of what was ostensibly a grassroots or bottom-up development. The political and social pressures brought to bear on this group, and the specific events which led to the groups' perceived demise, provide a critical evaluation of contemporary rural discourse and attempts at partnership between state and citizen.

'The West Awakes', and 'The Fight for the West', (O'Faolain, 1993a) were the headlines that signalled the emergence of the movement which hoped to bring about a rural revival in the West of Ireland. This resurgence of activism had set itself the goal, albeit a familiar one, of economic survival for the West. So what made this movement different from all the rest (Fr. McDyer's campaign for example)? Was it merely the involvement of the Bishops of the region which gave this initiative greater importance or at least more hope that its predecessors? Was it the way in which this organisation was being 'represented' as being different? Or, (just as importantly) was this phase of development actually different at all?

The DTWT group perceiving that the West of Ireland was in economic and social decline, sought to set in motion a populist movement and, in so doing, design an alternative approach to development within the region. Formed in 1991 and consisting initially of members of the local community and the Church hierarchy, DTWT could be described as attempting to

Retrospect and Prospect 129

renegotiate rural development in the West through, reproducing, representing and repackaging suggestions, ideas and alternatives for rural renewal. The name 'Developing the West Together', presented a somewhat fanciful collection of words, which tried to incorporate economic, social and individual objectives. This combination of goals was based on the concept that, for Ireland to develop, Irish people and Irish civic culture must change, and change rapidly. DTWT originated in 1990 when the Bishops of two dioceses[2] in the West of Ireland, Bishop Casey of Galway and Bishop Kirby of Clonfert were approached[3] by a number of small farmers from the south Galway area. These farmers had approached other organisations (local authorities, farming organisations, politicians) with little success before finally turning to the Bishops. The farmers expressed their concerns and their sense of alienation from the process of decision-making that affected their everyday lives and their economic prospects. The Bishops responded positively by expressing an awareness of the decline in the region and a willingness to join in efforts to combat this decline. The first step in the infancy of DTWT saw the Bishops drawing together a number of experts within the region. This Advisory Committee to the Western Bishops' Conference on Development (ACWBCD) was made up of professionals (academics, members of state agencies and business people) and a member of the clergy (of the 10 members there was only one female). The advisory body produced various papers and proposals to 'alert and shock politicians and people' (ACWBCD, Meeting Minutes 1991) as to the serious rate of decline in the West, with the debate *coming quickly to the conclusion that what was needed was a regional policy*'.[4]

The culmination of these reports was the organisation of a seminar in Galway on 4 and 5 November 1991. The twin aims of this seminar were to highlight 'the seriousness of the situation in the West of Ireland, and ... assist the process by which this situation could be addressed and remedied' (McInerney, 1992b, p.2). The line taken by the advisory committee was that new and imaginative policies would have to be devised. In particular, a comprehensive regional development strategy for the West of Ireland was to be designed and sufficient human and financial resources allocated for its implementation. The people of the Western region were to be fully involved if this process was to be successful (DTWT, 1991b). The seminar proceeded in November 1991, and as a route to some form of legitimacy, a number of the major 'players' in the field of rural and regional development were invited to attend. These included development agencies, statutory bodies, government departments, trade unions, women's groups and the unemployed, with a keynote address from John Hume (MP, MEP). McInerney (1992a, p.3) described the number and range of organisations represented as 'a clear indication, if further was needed, of the level of feeling and concern about the future of the West of Ireland [and] the willingness of the people of the West of Ireland to take an <u>active</u>

part in all the various aspects of the development of their region' (original emphasis). The seminar raised issues on education, greater transparency in decision-making, and the need for a collective voice (McInerney, 1992b, gives a more detailed account).

Despite positive reaction to the seminar, there seemed little scope for giving 'people effective local government which is relevant to their needs as perceived by themselves, not as seen by somebody from outside' (Hume, 1993 p.1–2). Instead, the presence of the extra level of experts, helped further disempower the local community (as indicated in conversations with DTWT members). The use of a 'panel of experts' was, it seemed, very much in keeping with the traditional path followed in development discourse generally. The seminar was however given a more progressive dimension by John Hume's keynote address which discussed the possibility of decentralised power and a 'Europe of the Regions'. This particular proposal was readily supported by some of the more active members of DTWT, raising their hopes for regional autonomy for the West.[5]

A further issue arising from the DTWT seminar was the importance of awareness-raising throughout the region and mobilising people into a populist movement. The strategy of putting *'bodies on seats'* (a phrase used by a member of the Advisory Committee) had the objectives of: informing people of the Bishop's concern for the West and of the initiative launched to challenge its decline. A number of public meetings were subsequently held. The first regional meeting took place in Sligo and was attended by approximately 490 people, almost double the anticipated attendance. Other meetings took place in Tuam (440 in attendance), Ballina (530), Ballaghadereen (630), Loughrea (430), Carrick-on-Shannon (450), Leitrim, Castlerea, Belmullet, Carraroe, Castlebar, Castlerea and Ballinrobe. In all, over 5,000 people participated in these meetings, in an attempt to put on record what they saw as the problems of their own areas, of the broader region and, more importantly, what they saw as solutions. However, the attendance by 5,000 people at a number of regional meetings, albeit promising, does not necessarily indicate a concern with the state of the region, and more importantly a willingness to do something about it. While the number was undoubtedly significant, sceptical observers might suggest that almost as many would turn out for an interesting county football match. Certainly, the importance attributed by DTWT to the volume of attendance at these meetings, led the group on a somewhat misguided path as to the willingness and ability of the people within the West to become involved in the planning and implementation of this new wave of development.

Eighteen core groups were formed throughout the West (Figure 5.5) to address the task DTWT had set itself. These core groups, while an important step in enabling grassroots involvement, did not have their potential fully realised. These groups were non-hierarchical structures made up of voluntary individuals who generally lived and worked in the areas they represented. The role of the core groups was to 'animate local communities and provide leadership, to encourage communication and involvement in making decisions – in other words, to try to 'make a match' between participative democracy and representative democracy' (Finnegan, 1995, p.3). That each parish in the region should have its own core group informing the 'experts' seemed plausible, yet how far this was a genuine achievement is very much open to debate. The short-term objectives of the core groups dealt with local issues (for example, the Sligo-Dublin railway improvement); while the longer term objectives were concerned with creating strategies for the future well-being of the region. A number of parish meetings were held and a large variety of issues were tabled by the core groups. These ranged from tourism, theme parks, golf courses and nature trails, to milk quotas and the need for tax exemptions.

Gradually however, concern grew regarding the sometimes divergent interests within the core groups pertaining to specific projects within their own areas. The use of the core groups as lobbyists, while originally encouraged for the benefit of all, became more concentrated on specific campaigns. This had not been envisaged, or encouraged, by DTWT. This type of activity, while understandable, flew in the face of Fr. Kelly of Drumkeerin's assertion that 'there's a new generosity in this region. People aren't just looking after their own little neck of the woods any more' (cited in the O'Faolain, 1993b). The concept of the core groups, admirable in intent, did not reach all the people. In discussions with co-ordinators of the groups, it was suggested that the groups did not get to the *'real people ... that we would've liked to have reached'*. The very nature of the groups' origins was perhaps one the main drawbacks as they had been put together *'by virtue of the local Bishop or the local priest being contacted and being told, – we want a core group together to organise this meeting [regional meeting], pick people'*. The inevitable result was that the people who were picked were generally already involved in community activities or in the local parish councils. In many cases, they were the local elite, the teachers, doctors, farmers and businessmen. That participants were generally male merely highlighted the lack of gender equality in Irish rural development. While not detracting from their sincerity, this type of participant began to represent what was called *'the M, M and M factor; they were dominated by middle-class, middle-aged men'*. The lack of gender balance, and poor representation by young people and other marginalised groups reflected the hasty origins of the groups and probably led to an excessively narrow perspective on development issues. While McInerney (1992a, p.7) argued that the 'best experts on the West of Ireland are the people of the West of Ireland themselves', the image of significant participation by the people of the region was misleading. In fact, those who did participate had their views structured by specific guidelines so as to ensure that the 'focus of the study is an identification of strategies and options for development, rather than the production of a list of individual projects' (DTWT, no date;a, p.1).

The role of the Church

The almost unconscious reference to DTWT as the 'Bishops' initiative' perhaps best reflected what was most hopeful (or most worrying) about this latest attempt to 'Save the West'. In many references to DTWT, by politicians, newspapers and local communities, the equating of the 'Bishops' initiative' with DTWT was commonplace. The profile of the Bishops as spokespeople was largely responsible for this, as was perhaps the use of the Bishops' 'name' originally an effort by the local communities to gain greater acknowledgement. Following the launch of DTWT, the role of the Bishops was seen as one of producing a collective voice to create an awareness of the high levels of unemployment and emigration in the region (Finnegan, 1994). The Bishops further emphasised that 'their competence was religious, not economic; and [they] were concerned with the ethical and human aspects of the problem' (ibid. p.129). Members of the Church's hierarchy saw themselves as 'facilitators of a process which [they] hope(d) [would] lead to constructive changes in the lives of [their] people' (Kirby, 1991, cited in McInerney 1992b, p.6). O'Faolain (1993c) suggested that the Bishops could not contain their pastoral role within the purely spiritual however, and as such, they had to get involved. The added dimension to the Church's involvement was their supposed ability to build on their 'base as the 'Church of the people' (Breen, *et al.*, 1990) yet the question remained, as to why it took so long for the Bishops to speak out, and whether it was coincidental that such profile raising had come when the Church was going through some difficult times.

DTWT progressed with the meeting of Bishops Casey and Kirby with John Hume and Bruce Millan (European Commissioner) in Strasbourg. This meeting discussed funding from the EC for a comprehensive study of the region, which would attempt 'to feed into a study at parish-level, and to shape it as much from the experience of ordinary people as by the knowledge of experts' (O'Faolain, 1993a). The word 'together' suggested Bishop Finnegan (1994, p.129) was very important, in that 'the Bishops believe(d) in a partnership approach, a partnership between public, private and local community interests'. This, he concluded, was 'one of the most important features of this [proposed] study, in that it [would] involve close consultation between the consultants and local development groups, both voluntary and statutory' (ibid., p.132). The sentiment of this statement was however, far from the outcome, as the participation of the core groups was not only flawed from the outset but also was, in any case, to a large degree ignored. The Bishops therefore went to Europe:

> Mitre in hand, claiming that the support of the 'grassroots' of the region was firmly behind them. They were up to Dublin to see Government Ministers. Nearly every one of the West's Dáil Deputies

and Senators turned up when they asked to meet them. Nobody dared dismiss them, as they would dismiss the people alone (O'Faolain, 1993c).

Politically, the response of the elected representatives toward DTWT seemed for the most part, positive. Few dissenting voices were heard, but in discussions with members of DTWT it was suggested that while the official correspondence received from Dáil deputies was positive and supportive of the actions of DTWT, behind this 'official line' there was nervousness. This nervousness was not only associated with *'the Bishops coming out and saying all these things about the region'*, but also nervousness whereby *'local activists from one political party had been instructed to get involved in the core groups and to take up positions of leadership in it'*. Essentially efforts were being made to exert some form of control or favourable direction on the core groups from the 'inside', rather than letting such groups challenge the traditional clientelism structure that was in place. Some dissenting voices were also heard which essentially suggested that the government, in any event, were actively pursuing initiatives regarding the economic and social decline of the West, and that the DTWT proposals would not make a lasting impact at government level.

A Crusade for Survival

> A question frequently asked ... in the course of this study is to whom is our Report addressed – the Bishops, the Government, the public agencies, the people in the West, the Commission? As I see it, our recommendations concern all of these groups. The scale of the problems in the West of Ireland is so great and the need for action so urgent that resolution of the crisis situation of which we speak in the Report demands a major partnership between all concerned. It is because of this crisis facing the people in the West that we have been prompted to refer to the efforts involved in its solution as 'a crusade for survival (Euradvice, 1994, p.vii).

The fervour generated by the regional meetings in the wake of the Galway seminar was followed by the dissipation of the radical edge of DTWT, as the main actors in the group (ACWBCD and the Bishops), endorsed Hume's (1991) suggestion to seek funding from the EC to undertake a major study of the region. There did not appear (at least officially) to be any debate within the group as to whether this was the only way forward. At the request of DTWT, *A Crusade for Survival* was the title given to the study of the West to be undertaken by a research team funded by the EC and the Department of Finance. The study was put up for tender, the Euradvice team (also involved in drawing up the proposals for the EC) were chosen, and the "chasing of funds" from Europe began.

What was the study for?

In the light of the deteriorating socio-economic situation of the West, and following discussions with the European Commissioner Bruce Millan, the Bishops of the region proposed that the EC fund a study which would:

> serve as a model for examining the problems of declining rural areas in so called 'Objective 1' regions whose development is lagging behind. The hope is that the lessons to be learned from the proposed study would serve as headlines for other disadvantaged rural areas both in Ireland and elsewhere in the Community, and that ... the West of Ireland could thus be identified as a 'flagship' for other peripheral areas within Europe' (Casey, 1992, p.3).

The *Crusade for Survival* proposed to be an analytical, participative and action-oriented study (Euradvice, 1994). Having supposedly learned from the failure of previous attempts to reverse the decline of the West region (for example, from the Congested Districts Board of 1891, to the 'Western Package' in the 1980s), the authors of the report indicated that they would be 'on their guard' in setting expectations for future development, by focusing on strategies for development, rather than individual projects (Euradvice, 1992). In the spirit of co-operation between private individuals and groups in the West, (which supposedly led the ACWBCD and the Bishops to call the initiative 'Developing the West Together'), the guidelines for those submitting tenders, required that 'the local contribution to the development process be fully taken into account by those carrying out the main study' (DTWT, 1992c, p.6). The core groups, which were formed by the Bishops, were seen as the main conduits for this dialogue.[6]

The geographical dimension of the study region (Figure 5.5) was also problematic. The regional expressions of Ireland (see Chapter 2) are for the most part confusing, if not entirely chaotic. After some deliberations the study area was finally agreed, between the Bishops and the ACWBCD, and covered the five counties of Connacht – Galway, Mayo, Sligo, Leitrim and Roscommon, and Co. Donegal in the province of Ulster. The official reason for choosing these counties purported to take into consideration a number of factors, the primary one being the level of rural decline in these areas, and the possible 'coincidence of the area with regional planning and executive organisations, including both national and local government functions, as well as monitoring of Community programmes' (Casey, 1992). While a certain degree of dispute (from Co. Clare) surrounded the extent of the study region, the proposers of the study defended its limitations and argued that they were well aware of the decline in other rural parts of Ireland, but that, with possibly the exception of Galway City, the province of Connacht and Co. Donegal: 'present(ed) a relatively homogeneous area of unrelieved rural underdevelopment

Retrospect and Prospect 135

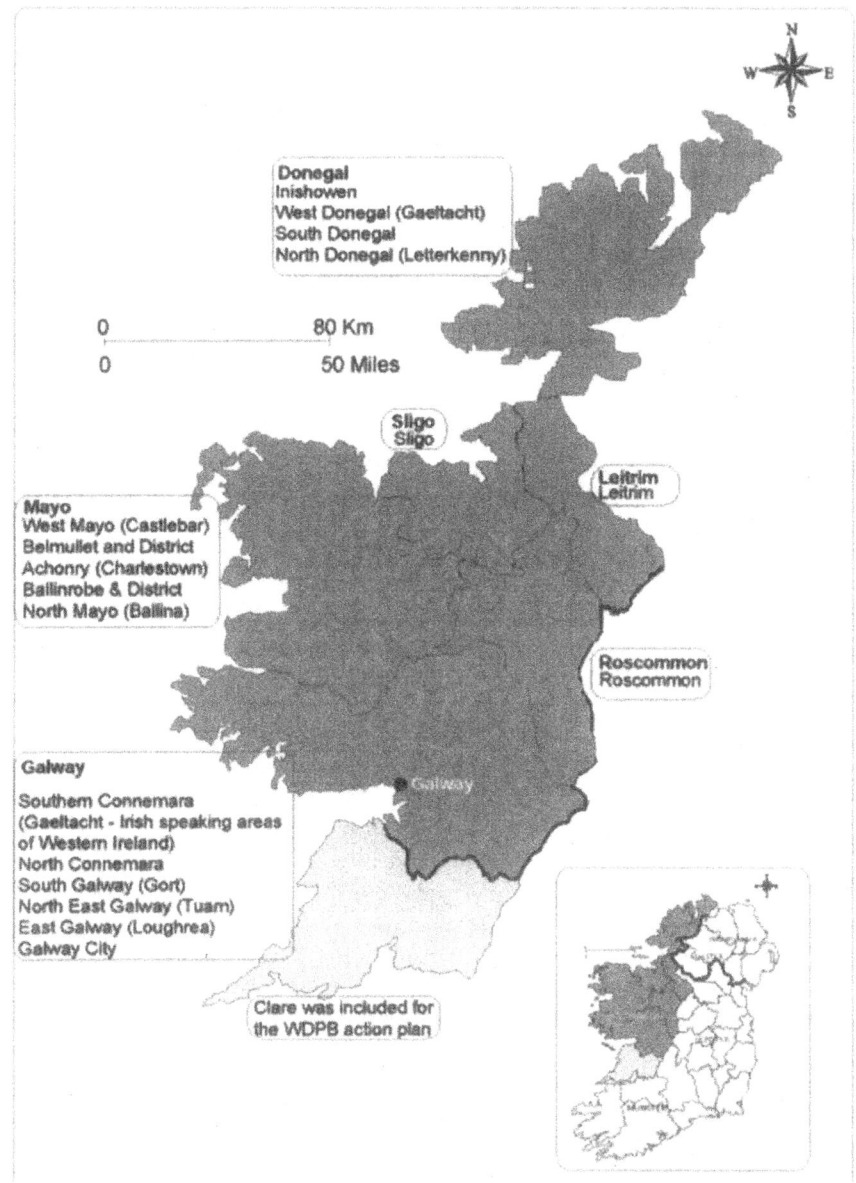

Figure 5.5 Developing the West Together study area and associated core groups

[which] correspond(ed) also to regional administrative structures which [could] be mobilised in assisting policy implementation in relief of rural development problems' (Euradvice, 1994, p.15).

Why do a study?

The idea that the report would generate productive economic activity and jobs in the West (Casey, 1992) was laudable. There were however a number of underlying limitations. The first is attributed to the fact that DTWT was simply following the guidelines laid down by European bureaucracy.[7] This was indicated in discussions with one member of the Advisory Body who suggested that *'the corporate strategy of Europe is that they need a major study that they have funded themselves before they accept movement'*. A second reason, more reflective of the broader discourses of Irish development, is the mind-set of extracting as much funding from Europe as possible, and then establishing a structure for its allocation (see also Boyle, 2000). In this way, the actual receipt of funds, rather than the use to which it is put, is deemed to be a kind of 'development' (see Commins and Keane, 1994). A third reason, could be attributed to the Bishops' viewing the study as an ideal way to 'tie up' their own involvement with the initiative, having being somewhat frightened by the level of momentum it had generated. A fourth possibility was that the funding allocation from Europe was seen as symbolic, particularly by some of the more radical DTWT members. The significant step was that a sub-region within Ireland (the main region), would be allocated "direct" funding from the EC, without sanctioning from the Irish government. Had this happened, a precedent for the other sub-regions would have been created, and the knock-on effect would inevitably have led to demands for greater regional control and (in the eyes of some DTWT members), eventual regional autonomy.

Drawing these issues together, it seems that the reasoning behind the study was a combination of all these perspectives. Essentially, the study was controlled by a 'clutch' of dominating elite; the professionals of the ACWBCD; some of the Bishops; and some members of the DTWT group. The fact that EC bureaucracy made it necessary to go through certain formalities, meant it was simply a path which had to be followed, rather than one deriving from any great belief by these parties that such a study would instigate alternative strategies to 'Save the West'. Where such strategies did develop, there was also little belief that they would, in any event, be taken seriously by the Irish government.

The study process

The study got off to a rather enigmatic start as there was much consternation, and indeed anger, that the 'job' of undertaking a

Retrospect and Prospect 137

comprehensive study of the West was allocated to a Dublin company, Euradvice Ltd. This resentment did not, as many of the organisers had expected, dissipate with time, and despite the request to Euradvice to allocate sub-contracts to firms in the West (and their co-operation with this request), in many respects the tension continued to grow. This underlying tension appeared to stem from the presence within DTWT, of regional activists who were pro-active in terms of pushing their own political agenda of regional autonomy for the West. The circumventing of Dublin in relation to funding was therefore seen as a potentially major triumph. Thus, whatever the talents of Euradvice, their Dublin base was seen as symbolic of the inability of the West to pull away from centralist control. There was a feeling among some members of DTWT that the enlisting of a team of 'Dublin Professionals' to inform the West how best to save itself was anathema to the group's objectives and ideals.

The dissatisfaction and ill-feeling surrounding the preparation of the study would seem to point to one conclusion; if DTWT had been really serious in putting together an action-oriented and dynamic study of the region, it would have benefited from a more focussed and energetic approach. Another crucial step would have been a study that would be capable of challenging the conventional developmental processes being followed by rural professionals and bureaucrats. The final product however was a 'safe-ground' report, penned by a respected professional, and a reinforcing the top-down ethos, which further disempowered the local communities. In short, a total contradiction to what DTWT had projected as its original objectives.

Possible outcomes

The urgency with which the study progressed was very much linked to 'chasing funds from Europe'. O'Faolain (1993a) suggested that DTWT had its eye on the European Structural Funds and this was further confirmed in Euradvice's tender proposal. Their approach, it was suggested, was strongly influenced by the necessity to contribute to the drawing up of the CSF for the next round of the Structural Funds, and their timetable was designed toward that end (Euradvice, 1994). Considering this in-built dependency in the Irish psyche, it was hardly unexpected that consultants with a track record and knowledge of European funding criteria be appointed. It is not the intention to imply that the Euradvice study team was unsuited to do a study of the region. Moreover, it merely illustrates how, from the outset, the study was geared in the direction of obtaining funds from the EC, and of compiling an 'economic' profile of the region. Such prioritising would suggest that the study was done more 'for the sake of it', than for any great desire to come to terms with the processes of rural development which were interwoven with rural discourses in the West of Ireland.

In relation to the study itself, the actual terms of reference (Figure 5.6) are less important than their interpretation. The terms, while claiming to embark on new initiatives, were merely a reconstituting of orthodox methods based on the traditional sectors of economy, demography, agriculture and infrastructure. There were no new or radical objectives, and in a sense, the West's situation was brought back to 'square one'. The notion that DTWT was to challenge the political and state system in relation to the West was swallowed up in politics and bureaucracy, and yet 'another' study. The study, ultimately conditioned by the professionals, was destined therefore to reflect the 'usual' professional discourses.[8]

Terms of Reference

1) Assemble and analyse the salient socio-economic facts as regards the state of development of the West of Ireland (demography, labour force, urban/rural structures, economic activity and income, social infrastructure);

2) Examine the contribution of past policy actions, at regional, national and EU levels to the present situation in the West and suggest ways in which public policies should support a strategy for development in the Region, taking particular account of the economic and social development possibilities identified at local and regional levels;

3) In the light of this analysis, review the requirements for economic and social development and for job creation within the framework of targets aimed at stemming the flight of population from the West;

4) As part of this review, consider different approaches to development, both in terms of how to modify or intensify existing measures and, also, of how to embark on new initiatives which might contribute to development in the West. The review should cover examination of proposals developed locally which might be included in the development plan for the West. A central focus would be the search for economically and socially sustainable business initiatives, projects and activities which would also contribute to solving the problems of unemployment and would take account of environmental necessities;

5) Assemble and analyse relevant information on comparative experiences in other Member States of the EU with a view to drawing lessons from such experiences for the benefit of the West of Ireland;

6) Draw up proposals for a plan for developing the West of Ireland and assess the financial implications of these proposals in terms of likely costs, both of private actions and public policies. This assessment should also cover the opportunity costs of not developing the West (Euradvice, 1994, p.15).

Figure 5.6 The terms of reference of 'A Crusade for Survival'

Retrospect and Prospect 139

The methodology employed in the study also contained three significant issues. These issues effectively created a microcosm of the larger political system, and centred on conventional discourses. In deference to the sense of urgency discussed earlier, a number of interim reports were prepared during the study to contribute to policy development and early action programmes. Reviewing how the subjects of the interim reports were selected, and by whom, it became evident that the decision-making powers rested in the hands of a few key actors and, to a lesser extent, the ACWBCD. The minor role played by local communities was already evident.

Centralist control personified

The apparent ambivalence that the Irish government showed towards DTWT initially, changed when it appeared that the group would obtain funding for a study of the region, directly from the EC. Recognising the precedent that this would set for the remainder of the sub-regions, and the inherent loosening of centralist control, political manoeuvring was quickly mobilised to reassert authority. The initial deputation to the EC (Bishops Casey and Kirby) had received a favourable response, yet it was only with a letter from Commissioner Bruce Millan to Bishop Kirby (1992), that the political manoeuvring and the 'fears' of the Commission began to emerge. The Commission, quick to reiterate that they were positively in favour of the study, and in its attempts to identify the problems of the West, outlined some obstacles. These 'obstacles' centred around what, Millan suggested, was the important belief expressed by Bishop Casey, that the results of the study should feed into public policy making and most notably into the preparation of the next CSF. To ensure this happened, the Commission suggested that 'it was essential that the study should be carried out in full co-operation with the Central Government authorities' (Millan, 1992). The culmination of the Commissioner's suggestion was that DTWT 'contact the Department of Finance with a view to obtaining the Department's agreement to the proposed study, its content and scope and its financing' (Millan, 1992). While this could be seen, on the one hand, as ensuring that the duplication of initiatives did not occur, it seemed to confirm the suspicions of some of those involved in the study that *'there was some political manoeuvring by the Department of Finance, which attempted to block the study on the grounds that they wouldn't have sufficient control since it was a study that was going to be totally funded by the Commission'.*

The involvement of the Department of Finance subsequently raised a number of questions. The role of the Department could be seen as being prudent in that a devolving of power to the region raised a number of issues, particularly those of funding and more significantly, the attachment of accountability and responsibility. In the absence of any popular mandate for the group, the issue of accountability and responsibility had been little in evidence in the DTWT campaign. However, while discussions with members of the Department (and former members) did not confirm these suspicions, it was felt by those working within DTWT that the Department of Finance's involvement was influenced by its desire to prevent the precedent of a sub-region within Ireland obtaining funds directly from the EC without government sanctioning. In effect, this was merely a reconfirming of the implicit centralised control exerted in Irish government (see also Boyle, 2000). That a compromise could not be found seems unlikely. Furthermore, the implications could have been far reaching in that had this funding of the sub-region occurred, it would have resulted in greater demands for regional control, a practising of subsidiarity, and the creation of collective forms of governance. DTWT (and its related organisations, the Council for the West and WDPB), were, instead, seduced by the intrinsic appeal of becoming involved in the decision-making processes. However, it would have been judicious to have obtained all the rules of the 'game' underlying this "spectacle" at the outset, rather than rushing 'blindly ahead and trading on the positive connotations of the idea of participation' (Shortall, 1994, p.253). Ultimately, this rash abandonment of ideals meant that the DTWT was easily absorbed by the established institutional structures.

Predictably the Department of Finance had to be taken on board, and although this was vehemently opposed by a number of the Core group members, it inevitably led to changes in the study proposal. One member of the DTWT argued that the Department had too much control and spoke with frustration of doomed attempts to retain power: *the battle we'd fought for two years, for that report, about the preparations, ... they were supposed to consult with us and take back our ideas ... and the battle we fought was trying to break the dominant influence of the Department of Finance ... we didn't succeed'*. The conditionalising, by the Department of Finance of the objectives of DTWT was therefore demonstrated in the issuing of proposed changes to the study. The Department described itself as 'positively disposed to the undertaking of the study', but it also had a number of concerns. These concerns were primarily that, the results of the study, as proposed, would be of "little practical value", producing some sort of medium term plan and a list of investment needs which could not be met, either by national or EC resources. The Department also disagreed with the allocated time span (twelve to fifteen months was too long), and the cost (too high). The most significant change, demonstrating the control which the government exercised, was that 'the main role in relation to planning for the region *vis-à-vis* the Structural Funds should be occupied by the sub-regional review committees and that the Bishops' study would only be ancillary to this, possibly in some sort of a 'background' capacity [and] in this respect the Department was willing to fund "a" study' (DTWT circular, No Date;a, p.1). Other proposals included the study being put out to competitive tender, the start up time being shortened, and the study monitoring committee including officials of the Department of Finance. Despite disagreements, in order for the study to proceed, the supposedly independent voluntary DTWT had to give way to the top-down bureaucracy imposed on it by the government. This consigned to the wastebasket any radical proposals that the report might have made in challenging the government.

Participation, consultation and conflict

The potential for creating challenging proposals was undermined by DTWT's interpretation of the term participation. The growth of DTWT, and its creation of 'core groups' supposedly allowed those at the grassroots to participate in the decision-making process. The more prominent ideas emerging from the core groups focused on: a regionalist approach; land policies; infrastructure; tourism; bureaucracy; job creation; information; and accountability. The regional polemic was perhaps the most debated issue, with dissatisfaction expressed about centralised power and decision making in Ireland. It was generally felt that this centralisation had strong negative effects on the West in terms of the ability to make decisions in the region, due to a lack of power and resources. Considerable disquiet was also expressed about the inequitable distribution of EC Structural Funds and repeated calls were made for the establishment of a strong regional authority for the West (McInerney, 1992a). These core groups, seen as major step forward in facilitating top-down and bottom-up integration, were deemed to be the most important aspect of the study, as they allowed those people living with the problems of the region to express their concerns. In the initial stages, the study was to be conducted in close consultation with the local communities, with the core groups providing this contact point. The longer DTWT continued, the more obvious it became that the policies and ideas being considered emanated from outside the region, particularly in relation to the moulding of the report. This firmly contrasted with Pyke's (1991) suggestion that for the initiative to be successful, development would have to evolve from within the region, as opposed to being imposed from outside (see also Kearney *et al.* 1994)

In keeping with the premise that organisations do not operate without hatred or passion, but are, instead, sites for the deployment and production of human emotions and meanings (Fineman, 1994), a further number of internal disputes arose within the organisation. These disputes highlighted the pitfalls involved in voluntary co-operation, and underlined the internal power struggles beneath the projected image of co-operation. The issues of contention centred on the perception that Galway dominated the West like Dublin dominated the rest of Ireland; the movement of the DTWT offices from Galway to Knock, and the role of the administrators in terms of involvement and commitment to the initiative. It was suggested that the real power of the movement was not vested in the core groups, but, because of their access to information, in the secretariat and Advisory Committee. A further alarming declaration was that the perception of those involved at the grassroots of the initiative was of a centrally-controlled, specialist-dominated organisation which if unchecked would foist a final report upon the voluntary sector.

The dwindling role of the Church

The first steps towards a decline in the role of the Church in DTWT began in April/May of 1992. In June of 1992, a meeting was convened between the core groups and the co-ordinator. At this meeting a strategy was thrashed out, requesting the continuation of the initiative beyond the time limit of the study, supposedly between the representatives of the groups and the co-ordinator. The proposal put to the Bishops was that, on a micro level, there was a need to put facilitators or animators in place at local community level (twelve were suggested), and that at the macro level (seen as the regional level), these workers could come together, share information, experiences, develop networks between communities and provide the potential for the creation of a strong regional lobby. Underlining the reluctance of the Church to carry the initiative beyond the phase of the study, the group's proposals initially received the go-ahead from the Bishops and, with funding proposals drawn up, was then dismissed the night before the group were due to meet the Secretary of the Department of Finance. The proposal was stopped and the decision taken to re-discuss the issues a few months later in May or June of 1993. This was a critical turning point for the future of DTWT, with the Bishops deciding to maintain the status quo, to keep on employing two workers with the only change being that they wanted the workers to move to Knock. The significance of this decision was that it underlined the reluctance of the Bishops to initiate a more pro-active approach in dealing with the development issues of the West. The reaction to the sudden case of 'cold feet' on the part of the Bishops was for the most part critical, not only of their failure to carry on the initiative, but also of their reluctance to indicate clearly their intended direction.

A Crusade for Survival – the launch

The launch of the longawaited report on the West came about in February of 1994, and wasted little time in rehashing the well worn phrase, that the 'West of Ireland is in crisis' (Euradvice, 1994, p.1). Archbishop Cassidy (1994b, p.1), speaking at the launch, extolled the major significance of the report and affirmed that the Taoiseach was 'underlying by his presence the importance of the issues [the report] raise(d), the opportunities it identifie(d) and the policies it propose(d)'. More sceptical observers saw the Taoiseach's presence as an indication that the prospects of change that they held out for were to be swamped by rhetoric and political pandering. The report itself signalled nothing new; it was content to deal in the conventional approaches of outlining the main problems and priorities of the region in terms of: depopulation; decreasing traditional agricultural production; centralist policy approaches by government; and the lack of integration between top-down and bottom-up approaches to development. The report attached 'considerable significance' to the role of the Church and DTWT, with calls for a participative approach, and an ongoing task for the Church, centred on 'providing the hope and inspiration for the last chance crusade for survival of the West' (Euradvice, 1994, p.6). The main recommendations called for the government: to give priority to the West in its development programme; to provide a Minister for the West; and to create a Western Development Board. Advocating what the study itself had failed to do, there was a call for the provision of 'administrative mechanisms which [would] enable local people to participate fully in the development process' (ibid.). Recommending a set of proactive, but traditional economic policies for the West, the report also called for the Church to continue its campaign for development and to 'take the initiative in establishing the Council of the West to co-ordinate the activities of local development groups in the development process' (ibid.).

A number of underlying themes can be drawn from the conventional and non-challenging aspects of *A Crusade for Survival*. There was nothing new or radical about the report. Indeed, rather than putting challenges to the government, it seemed to look for allocations that the government might sanction. The study did not, as it alleged, challenge the government and public agencies; one could go further and say that it disempowered those it was created to empower. The argument for a regional policy was one of the few solid issues, which the study did promote. The inconsistent treatment of the regions within Ireland was highlighted, and in one of the few real hints at a challenge to the government by the Church, Archbishop Cassidy posed the question:

> What were the grounds on which our successive governments looked to Europe for special consideration and extra finance? Surely on the grounds to some extent at least, that we were a peripheral, poorer part of the union and along with countries like Greece or Portugal deserving of greater support? Is the principle we held up to Europe to be hidden from our own? Are the grounds on which Ireland pleaded its case to be invalid in the West? I don't believe they are. Surely the West is to Ireland what Ireland is to Europe? The same principle applies right across the board. We make our respective but similar cases, not as parasites, not as mendicants, but as full members of a wider community that caters for the good of all (Cassidy, 1994b, p.4).

While this is a valid argument, the question remains as to why the Bishops did not seek to address issues such as this in the framework of the report, rather than paying lip service after the event. If the Bishops were serious about challenging the government on issues relating to the West, then the centralising dominance of the government would have been more strongly resisted.

If further evidence was needed of the demise of this populist movement, it was provided in the Taoiseach's virtual dismissal of the study's recommendations by referring, with great regularity, to the measures in the NDP, and the programmes of work being undertaken by the County Enterprise Boards. This particular tactic implied that the recommendations of the report had, in a sense, been anticipated, and that as such, the government had already put in place strategies to deal with them. Waters (1994, p.12), in referring to this dismissal of the report, suggested that the Taoiseach 'succeeded in appearing to make a response to the report while ignoring its main recommendations', and by way of this response, the central problem was defined in a very precise manner, in that 'nothing will be done except what is already being done. In other words: nothing will be done'.

The reactions to the report, varied from those who, in true political rhetoric, 'welcomed' the study, to the more vociferous, who dismissed it outright. The report was described by Cassidy (1994a) at its launch as 'the beginning of a new phase in the regeneration of the West', a report which if given active rather than album life could help create a sustained programme of development for the West (p.17). Other reactions to the report by members of DTWT were less enthusiastic and described the report as a poor investment for the financial outlay and not reflective of what DTWT had tried to achieve. Its only saving grace, it was suggested, was that it started a process in motion, a process which was recognised and acted on by the government (see later sections).

Report dead and awaiting burial!

A number of underlying issues moulded the criteria used in compiling *A Crusade for Survival*. The report, based on a traditional way of looking at development, raised a series of questions about the assumptions and discourses of development being pursued in Ireland. The traditional conception of looking at industry, agriculture, tourism and services, and seeing the creation of wealth in these sectors as having a knock-on effect in the other sectors of society (social exclusion, poverty), has been found wanting (see Commins and Keane 1994). In an article entitled 'Bishops' Report Dead and Awaiting Burial', Waters (1994, p.12) outlined why the study 'never had the slightest prospect of conveying the extent of the problem in a sufficiently urgent and unequivocal way' and suggested that it was not sufficiently innovative to encapsulate a strategy for 'saving the

West'. Waters attributed this failure to the overly-friendly relationship between the Bishops and the politicians, which inevitably led to a report which was 'hedged around with generalisations, unnecessary information, conventional wisdoms and a confusion of philosophies' (ibid.). He located the failure of the report in its lack of clarity in spelling out that the decline of the West of Ireland was due to a lack of democracy, and its refusal to identify the ability of the people of the region to control their own lives. This sentiment, Waters rather amusingly suggested, could have been documented for £249,999 less than the cost of the report (£250,000).

The lack of democracy, aided by the people who were moving the agenda along, and the Church-State relationship, were the underlying causes of the maintenance of the *status quo*. DTWT professed to be an organisation that was open to all, yet the people involved with DTWT represented (for the most part) a particular mode or style of development very much focused on economic development. Those involved were predominantly members of enterprise boards, LEADER programmes, statutory bodies, or were experienced community activists, journalists, retired civil servants and small business directors. DTWT was therefore 'semi-professional' rather than its membership being open to all members of the local communities. In this respect, the entire grassroots premise, on which the organisation had set itself up, was questionable.

The lack of unity within DTWT was exemplified by the core groups' increased preference for working in isolation. Somewhat symptomatic of the country as a whole, these groups moulded their objectives to fit specific funding criteria, while reinforcing the dependency culture and the narrow scope for development initiatives. Other factors also worked against the core groups as elements of a participatory development initiative. The first of these was their unrepresentativeness, and the fact that, for the most part, the core groups seemed to be 'hand-picked' by the Bishops and the local clergy. Likewise, the groups were cobbled together quickly and asked for an input to the study without being able to find their own collective feet, or develop a cohesion of purpose within their respective groups. Those directing the agenda of DTWT failed to provide enough opportunities for genuine participation, and there seemed to be an assumption by the Bishops and the ACWBCD, that, if they got people together in core groups, this would lead to some kind of unity. A further destabilising factor was the tendency of strong individuals to dominate groups. This resulted in more passive participation by others, and feelings that the groups were as centralist as the broader system they were designed to challenge. Such situations created disharmony within the groups and reinforced the dependency culture, which the initiative had sought to change. The widespread geographical extent did nothing either to promote cohesiveness within DTWT. As a consequence, participation in the decision making of DTWT became concentrated in dominant places, like Galway, and later Mayo.

Finally, it would appear that DTWT fell into the trap of dealing with the West as a unique homogeneous region, disregarding (or not realising) the significance of the informal power networks and the hegemonic discourses which are characteristic of all areas (be they social, economical or political). DTWT was more intent on a pragmatic approach, and this pragmatism became undermined by those more experienced community campaigners and rural professionals who participated, more for their own particular aims than for those of the region. Participation in DTWT, instead of being the panacea, became a focus for divisiveness and disharmony.

The credibility of DTWT was also further eroded by its inability to address the dependency that continued unabated within the region. Analogously, DTWT tended to address the issues of the West from a position of isolation, with little networking with other declining rural areas, either in Ireland, or in Europe. Its lack of strategy was highlighted by the fact that, while many of those involved in the group were anxious to keep the initiative moving after the study, they did not really know in which direction to proceed. This *ad hoc* approach mirrors, to a degree, the larger development processes pursued in Ireland, where there is more emphasis on a quick-fix solution, or on gaining a grant, than in any long-term cohesive strategy for development.

The Government Task Force Report

One of the outcomes of the regional study was the setting up of a government Task Force. *The fact that A Crusade for Survival*, did not put forward any radical proposals, rendered this concept of a Task Force to deliberate on the report's findings a political overstatement. The objective of this hyperbole, perceived as much in hindsight as from the impressions received, would appear to have been the government's wish to respond actively to DTWT proposals, while dictating the direction in which this initiative would proceed. A Task Force was set up and whether it was purely for "spectacle", it did have the potential to endorse innovative or radical policies for development in the region. The standard rhetoric was however delivered by the Task Force, as they 'agreed' that a more integrated approach was essential, 'recommended' that the views of local communities be sought, and 'highlighted' the need for the provision of adequate resources under the Structural Funds. These conventional responses were not only well-worn phrases, but were also unsupported by any strategy as to how these procedures would come about or be funded. The most significant recommendation, signalling the beginning of the end for DTWT, was that 'policy and action should be geared towards the goal of securing population stability for the region, on a county basis, at 1991 census levels by the end of the decade, and that this population should be a base for development at the start of the new Millennium'

(Government Task Force 1994, p.28). To achieve this population stability allegedly required the mobilisation of support, energy and creativity within the region, with a focus over and above that which was represented by the established regional authorities – that is, the creation of a Western Development Partnership Board (WDPB) – (Government Task Force, 1994). This new Board was given the responsibility of drawing up an appropriate 'action plan', designed on independent partnership structural lines, as part of the Local Development Programme. Members of the Board were appointed by the government, the majority being selected from nominations made by the County Enterprise Boards and LEADER groups. This selectivity reinforced the Board's professional composition, and raised questions as to its supposed independence.

The Council for the West

Before dealing with the WDPB, the Council for the West should be explored. Consisting of the 'elected, the co-opted and the ordained' (Cassidy, 1994a), the Council for the West also had its origins in the regional study *A Crusade for Survival* (Euradvice, 1994) which recommended that a committee be formed which would be:

> representative of voluntary organisations and local development groups in the region which would co-ordinate the activities of those groups. In particular it should be the principal body representing the voluntary sector in the negotiations for preparing and implementing the five-year plan for the region to be drawn up by the Western Development Board. The Council should be independent of Government and should be financed from resources raised under the auspices of Developing the West Together (ibid., p.35).

In combination with the WDPB, the Council was alleged to be 'the best option for a participative approach to planning for the region' (ibid., p.5). This claim is debatable however, not only because of the Council's questionable representativeness, but also due to a lack of cohesive strategy within its own objectives, and its lack of a specific mandate from the people it was claiming to represent. The recommendation that the Council raise funds under the auspices of DTWT also made it dependent on the Church and Church collections, inevitably undermining its independence as a representative of all voluntary groups and preventing it from challenging one of the major institutions in the country.

The Council for the West, launched on 22 October 1994 in Sligo, projected the image of a populist, apolitical and autonomous movement working in partnership with official agencies and local development groups. It claimed to derive its legitimacy from 'the views, concerns and aspirations of the 5000 people who attended a series of public meetings organised as part of the process of harvesting grassroots and voluntary sector opinion for the authors of *A Crusade for Survival*, and the members of the core groups who were duly elected by parishes and community-based groups – urban, town, village and rural – and who have in turn, elected half of the Council membership by due democratic process' (Council for the West, Press Release, 1994). It was to be aided in the discharging of these duties by the autonomy that it possessed, the populist nature of its origins and organisation, and its freedom to address socio-economic issues, on their objective merits, without political party bias (Hogan, 1994).

The recommendation to establish a Council for the West indicated little more than a tokenistic gesture to the local communities of the region, emanating as it did from the questionably grassroots-based DTWT. At the launch of the Council, the chairperson endeavoured to impart the focus of the Council's 'mission', by quoting the well-known advocate of local democracy, T.J. Barrington, who stated that it was:

> necessary to develop a real sense of citizenship for the simple reason that the success or failure of our society depends on the "spirit" of the people, the spirit of responsibility, of innovation, of enterprise and of tenacity. The major consequence of the concentration of decision-making at the centre is fragmentation – fragmentary decisions at the centre and fragmentary services to the consumer. The result is the bewilderment of the citizen and increasing acceptance of powerlessness – personal, community, and regional (Hogan, 1994, p.2).

While the sentiments expressed were admirable, it can be suggested that by the end of its first year, the Council had not only failed to reverse the national centralist regime, but in many respects had, albeit on a smaller scale, reinforced the centralisation of decision-making within its own structure.

The main functions of the Council highlighted the verbosity in which some voluntary organisations become enveloped, and the way in which they reinforce the rhetoric of rural development discourses. The functions of the Council were peppered with references to animation, self-help, cohesiveness, integration and pro-active development. The Council's success in incorporating these concepts was somewhat less vigorous. The structure, a series of sub-committees, under which the Council operated, also proved insufficient. From the outset, the fact that these committees were solely based on traditional sectoral lines – agriculture, tourism, industry – did not suggest that they were going to be either dynamic or innovative in their efforts. In reality, other work demands, lack of co-ordination and limits imposed by travel distances, led to a dwindling in interest and commitment in the committees.

The Council did recognise its shortcomings and saw its lack of success as rooted in its dispersive nature whereby it became increasingly involved with individual projects, while at the same time overlapping with other development agencies doing similar work. While this was the perception of the Council from (in a manner of speaking) the top-down, the views from the bottom-up were articulated in the reservations expressed at a Council for the West meeting that: 'the movement to develop the West began six years ago ... initiated by farmers. Yet for two and a half hours here today the word agriculture was not used once. The appointees on the Board do not reflect the bottom-up approach promised at the adoption of the report *A Crusade for Survival*. The Board's appointees should include people at the bottom of the ladder in agriculture' (Anon, 1994b). These comments underlined the unrepresentative nature of the Council, its lack of networking with the core groups, while further implying that the initiative was not organised, as professed, from the bottom-up.

A number of other factors curtailed the Council's potential. Primarily, there was the need for greater decentralisation, but not as would be expected, from the administrative and political system in Ireland, but rather from within the Council itself. It became evident that the power of decision-making rested within the hands of the elite group that comprised the Council. The second issue relates to the unreasonable time limitation. Clearly, the bringing together of different ideas, resources and objectives, could not be realistically achieved in such a short time span (2 years), when there was added pressure on the Council to be actively involved in monitoring the Action Plan of the WDPB. Finally, there was an evident lack of proper structures to enable local communities to become involved. There seemed to be a premise that, if there were core groups, then there would be unity of purpose. The upshot of this was that many of the core groups disbanded because of a lack of leadership. One group, in the latter stages of DTWT, expressed the opinion that the whole model was imposed from the top-down, forming a centrally controlled, specialist-dominated organisation.

If the Council did achieve anything, then it must be that it showed that in order for effective partnerships to take place, there must be integration, both in procedure and participation. Sufficient care should be taken to ensure that there is no confusion (intentional or otherwise) between consultation and participation, and that structures are proposed which ensure that local community involvement, in development issues, is more than just a token gesture, or a rubber stamp for policies and strategies already decided at statutory level (see Dillion, 1989). It is also important that voluntary groups do not become over-dependent on a select few members, nor that a select few members be allowed to dominate the workings and strategies of local community groups. Despite its failings, the Council did show the possibility of developing links, however tenuous, between the state and the voluntary sector. It is this potential which could provide rural communities with the impetus to come together, in an attempt to have an impact on the development of national policy.

The Western Development Partnership Board (WDPB)

It is debatable whether the government overestimated the staying power or influence of DTWT, or whether they were keen to be seen to be doing something. Irrespective of motive, the government, prompted by the recommendations of the regional study and the subsequent Task Force Report (1994) established the WDPB in October 1994. The remit of the Board was to produce an "Action Plan" for government within twelve months, which would 'indicate the type of policies and activities which [were] necessary in order to arrest population decline and to achieve population balance within as short a time-period as is possible' (Higgins, 1995b, p.1), in the five counties of Connacht, Donegal and Clare (Figure 5.5). The Board itself was made up of state and semi-state bodies. With the Board structured in this way, the question arises as to whom exactly the Board represented. If it were representative of the voluntary/community sector, then the argument is centred on why these sectors were so poorly represented, and, if the WDPB were speaking for the government, then the question arises as to why the Board had little power and even less funding. The question remains as to whether the WDPB was the voice of the local community at government level, or the eyes and ears of the government at local level. The low profile of the Board in no way helped clarify this confusion, with most communities not knowing what the Board was doing, or why it existed (McDonagh, 1997).

From the outset there seemed to be a number of question marks over the objectives of the Board and over its organisation. The main terms of reference were to target population stability and develop a plan, which would achieve population stability on a county by county basis at 1991 census levels. If nothing else, this could be seen as a unique mandate which the Minister for Western Development described as 'certainly exacting' (Carey, 1995a). The launch of the Board got off to a rather inauspicious start in that, for almost the first four months, it did not have a Chief Executive Officer (CEO). This reflected a rather astounding lack of urgency on the part of the government, as the Board had been set a tight time-frame of twelve months for the production of an 'action plan'. This lack of urgency could be adjudged as stemming from either the government's poor commitment towards the WDPB, or more cynically, that it was merely the subtle creation of a further obstacle in the progression of the Board (the only tangible knock-on effect of the delay in appointing a CEO was, that instead of the action plan being in the public domain in November of 1995, as originally timetabled, it did not appear until April/May of 1996). Thus, while the Board continued to meet during this period, the general consensus was that they were going nowhere, slowly. After appointing the CEO, the running of the Board was essentially in his hands, and the agenda of the Board, which supposedly met under the banner of a 'partnership', merely dealt with

Retrospect and Prospect 151

issues as they were presented to them. This concentration of decision-making and powers of direction, not only highlighted the politics that surround boards or organisations in Ireland, but also reinforced the dependency syndrome and the ease with which centralist control is accepted in the policy-making processes of local development. Ironically, this centralist control was a complete negation of the CEO's criticism of the 'curse of centralisation which exists in this country' (Higgins, 1995b. p.4).

The challenge

The challenges faced by the WDPB, or indeed the challenges that it supposedly would create, were indicative of the rhetoric that surrounds development issues in rural Ireland. It was alleged that the issues drawn up by the WDPB would challenge not only the state, but also the people of the region. The people of the West, argued Higgins (1995a, p.1), 'must react positively to the opportunities which are being given to them and [which] will be given to them through this plan', while the state must 'recognise the right of the West of Ireland to give its people an opportunity to live and work locally'. These sentiments, laudable in the world of political rhetoric, have pragmatically little place in the real life of rural communities, dominated by a centralised government with no inclination for greater inclusion of local communities. If nothing else, the strategy pursued by the government throughout the whole populist phase of DTWT, and its spin-offs, was to contain the earlier enthusiasm generated by the movement, and by a series of political moves, (the Department of Finance's involvement in the DTWT study, for example) to further reinforce the dependency mentality. Waters (1994, p.12) in recognising the inherent problems underlying the lack of participatory development and subsequent lack of democracy in Ireland, suggested that what was required both in terms of the West, and of Ireland as a whole was a 'transformation of the political consciousness which would up-end the present dependency mentality and replace it with a genuine participatory democracy', with Waters also recognising that 'this will not happen, because we have yet to acknowledge that it is even a necessity'.

The WDPB continued to talk about operating on the principles of subsidarity, partnership, and reducing bureaucracy, but such sentiments can only be viewed as a kind of hyperbole; these concepts already having been shown, in DTWT and the Council for the West, as non-events in relation to government policies. As Faughnan and Kelleher (1992, p.89) suggested, 'past experiences, the ethos of state agencies and the perception that the state did not trust the voluntary sector', all combine to affect adversely any structured consultation which might take place between the state and the voluntary sector. The Board's CEO continued to make all the proper statements, in terms of demanding greater participation for local communities, and the creation of a more decentralised system of administration, where 'the state would have to yield power to the regions ... and reduce the massive curse of centralisation' (Higgins, 1995b, p.4). Behind these aspirations there existed quite a dismissive attitude to what the Board was trying to achieve. These attitudes stemmed not only from those outside the Board, as for example in references to *'the idiotic mission statement about stabilising population'*, but also from a lack of conviction within the Board in relation to the terms of reference given.

The image projected by the WDPB loudly proclaimed itself not to be the source of another report which repeatedly stated and restated the region's problems (emigration, depopulation and unemployment), but instead, the creator of a blueprint for 'action', and an end to the need to produce other reports of a similar character (WDPB, 1996). Although the Chairman of the WDPB suggested that the year-long time-frame which it took to complete *The Challenge: A Positive Future Through Action* reflected 'the careful thinking and consultation which took place in its preparation' (ibid., p.3), there were those who felt that the so-called "action" plan, was yet another report (Figure 5.7) which would be shelved alongside that of *A Crusade for Survival*.

A positive future through action

What was termed the process of bringing the study *A Crusade for Survival* (Euradvice, 1994) to *A Positive Future Through Action* (WDPB, 1996) was launched on 15 May 1996. The newspaper headlines surrounding the launch of the plan were very positive. Attention was focused on the strategies of the plan to create over 15,000 new jobs, the plan's call for a defined regional policy for the West, and its demands for a twenty year commitment from the State towards the West (MacConnell, 1996, MacDubhghaill and O'Sullivan, 1996, O'Sullivan, 1996b, Rice, 1996). Empowerment, and participation of local communities, were among the key themes expressed in the plan, where that inevitable part of the rural tradition, the concept of self-help, was seen as having the potential to solve the problems of the region. In synthesis, the plan suggested that the future of many rural communities would depend on its inhabitants' ability and willingness to help themselves:

> most important of all in terms of a justification for having a specific plan for the West of Ireland is that people from the West of Ireland have a loyalty to the West, to being people of the West and wanting to put something back into the West, that does not exist in other parts of Ireland (Taoiseach Bruton, speaking at the launch of WDPB Report, cited in O'Sullivan, 1996b).

The action plan proposed a challenge to the people of the region to, 'accept responsibility for the development of the region [show] a willingness to take a pro-active role in the development of their own areas and to confront the attitudes which inhibit the region's development' (WDPB, 1996, p.21). This advocacy of the self-help concept is allegedly justified by the policy makers because of their desire to unlock the pent-up self-help resource which supposedly characterises rural society (see McLaughlin, 1987). What was a contradiction in terms however, was that while the WDPB urged local communities to confront the attitudes which were limiting development in the region, by their own recommendations they were further reinforcing those attitudes, through centralisation, bureaucracy and a dependency culture.

The WDPB report's call for a commitment from the EU and national government for development supports and incentives to achieve subsidiarity, cohesiveness, and the development of alternative forms of economic activity (WDPB, 1996, p.14), is characteristic of Irish development discourse. The belief that supports and incentives are *the* means needed to achieve subsidiarity and cohesiveness underpin the majority of development programmes. It is ironic that the WDPB, a group designed to develop a sustainable plan for the people of the West to take control of their own lives, automatically nail their colours to the masts of the need for greater commitment from the government and the EU. This reaction would seem to perpetuate the notion that in order for the bottom-up to become 'empowered', it must in some inevitable process be structured from the top-down (see also Chapter 4).

Acknowledging the confusion and apathy which existed among the general public regarding the plethora of agencies and the duplication of delivery systems, the WDPB (1996) allegedly sought to put in place a development process which would be; 'effective', 'easily accessible', and 'minimally bureaucratic'. To do this, they proposed creating a Western Development Commission; a Western Investment Fund; a Western Social Development Unit; a Programme for Identification and Linkages of Opportunities and the innovative approaches and Technologies (PILOT), and Local Enterprise Networks (LENs) (Figure 5.8). These recommendations contradicted the Board's minimally bureaucratic process of development, and if nothing else, further complicated the delivery systems in the region, being additional rather than replacement agencies. Overall, the action plan described itself as seeking to put forward the case for a specific regional policy which would 'achieve a more balanced regional pattern of growth and development' within the West of Ireland (ibid., p.16). This policy it was claimed was justified on the grounds of market failure, where free and unregulated markets failed to deliver an efficient allocation of resources.

No surprises

The end result of the WDPB was, that while they did not 'state and restate

154   Renegotiating Rural Development in Ireland

Figure 5.7   The cover of the Western Development Partnership Board Report. The image projected on the front cover of the WDPB report (1996) says a lot about the development discourses pursued in Ireland. The traditional industries of the region; agriculture, fishing, tourism, telecommunications and food production are depicted, and, more interestingly, the illustration presents the male population, with sleeves rolled up and smiles on their faces 'working' and toiling in their economic professions, while the female contingent are cheerfully minding their children or on holiday.

The **Western Development Commission** was to incorporate a legal entity, have executive powers, and although reporting directly to the Department of the Taoiseach would also have a 'straight-line communication to local communities via the propsed local networks' (WDPB, 1996, p. 26). The WDPB described the commission as becoming a 'power-house of regional economic and social energy ... provid(ing) a unique exercise in defining regional policy in Ireland' (ibid.). The commission was to be made up of no more than fourteen members, nine of which would be nominees of the Department of the Taoiseach (for a three year period), the remaining five representing the somewhat orthodox Sectoral Advisory Councils consisting of experts from state agencies, third level institutions, financial and private business sectors, established for five strategic areas of development - natural resource-based products; manufacturing; the marine; tourism, Arts and heritage; and information technology and telecommunications(see also Chapter 6).

The **Western Investment Fund** would encourage growth in the region by making 'medium and long-term funding available to stimulate and foster commercial and social enterprises in the western region' (ibid., p.32). The expected funding is envisaged as coming from the Irish Government (25% - £5 million over 5 years), the EU (25%), the European Investment Bank (25%) and from private depositors (25%), leveraging a gross investment of over £200 million in five years. The possibility of the government "investing " £5m in the West was not as straightforward as these proposals suggest, as there was a reluctance to input financially with the government being more content with symbolic gestures like a Minister of State for the West.

The **Regional Social Development Unit** for the West, had priority areas of pre-development, measures to combat social exclusion, the potential of the social economy, public service provision and the development of greater participation and child-care (ibid.). The interesting aspect of the unit is that two of its key functions:

(1) the implementation of strategies to enable greater participation by voluntary and community groups in policy and decision-making; and

(2) developing mechanisms for the support of the voluntary and community sector in the region (ibid., p.43-44);

would seem to have brought the initiative full circle in that greater participation in decision making and greater support for the community sector were the two most fundamental objectives underlying the DTWT initiative.

The **PILOT** programme would 'co-ordinate the role of all key players leading to the establishment of new enterprises in five strategic sectors (natural resource-based products; manufacturing; the marine; tourism, arts and heritage; and information technology & telecommunications)' with a remit of linking state agencies, educational and financial institutions and the private sector, in specifically identifying new business opportunities, to provide 'hands-on' support and to ensure that the best advice is available to promoters of projects (ibid., p.30).

Local Enterprise Networks (LENs), are to 'mobilise widespread support for enterprise at local community level', promoting investment and trade and ending the isolation of the would-be entrepreneur (ibid., p.38). The LENs, consisting of executives of large employers and 'enterprising individuals from all walks of life and the unemployed' (ibid., p.38) set, as their objectives, the promotion of greater co-operation between businesses, encouraging greater local ownership, increasing trade and investment opportunities and ending the isolation of entrepreneurs.

Figure 5.8 Proposals submitted by the WDPB

the problems of the West', their recommendations did little else in terms of action but thrust responsibility back on the local communities without putting in place the necessary support structures. In terms of action, nothing of any significance took place, apart from the creation of more boards and more committees, with no clear commitment to funding or to any long-term strategy from the government. That the Taoiseach of the day, launched the action plan (16 May, 1996), welcomed its findings and the role which it was to play, was perhaps a sufficiently telling comment on its likely contents and indicative of its lack of radical proposals. Refering to the WDPB's action plan as being an important 'reference point for economic and social development in the region' (Bruton, 1996), the Taoiseach appeared to welcome the report, yet at the same time, essentially dismiss its importance in the decision-making processes (similar to the previous Taoiseach's dismissal of *A Crusade for Survival*). The Taoiseach acknowledged the valid case put by the WDPB for a regional policy for the West, agreeing that the West had 'particular economic and social problems, its peripherality, its community's sense of isolation from decision-making, the concentration of small agricultural holdings and lower standard of infrastructure [which] all demand a particular response' (ibid.). Putting the onus back on the community, the Taoiseach suggested that the most important aspect of the Plan, was that it 'did not in any way come down from the top. It has come from the grassroots in the West of Ireland. It is a product of the people' (Rice, 1996, p.3).

Manipulating this line of argument further, it was suggested that the future of the West lay in the hands of the people, and that supporting this action plan would demonstrate clearly that the people of the West were ready to accept the challenge. This turning of responsibility on to the community sector echoed Varley's comments that such a proclamation could be seen 'either as a rhetorical device that serves to legitimate an array of new state measures or [as] push(ing) responsibility for local development, and employment generation onto localities themselves' (Varley, 1991a, p.84). Whatever the interpretation, the Taoiseach attempted to reassure the West of the government's commitment to its well-being, the evidence of which he suggested was in the 'allocation of a political spokesperson for the West, a Minister who would provide a political focus at the heart of government for dealing with particular problems of the West of Ireland and unlike the situation in any other region in Ireland, an indication of a priority for this part of the country in the light of the decline in population that has occurred here' (Bruton, 1996). The sceptical interpretation of this appointment was however that it seemed easier to commit a Minister to the West, than to commit financial support.

A new vocabulary and the same old problems

Rafferty (1992 p.60) suggested that 'there have been many initiatives which were prefaced with the word 'community', but [they] neither came up from that source nor involved the local people, and when the contract period of whatever the project was up, so too was the framework, and the professionals left the area in a puff of smoke. The locals, if lucky, were left with an evaluation document, a new vocabulary, but the same old problems remained'. The fate of the DTWT initiative seemed to follow such a path. However, commentators such as Rolston (1992) also suggest that were it not for the pressure from such groups (as the DTWT and the Council for the West), there would be no drive to raise the spectre of partnerships in rural Ireland. It has however also become increasingly apparent, that the involvement of the voluntary sector in any government deliberations in Ireland is more by way of legitimising decisions already made, and fulfilling the spectre of consultation between state and community. While the Irish government seems keen to espouse the important role of voluntary community groups, the actual outcome is somewhat different. For any community/voluntary initiatives to proceed, funding and direction, in the majority of cases, comes from the top-down. This controlling of the agenda was particularly apparent in the WDPB. While the WDPB called for a reduction in bureaucracy, its action plan seemed to increase it; its calls for a reduction in the number of agencies dealing with development issues resulted in even more agencies being proposed; its calls for radical and innovative approaches resulted in orthodox and conventional responses. Further, its calls for greater government commitment resulted mainly in platitudes and the allocation of a Minister of State for the West with little or no budget funds; its call for greater community participation seemed fairly hollow in the light of the lack of recognition that its action plan gave to this sector, particularly reflected in the lack of meaningful consultation between sectors, during the compilation of the report. The objectives of the Board, therefore, appeared to be too concentrated on a particular mode of development, raising the question as to whether particular assumptions about development in Ireland need to be challenged (see Chapter 4). This situation was characterised by strong input from the statutory bodies, which inevitably led to a particular style of development being pursued by the Board, very much focused on the economic aspects.

The so-called populist organisation DTWT, was also shown to be a microcosm of the larger political situation. It was centrally run, dominated by professionals, and preserved the *status quo*. DTWT could essentially be described as a local top-down agency, with the community-government partnership being merely a spectacle for legitimising government policies and proposals. The participative ideals promoted were given little practical effect, and while it was easy to espouse the principle of participative development, many factors militated against its concrete attainment. The degree to which the rural development agenda was set by local interests was therefore extremely limited. Further, the outcome of DTWT, and subsequently the WDPB, indicated the lack of any real democratic process in relations between state and community. The failure of these organisations reflects the frustration of bottom-up development in rural Ireland, and highlights the dominant role played by civil servants and government in controlling development policies in rural Ireland.

The importance of the Church in rural Ireland has also diminished. Small but perceptible shifts in the power structures of rural Ireland are illustrated in the demands by new social movements and grassroots groups for new ways of determining their own development paths. This move, away from the traditional paternalistic Ireland, has led to a smaller role for the Church, while alternative development strategies with more participative and partnership orientations are sought. Despite its apparent solidarity with its flock, the Church seemed equally involved in the development spectacle, providing little of substance in terms of their support for DTWT. For all its outward show of commitment to the economic and social progress of the region, the Church was ultimately comfortable with the *status quo* and reluctant to enter into conflict with the state. By the very nature of its large outreach, covering thousands of communities and parishes, the Church made an ideal advocate for change, yet it largely failed to engage in the developmental issues at grassroots community level. The fate of the DTWT initiative highlighted the non-confrontational relationship between Church and State, reinforced the dependency culture, and confirmed the narrow scope for development initiatives in Ireland.

The type of development phase that the DTWT initiative sought was prevented by the government's ability to quell growing devolutionist calls, by bureaucracy, and by following the kind of orthodox and traditional routes which become lost in the milieu of political rhetoric. The entire process can be described as a journey where the communities of the West started out looking for local democracy, were directed onto the political/ bureaucratic roundabout, lost sight of the exits for increased participation and community involvement in the decision-making process, and, with their sense of direction confused by the bureaucrats, ended up back on the road of a centrally controlled development agenda. The aftermath of the study, particularly how the influence of the government and the state agencies enveloped the voluntary process within a thinly disguised veil of political bureaucracy was underpinned by the rhetoric of being "seen to be doing something". The three main elements borne as a consequence of the regional study, followed the traditional and orthodox approach and created yet another government appointed Board and produced yet another report. DTWT subsequently concluded by attempting to treat the symptoms of the problems of the West (depopulation, emigration, and unemployment), while leaving the real problem, a lack of participative democracy, largely untouched.

Where to next?

Development discourse, despite enormous continuity over time, changes its language, strategies and practices. Now, over five years after its decline, the brief exploration of DTWT carried out in this chapter clearly illustrates the frustration of bottom-up development. This narrative provides a useful insight to the inadequate nature of rural development policy in Ireland, and the need for human development to be placed at the centre of the equation. The necessary change in structures highlighted by DTWT include; alterations in organisational frameworks; changes in the mind set of those people who create and administer policies of change in rural areas, and changes in those who are affected by these policies. While the Irish government encourages participation, partnership and integration, local communities, even when they show a willingness to become involved, remain largely unable to do so. Consequently rural development in Ireland must undergo a significant reorientation. Local communities must be given the means to participate as main players, identify their own problems and develop their own strategies for development. Against a tradition of paternalism and cultural conservatism, the real challenge is to put such a system in place. It will take new forms of rural organisation 'to break out of the entrenched patterns of patronage and exclusion and focus collective efforts on problems common to all groups' (Wilkinson, 1992, p.34). The findings of the DTWT study clearly demonstrate the need to formulate and implement development policies to match local needs, with the pre-requisite of greater co-ordination between the various actors, and the development of the local capacity. In this move towards developing the human capacity to instigate, lead, and control development (Ó Cinnéide, 1996), there is a need to dispel feelings of powerlessness and hopelessness, through programmes of social animation (Melo, 1992; Ó Cinnéide 1993b).

Ultimately there is no 'magic potion' which will transform people, who have been used to staying in the background (see O'Faolain, 1993b), into people willing and able to stand in the spotlight. The sentiment that calls for a high degree of participation is laudable, but regional or local partnerships will only be meaningful under decentralised conditions. Each region must have its own co-ordinated strategy, backed up by a programme of capacity building within local communities. For the successful animation of local communities, there is a need to provide not only the requisite hardware (communications, infrastructure, and housing), but also the software (people's skills, knowledge, and attitudes), for meaningful local participation. The major consequence that this poses for rural development in Ireland, is that despite the current difficulty in achieving any degree of devolution of power level, this may be coming to an end as the rest of Europe devolves. Devolution of responsibility to the regions is becoming a key element in future European development. The recent changes to the regional status of Ireland, with the introduction of two regions (Figure 6.1) in order to retain Objective 1 status (in at least part of the country), will provide a significant test for the Irish government and their steadfast reluctance to devolve power from the centre. This growing trend is proving influential. Community-led development and partnerships are also assuming a considerably raised profile. Increased dissatisfaction, and a growing tendency towards self-reliance, has forced the bottom-up approach to development to become an accepted and necessary ingredient for development in the majority of rural communities (Ó Cinnéide, 1986; O'Cearbhaill, 1992; Murray and Dunn, 1995). Consequently, however embryonic the move towards new forms of governance, greater decentralisation and regionalisation, seems inevitable. As part of this dynamic, the emergence of new forms of rural governance indicates a move toward a more radical and challenging concept of integrated planning and partnership that will eventually determine the future of rural areas in Ireland. In the next chapter this changing focus from government to governance in the Irish arena is explored more deeply.

Notes

1. Healy and Reynolds (1991, p.47) have suggested that 'the National Development Plan which was drawn up to benefit from the EC Structural Funds is a good example of the tokenism that surrounds many of the so called consultative and participative processes in development [and] if the resultant scepticism is to be eliminated policy makers need to appreciate and use processes for the participation of the maximum number'.
2. The other bishops within the region were all subsequently involved but the main figureheads were initially Bishop Casey and subsequently Bishop Finnegan.
3. The approach to these specific Bishops could have been made because of their relative popularity within the region, or, in the case of at least one, the fact that they were known to the people concerned.
4. The use of *italics* in the main body of text indicates personal communication. Names have been omitted to ensure confidentiality.
5. This desire continued after the DTWT with its spin-off, the Council for the West, calling for the retention of Objective 1 status for the West region to 2006 and for a comprehensive regional policy to be put in place (letter to the *Irish Times* (20-1-1998) from Marian Harkin Chairperson of Council for the West).
6. In Euradvice's tender proposal, this allusion to participation was endorsed, with the consultants intimating that such consultation would 'enrich our studies and assist in drawing up worthwhile practical proposals for inclusion in our report' (Euradvice, 1992).
7. This notion reinforced the selection of Euradvice as the Study Team as they were acknowledged as being conversant with the policies and strategies of obtaining funding from European sources.

Retrospect and Prospect 161

8 The standardised discourses with which the interim reports dealt included the 'Economic and Social Situation of the West of Ireland' (November, 1992); an 'Assessment of Policies Affecting the West of Ireland' (March, 1993); the 'Development of Information Technology, Telecommunications and Business Services in the West of Ireland' (June 1993); and the 'Development of Marine Resources of the West of Ireland' (July, 1993).

6 The Emergence of Rural Governance in Ireland

The contested concept of 'rural development' and the so-called 'new' approach to it recently emerging (Commins and Keane, 1994) are integral to forming understandings, judgements and 'answers' about rural development in Ireland. The theoretical constructs which underpin development discourse and the changing perceptions, interpretations and ideals that play a part in the type of development pursued provide an important conceptual framework for understanding and evaluating rural change. In this chapter, the need for alternative channels between state and community to raise economic, social and political productivity is explored. The chronology of Irish rural development policies examined in Chapter 4, provides a sound benchmark for understanding the current emergence of area-based programmes. As has been suggested however, Irish rural policies are more likely to be reactive rather than proactive, to be fund-driven and Brussels-generated rather than dynamic and contrived in Dublin. The determining question is whether the centralised and bureaucratic Irish system of administration can adopt the more radical and challenging concept of integrated planning and partnership, on which the future of rural areas would seem to depend.

The emergence of rural governance in Ireland

The ways in which rural areas are governed have undergone a number of changes in recent years. This is particularly apparent in the UK and many European countries. Ireland, while less marked, is also beginning to show some change in state structures and a movement from government to governance. This latter shift is particularly topical as the current political climate promotes the regional and local as important elements in forging paths for rural, economic and social development. The growing importance of the local and regional level has yielded a reconfiguration of rural development policy and the administrative nature of these policies. The complex set of relationships between different actors and networks now emerging characterises this shift from local government to local governance (Stoker, 1997). The concept of contemporary rural governance is however particularly heterogeneous and there is considerable discussion about how the 'transition from government to governance should be

The Emergence of Rural Governance in Ireland 163

conceptualised' (McCafferty and Walsh, 1999). This complexity, has increasingly become a focus for rural research agendas and for those academics and policy makers who seek to explain the shifting nature of power structures and their repercussions in rural areas. The search 'for an efficient and effective blend of governmental and non-governmental forces' (Goodwin, 1998 p.5) involves a range of new agencies and institutions with public, private and voluntary sector inputs (for example LEADER groups, Development Boards and Enterprise groups). This array of local initiatives 'throw up a multitude of discourses and interpretations of development' (Edwards, 1998) and form part of a shift from the 'natural' need to develop, to one where communities can experiment with different ways of organising societies and economies (Escobar, 1995). The recognition by the Irish government of the 'considerable community and voluntary effort which can be mobilised to promote economic and social development in rural areas' (Department of Agriculture & Food, 1999, p.48) is increasingly widespread. In the context of rural development discourse in Ireland, this changing focus from government to governance subsequently advances a new set of questions for the future of rural areas both in terms of policy and administration restructuring. Moreover this restructuring of rural Ireland is set against an administrative and institutional background that historically has created barriers to a more inclusive or collective regulating of society.

The administrative context

Ireland has a 'unitary' government system, with power residing with the national (central) government. There is a tier of local government, with twenty-nine county councils and fifty-nine urban authorities of various sizes. These are not as powerful, or well-resourced, as those found in other European countries. In more recent years changes have taken place with the establishment of Regional Authorities for strategic planning purposes and also the introduction of two Regional Assemblies associated with the division of the country into two regions for the purpose of EU funding. Nevertheless, attempts to create a regional tier of governance in Ireland is invariably resisted by the 'symbiotic' relationship of national and local governments, that the Irish political tradition has forged, and which the electoral system has underpinned (Chubb, 1992). As Ireland operates a single transferable vote form of proportional representation (PR-STV), voters are able to rank their preferences for all listed candidates and are furthermore able to vote for candidates of different political parties. Consequently members of the Dáil are often 'much more concerned about doing favours for their constituents than they are with initiating or debating national legislation' (McDonald, 1989, p.37). This oldest of traditions in politics, that of 'clientelism', is one of the most accepted elements of Irish political life. It creates a dependency syndrome in the Irish electorate, and is one of the root causes of apathy towards local democracy and local government. Put simply, clientelism involves ordinary people seeking out their local TD, or similarly placed elite, to acquire some benefit or service, which they feel they would not receive by their own or their group's efforts (Bax 1976, cited in Hazelkorn, 1986). There are two main forms of clientelism, that of 'patronage', which dispenses favours (jobs, grants) directly, and secondly that of 'brokerage', which alternatively places the 'client' in contact with people who control the (first order) resources directly (Hazelkorn, 1986). The impression that the politician's main task is to provide the solution to various problems has been encouraged, if not fuelled, by the centralist nature of government policy. Few politicians describe themselves as legislators, and prefer to see themselves as representing or servicing their constituents. The government's centralised and bureaucratic approach is reflected in local government and is partly a reaction to, and reinforcement of, politicians' self-interest and indifference to the wider local issues (Hazelkorn, 1986). Chubb (1982) rounded on the influences of Britain, nationalism, Catholicism, a dying peasant society, authoritarianism and anti-intellectualism, and suggested that 'these factors, coupled with the country's smallness and rurality, had fashioned a society where priests and politicians reigned and [this] reinforced intellectual and political passivity' (cited in Hazelkorn, 1986). Moreover, Higgins (1982, p.114) suggested that for 'generations, Irish people saw that to get the benefits that public authorities bestow, the help of a man with connections and influence was necessary [and] all that democracy has meant is that such a man has been laid on officially, as it were, and is now no longer a master but a servant'.

With such complex origins, it is clear that the structure of national and regional politics has to alter, if any degree of local or regional autonomy is to be forthcoming. Local planning is *ad hoc* and project-oriented, and is more 'adapted to obtaining funds from the government (and/or from the EU) than to developing self-reliant local strategies for local development' (Amdam, 1996, p.6). In comparing strategies with Norway, Amdam (ibid.) described the Norwegian system as one of 'planning without money', where the 'local' influences the 'national', while its equivalent in Ireland was one of 'planning to obtain money' without any long-term strategies in place. This type of planning approach is very recognisable in the strategies pursued in terms of rural development. These are more likely to be 'reacting' to a crisis, rather than anticipating or planning future actions. For successful devolution of power to the regions, and the creation of meaningful local authorities, it will be necessary for the entire structure of local government to be reformed 'with substantial devolution of power from the centre to the level at which people live ... with the work of deputies firmly focussed on national issues while the

The Emergence of Rural Governance in Ireland 165

local authorities get on with delivering local services' (McDonald, 1989, p.38). The question remains however as to whether a centralised governmental administration, such as that which exists in Ireland, can contemplate running alongside a commitment to community development, partnership and participation as currently promoted (see particularly Chapter 5)? From this vantage-point, in the next sections, the quest for new forms of governance and the move toward a more inclusive regulating of society will be critically assessed.

The first layer – the local authorities

> Ireland does not in fact have local government ... merely local administration. Local councillors and officials are treated like children, and they are not regarded as capable of making even the most minor decisions (McDonald, 1989, p.36).

Regional politics and local government in Ireland are out of step with the systems of many other European countries (Hussey, 1993; Chubb, 1992; McDonald, 1989). The Irish government is one of the most centralised administrations in the EU, and is often criticised by those who advocate greater regional control. While there are current attempts to review the operational structures of local government, this centralist system, often regarded as a legacy of British colonialism when power was administered from Dublin, has not changed since Independence in 1922, and has been followed rigidly by successive Irish governments. 'Neither local nor government' is often the description given to the *ad hoc* fashion in which local government in Ireland is administered. Barrington (1992) perhaps one of the best known campaigners for greater local government authority, suggested that, 'no people have had to endure as much frustration as the Irish for lack of opportunity to govern their collective lives' (cited in Hussey, 1993). Barrington's report on Irish local government (published in March 1991), would, if implemented, have changed the entire structure of local politics in Ireland. Given the long history of Irish government declarations of intention to reform, and subsequent inaction in this area, not too much was expected, and not too much happened (Hussey, 1993), at least up to the latter part of the 1990s.

The specific functions allocated to Irish local authorities by central government are considerably fewer than in most western democracies. In a list of fourteen Council of Europe members in 1991, Ireland was bottom of the list with regard to local responsibility (ibid., p.100). Due to a lack of power (e.g. no financial autonomy) local authorities are constrained in their ability to foster such things as local economic development or to plan effectively in a number of areas. In comparison with Norway for example, local government in Ireland is responsible for few activities, bar land-use planning, development, and some infrastructure and housing provisions. Direct engagement in local economic development is a voluntary activity for local government, dependent upon co-operation and partnership with state-sponsored bodies, and on funding from the EU or national sources. In contrast, most of the 'production of public goods (except for defence, police, universities) in Norway is delegated to communes and county communes under combined national and local democratic control, the responsibility for such production in Ireland is mostly delegated, if at all, to state-sponsored bodies under central, direct political control' (Amdam, 1996, p.2).

Local authorities are dominated by non-elected officials and, as such, lack a popular mandate. The range of functions and powers associated with this level of administration is mainly concerned with planning, development and environmental management and control, with effectively no involvement in major policy areas like agriculture and education. As a matter of course, Irish local councillors have very little power. The fact that local authorities cannot change a local speed limit without approval from the Minister for the Environment, indicates their lack of responsibility and reinforces their role as mere agents of central government (McDonald, 1989). In comparison with the Danish system which contains almost '300 local authorities, with responsibility for spending two-thirds of the national budget on a whole range of services, from planning to health and education' (ibid., p.38), the limited powers of the Irish regions are being whittled away year by year.[1]

At the lowest level each county has its own local authority (county council), though some of the larger urban areas like Galway also have a Borough (City) Corporation. This is the basic unit of local administration, making up the core of the local administrative system in terms of powers, functions and finance, all of which are limited by the centralised power structures of the state. One of the main criticisms of this administrative system is its lack of integration, both horizontally and vertically. This lack of integration was highlighted in a recent study of twenty-four state agencies and semi-state organisations which revealed 'that fourteen had different numbers of regions [and] even where two or more bodies had the same number of regions, in no instance were the geographical borders the same' (Rural Development News, 1992, p.1).

The elected bodies of the local authorities consist of: Town Commissioners (26); Urban District Councils (UDCs) (49); County Boroughs (5); County Councils (29), and Boroughs (5). Each local authority has two sections, the elected council and the executive, which respectively, make and implement policy. Until the mid-1990s, only twenty-seven County Councils were in existence, two in Co. Tipperary, and one in each of the remaining counties in the Republic of Ireland, but in 1994, Dublin County Council was reorganised into three administrative units to cope with the huge increase in population (see Coyle, 1996). All the above councils are elected by their constituents and the number of councillors is determined by order, with the exception of the Boroughs and County Boroughs where the number is fixed by statute. Elections are held every five years with between twenty and forty-eight councillors elected to their post in the County Councils; between fifteen and fifty-two members are elected to the County Boroughs; usually twelve members are elected to the Borough Councils, with nine members elected to the Town Commissioners, and nine members elected to the UDCs (Dooney and O'Toole, 1998). All of the local authorities are run by a county or city manager who administers the authority in conjunction with the elected council. The manager is appointed on the recommendation of the Local Appointments Commission and internal appointments are not permitted. The same person acts as manager for all County Council, Boroughs, urban districts and towns in the county, for a maximum of seven years. Technically the county manager undertakes executive functions of the local authority[2] while the elected members undertake the reserved functions.[3] In reality there is closer contact between both, with the manager taking part in council sessions, although without the right to vote (see Dooney and O'Toole, 1998). The Town Commissioners have limited responsibility with respect to the above functions. The services provided by the local authority can be divided under eight broad headings: housing; roads and traffic; water supply and sewerage; development plans; environmental protection; recreation and amenity; education; miscellaneous (ibid.). The funding required for the above functions comes from four sources: central government grants; rates on commercial property; charges for the supply of goods and services; and motor tax (see Dooney and O'Toole, 1998; Coyle, 1996). The reliance on funding from the Exchequer has severely curtailed local authority autonomy, particularly since the decision to abolish domestic rates in 1977 and the subsequent abolishment of agricultural rates (Coyle, 1996). Unlike local authorities in other European countries, Irish local authorities have no policing function, no responsibility for tackling poverty and no control of the health care system within their areas.

There are myriad reasons for serving on a local authority. Some suggest the motivation stems from the personal satisfaction gained from serving the community, the more sceptical might see it in a less altruistic light, as a stepping stone on the road to Dáil Éireann. In recent years the profile of such positions has improved with central government instituting a number of reforms, including legal recognition of the role of local government in the constitution. Each local authority has a statutory duty to produce a development plan for their county with a review every five years. These plans cover such areas as land-use, environmental protection, provision for new infrastructure etc. While this can be seen as a move in the right direction, there is still a considerable amount of change needed if Ireland is to have an effective local government system.

More recently, local authorities have also been encouraged to develop links with the local development bodies active in their area. In this way, much of the local development function of local government in Ireland is shared with other bodies, such as state agencies,[4] local community-based groupings – 'partnership companies', LEADER groups and others funded by EU Structural Funds. An example of a partnership approach between local government and the bodies listed above can be seen in the form of the County Enterprise Boards (CEBs), which were set up with the aim of providing a new forum for the promotion of local indigenous development. How successful these CEBs have been remains debatable, particularly in relation to attracting or retaining industries in the more rural areas.

The second layer – the regional authorities

In January 1994, the Irish government established by statute eight Regional Authority areas (RAs). These consisted of amalgamations of counties, the fundamental units of the local government system known as NUTS III regions. The remit of the RAs is to promote 'the co-ordination of public services in each region and encourage joint action between the different agencies responsible for the provision of public services, including the local authorities' (Walsh, 1995, p.1) and 'to advise and monitor on the implementation of EU funding in the regions' (Department of the Environment, 1996, p. 66). The RAs are indirectly elected, have no taxation powers and consist of city and county councillors from the regions, appointed by the constituent local authorities to the RAs. Their numbers vary between twenty-one and thirty-seven. An operational committee that includes the relevant county and city managers and the executives of public agencies support the board of the RA. In addition to the tasks already outlined, the RAs also 'advise and act as a consultative forum for the newly established Regional Assemblies' (Department of Agriculture and Food, 1999, p.28). The main tasks of RAs are to:

- Promote the co-ordination of public services in the region and integrate the policies of central government ministers at the local level;
- Produce their own regional reports;
- Review the development plans of the local planning authorities with regard to consistency and the implementation of the EU-funded programmes; and
- Review/monitor and advise on the implementation of the Structural Fund and the Cohesion Fund programmes at the regional level, i.e. to ensure a regional input.

The irony in the remit of the RAs is that the task of 'promoting co-ordination' comes at a time when there is a significant lack of co-ordination within government policies, well illustrated by conflicts in the NDP 2000-2006 (Department of Finance, 1999) and the White Paper on Rural

The Emergence of Rural Governance in Ireland 169

Development (Department of Agriculture & Food, 1999). The description by the Department of the Environment (1996) of the RAs as operating on a 'modest scale' with a 'non-invasive role' with respect to the services delivered by other regional structures indicates the lightweight nature of this tier of administration. This impression is further reinforced by the paltry annual expenditure ranging from £100,000 to £200,000 and staffing levels which typically include a secretary and one or two other employees. Compounding the lack of weight which the RAs possess, Walsh (1995), also highlights the potential demise of these RAs as this regional system was largely created for pragmatic, rather than idealistic reasons. This artificial creation of 'regions' has no basis in regional identity, tradition, culture or economic divide and as such lacks both popular recognition and support. The one positive attribute than can be gleaned from the creation of the RAs is that they have yielded a new interest in regional planning which recognises that 'rural development requires a regional planning framework which can set out key long-term objectives and strategies and achieve the co-ordination of certain policies at regional level' (NESC 1994, p.34).

The third layer – the regional assemblies

The EU's promotion of an increased role for local and regional actors has made very little impact on administrative or institutional structures in Ireland. With the EU so actively concerned with reducing disparities between regions, it is ironic that concern with regional development in Ireland, is treated with a minimalist attitude at a time when the country is receiving (as in the past) major EU benefits from the European Regional Fund. The creation of two regional structures in Ireland in March 1999 suggested a move toward a less centralised form of government. The apparent change in thinking that brought this about was not due to any desire to promote regional actors in the state, but rather a direct result of Ireland's growing economy and concerns for the potential loss of EU funds. The Irish government's dedication in chasing the EU money train led to the creation of two 'super' regions within the former 'one region'. The indisputable statistics of growth and prosperity in southern and eastern Ireland would demand a reduction in payments and a movement to 'Objective 1 in transition' status, if Ireland were to remain as one region within the EU. Was this threatened loss of EU funding finally sufficient motivation to push the Irish government along the road to regional devolution? Or would it be the case that the government would forgo Objective 1 status 'rather than concede to direct regional negotiations with Brussels as such negotiations would take power out of the Departments hands' (Senator B. Ryan, Labour, Seanad Debates, 3/06/1998). The answer was neither. The Irish government did not forgo Objective 1 status (at least not totally) nor did it devolve power to the

170   Renegotiating Rural Development in Ireland

regions. Instead, yet another layer of bureaucracy was created with the decision-making authority still remaining firmly with central government.

Boyle (2000) rather amusingly traced the 'stroke politics' which unfolded during this period. The relationship between Ireland and Brussels was firstly undermined by issues of alleged payments to politicians for planning favours, culminating in what became known as the Flynn affair which led to a rather heated and public row between the government and the Irish member of the European Commission, Mr. P. Flynn. This did nothing to increase the Irish government's bargaining power at the then upcoming Berlin summit. Consequently, the contentious debate on dividing the country in to two regions gathered momentum. One of the central figures in the debate was the Independent TD for South Kerry,

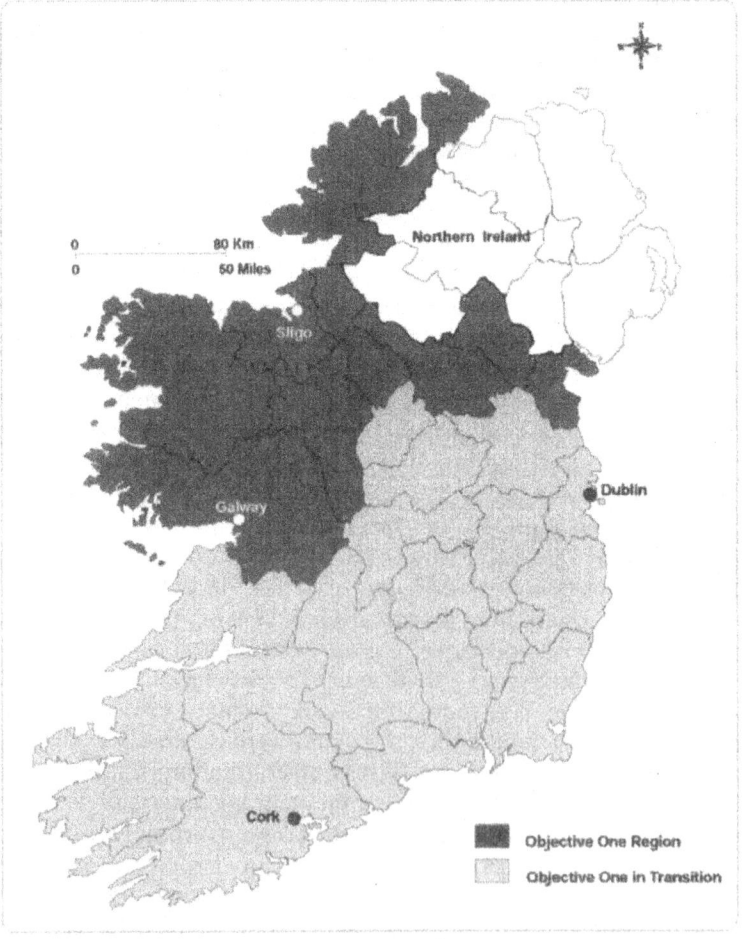

Figure 6.1 Reconfiguring Ireland's regional status – the creation of a new 'Objective One region' and an 'Objective One region in Transition'

Jackie Healy-Rae and his alleged trading of support for the government in return for the inclusion of Kerry in the new Objective 1 region (Clare would also have to be included as Objective 1 regions had to be contiguous). A report in *Ireland Today* (1999) suggested the inclusion of Clare and Kerry in the government's first submission to Eurostat was a masterful negotiation strategy by the Irish government. Their reasoning was that this allowed the government, not only to attain the support of an Independent TD, but also allowed it a negotiating position with the EU, that is, by subsequently 'giving up something' and agreeing to exclude these counties from the final agreement. The EU Commissioner for Regional Affairs, Monika Wulf-Mathies (1998) declared in an interview on the Irish position, that devolution should take place in Ireland not only to get more Structural Funds but also to bring about 'real change in the legislative and regional make-up of the country'. The vision of regional governance held by Wulf-Mathies and the EC was however far different to that of the Irish government, with its questionable preparedness to give 'any new regional structures a real role in the preparation, management and monitoring of the regional components of the National Development Plan' (McCreevy, 1998). The political meandering and lack of desire for regional devolution was further highlighted in the Dáil Debates up to March 1999, when after the rejection by Eurostat of the regional groupings (which included Kerry and Clare), the government rather readily agreed to omit these counties in the hope of retaining Objective 1 status for the remaining thirteen counties in the Border, Midlands and West areas. The two new regions created were the Border, Midlands and West Region (BMW) and the South and East Region (S&E) (Figure 6.1). The BMW region has its headquarters in Ballaghadereen in Co. Roscommon and is made up of counties Galway, Mayo, Roscommon, Donegal, Sligo, Leitrim, Cavan, Monaghan, Louth, Longford, WestMeath, Offaly and Laois. The S & E region has its headquarters in Waterford City and is made up of counties Meath, Dublin, Kildare, Wicklow, Carlow, Wexford, Kilkenny, Waterford, Tipperary, Cork, Limerick, Kerry and Clare. The fact that this decision to jettison two counties was so easily taken, suggests a lack of commitment by the government toward delegating power to the regions and showed the political manoeuvrings to be little more than horse trading in the EU money pit. The acceptance by Eurostat of the revised regional structures signified yet again the ability of the Irish government to maintain centralised control while maximising its EU subsidies. The Berlin summit negotiations of March 1999 accepted the two new regional assemblies and confirmed funding for the coming seven years, for two separate regions in Ireland - a cosmetic exercise in regionalisation that would net the Irish government some extra 590 million euros. All in all, the new two-region bargaining tool proved successful, even lucrative.

This newly established NUTS II level in Ireland, created for the purpose of maximising EU funding beyond 2000, is subsequently one of the more contentious of regional expressions. What is perhaps of most concern is that at a time when the EU could have forced the hand of the Irish government into a reconsideration of the role of regional governance, it instead accepted a tokenistic, non-threatening version with only the veneer of regionalism. Murphy (1991, p.84) writing prior to the creation of these newly formed regions, suggested that even as things stood in the 1990s there was a contradiction between the 'centralised State's hostility to any meaningful regional policy within its own jurisdiction and its insistence that the EC should apply regional policies to the Republic as a peripheral region of the Community'. Without the insistence of the EU for greater regional powers and the lack of a strong lobby from the regional actors themselves, the establishment of the two Regional Assemblies signified nothing more than a cosmetic commitment toward regional administration and a further step in reinforcing this 'spectacle' of development and the 'subsidy shopping' that is characteristic of Irish rural development policy and practice.

The remit of the Regional Assemblies themselves is that they are to be funded from central government and are to be the lead agencies for the Regional Operational Programmes. In addition to a full time director, the Assemblies will have a staff of between fifteen and eighteen, with six meetings scheduled to take place annually over the life of the Assemblies (that is, five years). The Assemblies will form part of the Monitoring Committees on Expenditure. The Western Development Commission, the social partners, community groups and representatives from central government will also be represented on the Monitoring Committees on Expenditure for the Regional Operational Programme. The Assemblies will be represented on the Inter-Regional Operational Programmes' Monitoring Committees and will play a role in the creation of the NSS (Department of Finance, 1999). The essence of the Regional Assemblies is one of being 'assigned the functions of promoting co-ordination of the provision of public services in their regions ... and will also retain a significant co-ordinating role in relation to the eight existing Regional Authorities which will remain in place' (Department of Agriculture and Food, 1999, p.28). Finally, although these assemblies are now set up, it is still unclear whether they will have funding authority or merely be advisory bodies. In keeping in line with other NUTS II regions in Europe which have considerable powers devolved to them, it would be expected that the Regional Assemblies would have a funding and administrative role. This was very much the idea presented by the Fitzpatrick Report on *Regional Development Strategy 2000-2006*, which proposed such a devolution of power with a blueprint for development in these two 'super' regions, including £7.4 billion to be spent on infrastructure in the West and Border Regions. Since the issuing of this document, there has been little or no response from the Minister for Finance apart from a report in the *Irish Times;* (1999) to the effect that the Minister saw the Regional

Assemblies overseeing the spending of £3.5 billion (of the total £35 billion). The Regional Assemblies limited powers of monitoring and administration in relation to the NDP reconfirm the view that the new two region division was more to do with maximising funds from the EU than any great concern for balanced regional development. Consequently the current NDP 2000-2006 commitment to promoting balanced regional development seems hollow, with little specific effort made within the Operational Programmes towards concrete action. Whether the enforced changes to the regional status of Ireland will provide a significant test for the Irish government and their steadfast reluctance to devolve power from the centre, remains open to debate. The indications at present would suggest business as usual.

Local development in Ireland and issues of governance

Reviewing recent literatures (Keane, 1990; Healy and Reynolds, 1991; Varley, 1991a; Varley, 1991b; Ó Cinnéide and Grimes, 1992; Ó Cinnéide and Cuddy, 1992b; O'Cearbhaill and Varley, 1993; Ó Cinnéide, 1993b; Commins and Keane, 1994; Frazer, 1994; Kearney et al., 1994; Amdam, 1996), it becomes clear that there are many misconceptions and different understandings of what development discourse entails with respect to public, private and voluntary sectors. The discourses of development in Ireland have toyed (at least more vociferously in recent years) with the concepts of partnership, changing approaches to rural development and acknowledging the need for community as a basis for rural activation. This section (see also Chapter 5) explores further these issues of governance and the emergence of new mechanisms and structures of governance (such as LEADER) and ask the critical question: 'who has been involved in new forms of governance and who hasn't, and why this is the case' (Goodwin, 1998 p.10). Further, the section offers a critique of the discourses of development (for example, those of participation, partnership and community) and an interpretative commentary on the value of the discourses in the narrative of Irish rural development, with an eye to the concept of development as 'spectacle'.

The concept of governance has begun to enter the vocabulary of elected and un-elected officials alike as the 'search for reductions in the resource commitment and spending of government' (Stoker, 1997 p.6) gains momentum. The reasons for this are many. The traditional use of the term governance has been very closely linked to that of government. While the term can be often more rhetorical than substantive, Stoker (1997) suggests that its emergence has come about from a recognition of the limits of government. Previous definitions of governance have now given way to more progressive interpretations like 'a change in the meaning of government, referring to a new process of governing; or a changed condition of ordered rule; or the new method by which society is governed' (Rhodes, 1996, p.652). Stoker (1998, p.18) further suggests that there are five main complementary (rather than contradictory) aspects to this new pursuit of governance, namely that:

- Governance refers to institutions and actors drawn from, but also beyond, government;
- Governance identifies the blurring of boundaries and responsibilities for tackling social and economic issues;
- Governance identifies the power dependence involved in the relationships between institutions involved in collective action;
- Governance is about autonomous self-governing networks of actors; and
- Governance recognises the capacity to get things done which does not rest on the power of government to command or use its authority. It sees government as able to use new tools and techniques to steer and guide.

There is no easy mixture of these ideals, and in many cases, as for example in the blurring of boundaries and responsibilities, the issue of scapegoating or blame avoidance can surface (ibid.). In essence the movement towards new forms of governance is largely concerned with inclusive or collective regulating of society. That is, an increased role for different private, voluntary and community groups in the strategic development of their locales and in the decision-making process that affects their lives rather than the more centralised exclusiveness of government control. The 'steering rather than rowing' (Osborne and Gaebler, 1991) envisaged for local government would allow local authorities for example, to be 'more entrepreneurial, flexible and responsive to community needs' (McCafferty and Walsh, 1999).

The issue of governance is therefore not only complex in its conceptualisation, it implies more significantly a major change of emphasis, specifically in the changing relationship between the state and its society. This change, while welcome, particularly in the responsibility being shifted more toward voluntary, community and citizen, also provides for what Stoker (1998) describes as the 'blurring of responsibilities'. For example, if local communities are to have more autonomy in looking after their own economies then, if things go wrong, who is responsible?

How can this be applied to Ireland or can it be applied at all?

One thing beyond dispute is that there are changes taking place in how a society is run and these changes, while working differently in different places are worthy of consideration and debate. While the debate on governance is gaining pace particularly in the UK, not all commentators are convinced that this trend is an entirely recent phenomenon. Imrie and Raco (1999, p.46) for example suggest that this 'new' form of governance is anything but new, and 'is not dis-similar to the substantive policy objectives or procedural policy styles of the 'old' modes of local government'. Furthermore, although Imrie and Raco (ibid.) acknowledge the changes in local government/governance in the last number of years, they also question the so-called new directions that are emerging and call for more emphasis to be given to the continuities in local government/ governance. Linking this new perspective of governance to the Irish system is somewhat more problematic, not in the least due to the considerable differences between Ireland and the UK in terms of institutional and administrative systems. McCafferty and Walsh (1999) suggest that among the most significant of these differences is not only the historically more restricted role of Irish government in relation to issues of welfare and privatisation in the local economy, but more significantly, that 'Ireland did not experience the surge of institutional change and associated legislative activity flowing from an ideologically driven political agenda, as occurred in the UK in the 1980s' (p.4). While this may still be the case to some extent in Ireland, the last decade has seen change, if not in practice, then most certainly in thinking. This is particularly so with regard to issues of local government and the increasing role being placed on the community and voluntary sectors to provide for their own economies. The strategies as envisaged by the government in the White Paper on Rural Development (Department of Agriculture & Food, 1999) lend temselves to the notion of the emergence within Ireland of this form of governance, where the local has an impact on the national and where the community has a role to play in its future direction and development. For example, the Irish government suggests that it is 'committed to implementing a strategy for rural development on the basis of an inclusive approach to sustainable development, the integration of policies, a regional dimension and partnership with the rural community' (p.7) and further, that it is committed 'to encouraging, supporting and empowering active rural communities to plan and contribute to the development of their own areas' (p.49).

Consequently support for local area-based initiatives that promote community empowerment, participation in decision-making and control over resources, has allegedly become central to rural and local development policy as envisaged by the Irish government (Department of Agriculture & Food, 1999). The recognition by the government of the 'considerable community and voluntary effort which can be mobilised to promote economic and social development in rural areas' (ibid., p.48) has led to the creation of a plethora of area-based partnerships, committees and development boards. The Irish government has declared its intentions to implement programmes which fund voluntary and community sectors such as the Community Enterprise Schemes, the Community Development Programme, the Programme of Core-Funding for locally-based Community and Family support groups, and the Family and Community Services

Resource Centre Programme, in order to maximise the potential success of these partnerships and community groups in addressing social inclusion (ibid.).

Within this rhetoric, further changes recently occurring in Ireland, include those of the operational structures of Local Authorities (with more forthcoming) and a growth in local development activity. The reasons for the growing emphasis on local development and the partnership approach can perhaps be reconciled with an emergence of the historical traditions of community in rural Ireland (the Meitheal system for example) with McCafferty and Walsh (1999) suggesting that other factors include:

- Identification of new areas/groups with major social need;
- Desire to improve the local delivery of national welfare services;
- Potential of local initiatives to generate employment;
- Official support for community development and participation: and
- Involvement of the national social partners in the local implementation of policy (p.5).

From a more pragmatic (perhaps cynical) stance the emergence of this new policy emphasis on local development is more likely to have been directed via the EU and its promotion of local development through such Community Initiatives as LEADER, URBAN and the Poverty Programme. Through these programmes and the EU's recognition of the role of local actors in rural development, local, regional and national actors have been required to develop new structures to administer rural development programmes. Subsequently Ireland's chasing of Structural Funds has guided them down the path of partnership, local development and new systems of governance.

New mechanisms and structures of governance

The Pilot Area Programme for Integrated Rural Development (IRD) 1988-1990

This pilot programme, initiated by the Department of Agriculture and Food in 1988, was seen as the first significant attempt at integrated rural development in Ireland. The programme was based on the need 'to extend interventions beyond agriculture and to incorporate mechanisms for linking local initiative to statutory action' (O'Hara and Commins, 1991, p.32). The aims of the IRD strategy were to 'initiate and foster development designed to lead to improved economic and social conditions through the establishment of commercial self-sustaining enterprise and the encouragement of a community-based attitude of self help' (Commins and Keane, 1994, p.163). The programme covered twelve sub-county areas

(6,000-15,000 inhabitants) and was served by a co-ordinator/animator, who organised local groups, determined their development priorities and facilitated interaction between the groups and the various statutory agencies involved. The most notable (non)feature of this programme was the minuscule amount of funding allocated. Used mainly for technical assistance, these minimal funds were allegedly designed to help 'to advance projects to the stage where they could tap into other 'mainstream' funding sources' (ibid., p.163). In this 'new' expression of Irish rural development, there was a strong emphasis on a 'shared learning' approach, with the main objective of the programme being to enhance local integration in the sense of developing activities that were mutually reinforcing and complementary. The outcomes were characterised by Varley (1991a) as resulting in a heavy focus on exploiting local tourism potential and on alternative agricultural enterprises.[5]

Varley (1991a, p.99) critically suggested that such initiatives as the IRD programme showed a rather narrow view of community development by the Irish state whereby: 'community groups are seen not as entities with their own special attributes and needs but as capable of being mobilised for special purposes - the conferring of popular legitimacy on area-based state interventions, job creation, service provision - and, for all the rhetoric, they turn out to be anything but major players in the newest generation of area-based development programmes'. While it would be an exaggeration to claim that the IRD type of programme could transform rural Ireland, it did have a limited success; approximately 604 jobs were created (O'Malley, 1992), making a useful contribution to the social and economic development of the areas in which it was pursued. O'Malley (ibid.) suggested that the main obstacles to the IRD programme were its short time frames and its financial and technical constraints, which in some cases led to viable projects not getting off the ground for lack of support. In looking at how the IRD pilot programme encouraged a partnership-based development, Varley (1991a, p.98) posed the question as to whether new life could be breathed into 'community participation' by means of 'partnership from above'. He suggested that the legacy of the IRD pilot programme, and a significant shift in emphasis from earlier programmes, was the recognition 'that local communities cannot proceed very far individually; only when they are brought together on a larger area basis, and their activities co-ordinated and 'integrated' are they likely to make a significant developmental impact' (ibid., p.98). The positive soundings of this programme seemed feasible, yet the reality was the need for the pilot scheme to be successful in terms of end results. As a consequence, Varley (1991b) suggested there was a pressure to 'pick winners' in the form of small groups of experienced core activists. This trend seemed to account for the relative success of some areas, in comparison to others, in terms of jobs and other issues. Ultimately, despite the very limited resources devoted to it, the IRD did succeed in providing a basis for harnessing local resources and empowering some communities, and in this way, represented an important contribution to rural development in Ireland. Commins and Keane (1994, p.164) duly observed that 'if community-based development [was] expected to address the difficult issue of economic and social development then attention must be given to the more basic process of development, *viz.*, a 'pre-development' phase involving the animation of local groups and the generation of a capacity among local people to work purposefully in collective action'. It would follow from this however that instead of being empowering, the IRD pilot programme and other similar types of state initiative can often be debilitating for community groups, with their stop-go type development and one-off funds often leading to cynicism amongst community volunteers and workers alike.

Area-based partnerships

The quest for 'new forms of governance', stems from the increased realisation that economic growth will not in itself improve the prospects of vulnerable and marginalised groups. Further, the view that national partnerships or specifically targeted programmes will also be insufficient, has led to the configuration of public-private area-based partnerships to address area-specific issues and to set in motion policies to tackle these issues. The recognition that an important spatial element exists in the increasingly diverse world in which we live and the many issues that governments have to address, like competitiveness, unemployment, poverty, social exclusion, has led to the promotion of (allegedly) more effective delivery mechanisms in the form of area-based partnerships. For some however, the assumption that area-based approaches to rural development will create sustainable employment remains an 'open question' (Matthews, 1995), while for others such partnerships are promoted as being flexible, decentralised, participative in their administration, and the core of a new localism in Ireland (see Sabel, 1996). The traditional Irish attachment to centralised administration suggests that the devolving of decision-making to a local level can be viewed as an innovative step. Despite the growing acceptance of 'partnerships' as being able to tailor their activities to the local problems they encounter, they will still require a great deal of political good will and commitment if they are to succeed and become a meaningful reality in the lives of those, who up to now, would be classed as excluded. In this light the concept of partnership is a challenging process.

What are partnerships?

Partnerships create a framework for the voluntary-state-private sector to work together. The debate on what partnership seeks to achieve, involves a number of key issues (see OECD 1990; Combat Poverty Agency 1995; ADM 1997; 1997a; Mernagh and Commins 1997). The concept that partnerships allow for better targeting of resources is strongly promoted. It is argued that people 'on the ground' are far more effective in recognising issues like unemployment and social exclusion than those in centralised administration. Partnerships are seen to allow communities to bridge the gap between local and state agencies and encourage people to become involved in their own areas (local ownership of actions) by promoting principles of equality, and enabling the empowerment of the marginalised and excluded groups through the development of skills and knowledge (ADM, 1997). In Ireland twelve partnership companies were created in 1991 under the Programme for Economic and Social Progress (with the use of Structural Funds). In 1995 an additional twenty-six disadvantaged areas were added to provide thirty-eight area-based partnerships in urban and rural communities. Essentially, partnerships pursue area-based economic development that is primarily targeted at problems of unemployment and underemployment and at reaching other disadvantaged groups within specific areas. These problems are addressed in ways which central government may not be able to pursue. Legally, partnership companies are independent, with a Board of Directors comprising representatives from community and voluntary groups, state agencies (departments concerned with training and education), social partners (trade unions, business associations) and, in rural areas, farming organisations. In practice, this amalgam comes about by the state agencies nominating regional officials whose work is of local concern; social partners nominating the local representatives and the community groups electing or selecting people who are 'well-respected' in the community. The obvious drawback, particularly in relation to the social partners, is that people are nominated to take a seat on a partnership board by virtue of their position in a given organisation, rather than any burning desire to help the community in question (McDonagh, 2000). ADM (Area Development Management) is the main body responsible for the partnerships. Established in 1992 by the Irish government, ADM is an intermediary company supporting local social and economic development through evaluating local partnership plans, allocating funding, monitoring performance, assisting in setting up partnerships, and providing information, guidance and advice on financial controls.

Partnerships are difficult to describe in broad terms. Fundamentally, they are all based on the same principles and are subject to the same rules. It is also true that each partnership is characterised by a combination of varied and evolving projects. In a sense 'partnerships are the projects' (Sabel, 1996) and as the projects change and evolve, so to do the partnerships. For the most part, while partnerships are one-dimensional in their primary objectives (that is, to re-integrate the long-term unemployed back into the workforce), their initiatives soon become multi-dimensional with inputs from education and training, enterprise, community development, environment and infrastructural issues. Furthermore, large scale differences are observable between the Action Plans presented by the local development groups at the onset, and what these partnerships subsequently pursue (see Sabel, 1996).

Despite their obvious success (for example, the number of business start-ups and people returned to employment was twice that expected) a question mark hangs over the achievements of partnerships. These questions include for example, whether the people placed in jobs keep them over the longer term or, whether the new businesses created survive beyond the funding phase? This undoubtedly important aspect may be overlooked due to the indirect nature of partnership interventions, for example, increasing entrepreneurial abilities and capacity building, which are difficult to quantify. Therefore a comprehensive overview of partnerships in Ireland is needed particularly in relation to their evolution (in their own localities); the relationship between the various partnerships, and the influence (if any) which partnerships have on a national scale. Further, there is a need to determine which connections between partnerships, local government and national agencies work best and under what conditions (Sabel 1996).

The importance of partnership

It is widely recognised that partnerships suffer from a lack of training, support and resources. The responsibility placed on these groups to promote economic and social development in rural areas (see Department of Agriculture & Food, 1999) is therefore questionable. Partnership, is generally understood as being synonymous with equality; a coming together of two (or more) sides/groups both of whom would have an equal share and input (Dillion, 1989). While all 'sides' may, understandably not come from the same resource power base, there is the implication that all would be in a position to make equally important contributions. For such partnerships to work, two basic requirements would seem to be: a commitment to work together and, a willingness to ensure equality in the decision-making process. As such, partnership may be defined as a relationship between equal but different partners. Partners will probably differ in their origins, goals, activities, structures, resources and contributions, but they nevertheless are integratively essential to the process. Partners, at least in theory, should have equal status within a group and as such they should have equal say on where resources are directed or where money is spent. The make-up of a successful partnership should therefore include consultation, community involvement, communication, commitment and control (Craig, 1995). Control of decision-making should be exercised for the benefit of the community and individuals should not be allowed to influence the process for their own agenda. In reality, such equality rarely exists, with the more experienced and the representatives of larger (more powerful) agencies having far more power than others (McDonagh, 2000). In many cases, partnerships become dominated by the more powerful groups and the partnership is effectively transformed into a donor-recipient relationship. Clearly there are several key issues at play within the mechanism of partnership: what the so-called partners have to offer; what is their agenda; what each organisation and individual can contribute to the partnership. There is an urgent need to re-evaluate the whole concept of partnerships within this specific context.

The local community, partnership and participation

The ultimate target of a partnership is the local community it serves. A continually professed desire of partnerships is to get local people actively involved in their communities and the decision-making process by helping develop their ability to take part in this process, through capacity building. The demand for active participation has been fuelled by greater access to information, higher education levels and a realisation that these activities have a large impact on the quality of people's lives. Participation as a concept however appears to be almost intentionally vague. It can mean everything from being informed of certain events, being consulted about others or even having the ability to stop or control proposed directions of a group and/or situation. As such, the nature of involvement of the local community in a partnership is often very unclear. In exploring one particular partnership in the west of Ireland, McDonagh (1998) highlighted a number of issues including: the lack of clarity on what partnerships were trying to achieve; the lack of involvement by the community sector in the decision-making process; the lack of clear guidelines on the role the local community has to play, and the lack of a proper feedback mechanism. If partnerships are to continue to progress they must harness all elements of the rural base, the private sector, local co-operatives, community groups, the local county council, FÁS and other state agencies, the farming, fishing and forestry communities. It is essential that partnerships regularly relate to their original aims and objectives and critically assess whether they are staying true to these goals (and whether some objectives need to be changed, modified or dispensed with) through evaluation of projects, particularly in relation to their relevance, quality, efficiency, and impact.

Partnerships are unlikely to benefit from their innovations until the broader political elite addresses their long-term future. Current uncertainty with regard to funding encourages short-term gains to the detriment of long-term strategies. The types of 'competition' partnerships are forced to engage in, are reflected in the type of projects that partnerships endorse. Although project choice may be influenced by the broader political constraints of partnerships in general, there seems a distinct emphasis on 'concrete' short-term projects and a shying away from experimental and innovative ones because of their uncertain outcome. Partnerships, in order to fulfil their potential, need to concentrate on targeting innovative projects; on looking at new ways of doing things and ways of influencing state agencies. Only by observing such a focus can they avoid the risk of becoming small grant-giving agencies. Partnerships need to be judged less in terms of tangible projects, and more in terms of the contributions they have made to developing the human capacity and community spirit within any given region. The lack of horizontal diffusion of information and beneficial learning (i.e. best practice) between partnerships is also a drawback with partnerships pursuing similar types of objectives, but employing different strategies. These strategies would be more effective if they worked together in a co-ordinated and harmonious way. To this end the commitment in the latest NDP to continue funding for partnerships and community groups to 2003, while welcome, is still inadequate to support the long-term strategies required for local development. While current discussions and negotiations are trying to integrate partnerships more closely with local government, the uncertain position of local government itself would seem to indicate a correspondingly uncertain future for partnerships in Ireland.

In addition, the profiles of the partnerships need to be heightened and promoted. The outside perception of partnerships is often that they are small grant-giving agencies. While this is an inevitable part of the process of partnership, the fact that they are seen only in this light (as much from within, as outside) is particularly worrying for their long-term future. A significant danger would be that partnerships become 'mini-bureaucracies' and effectively become another part of the problem rather than part of the solution. Partnerships have other risks to contend with: the longer-term survival, the vulnerability of funding, the financial support from the EU and the position of the partnership programme within public administration are all significant concerns. This is particularly so in relation to institutional legitimacy, democratic legitimacy and calls for rationalisation, which individually or collectively could threaten the continued existence of partnership groups (Sabel, 1996). Nowhere is the control of resources for example, that the partnerships exercise, governed by precise administrative rules or sanctioned by a popular vote of the community. Subsequently, partnerships have an uncertain legitimacy, which has serious implications for their accountability in the eyes of the general community. Furthermore, often partnerships with similar objectives do not appear to benefit from each other's knowledge and experience. Informal episodic exchanges between partnerships are not really sufficient. The role of partnership *vis-à-vis* other local development groups is also a hazy area offering little guidance as to what these roles entail or how they could be integrated. The significant pool of experience

The Emergence of Rural Governance in Ireland 183

formed by the various agencies is not currently being exploited as a potential learning resource on which to base new forms of collaboration. Those in authority do not seem to be systematically monitoring the results, successes and failures of partnership groups, nor the underlying reasons. As a result, these agencies are not well placed to learn from, and disseminate, best practice cases; that is, specific projects undertaken by partnerships may be very successful but the overall experiment may fail. Ultimately, in an ironic parallel, the role of partnership in Ireland is close to Ireland's own role in relation to EU Structural Funds, which places it as 'one beneficiary among many, of a programme designed to foster decentralised innovation' (Sabel, 1996, p.98).

The LEADER Initiatives

LEADER I

'The LEADER Programme represents one of the more positive developments to be introduced in rural Ireland in recent times' (Alan Gillis, former IFA President).

'As experience is shared and rooted deeply in the community, this integrated process is becoming unstoppable and offers a real basis for confidence in our future' (Phillip Mullaly, Enterprise Trust).

(Quotes taken from the 'Irish LEADER Network', no date)

The EC DGVI first launched the LEADER programme in 1991. Since the initial pilot programme of LEADER I, there has been LEADER II (1995) and LEADER + (2000). LEADER from its inception, promoted the notion of local participation in the designing and implementation of rural development projects in specific territorial areas. The EC defined the scope of the programmes as a guiding set of principles rather than technocratic or sectoral measures. The local targeting of funds from the EU Structural Funds was manifest in the participatory nature of the LEADER programme and the community-based strategies it sought to engage. This move toward a bottom-up developmental phase was part of the EC desire for a more integrated (both horizontally and vertically) rural development package in the member states of the EU.

The LEADER programme essentially involved the transfer of EU grants directly to designated groups through an intermediary, which in Ireland's case is the Department of Agriculture, Food and Forestry (now the Department of Agriculture, Food and Rural Development). LEADER is seen to have been very influential in Irish rural development policy, indeed Ireland is believed to be the best example of local community participation in local development (Jouen, 1999). The LEADER initiative did focus much needed attention on some important priorities, for example, the increased desire for communities to become involved in their own development; the development of confidence and capacity-building in rural communities, and, if nothing else, the elevation of development in rural areas on to the national and EU stage. However, there were also some cynical reactions to the announcement of the LEADER initiative. The discourse from politicians and policy makers that a 'bottom-up' or community action approach was part of the panacea to rural ills was suggested in the statement of Joe Walsh TD, Minister for Agriculture, Food and Rural Development; 'given the opportunity, rural communities have the talent and the ability to contribute in a major way to their own development [and] this fact is certainly evident from the experience of LEADER' (Irish LEADER Network, no. date, p.22). This 'opportunity' was however seen by many other commentators as being merely well intentioned rhetoric, and in reality was no more than 'just another scheme to distract us all from the inevitable decline of the countryside and its people' (McGuinness, no date, p.23). As such, the rural development path pursued by the Irish government can be questioned particularly with regard to the quite limiting rules of engagement for those local communities encouraged to become involved in this programme.

The main objective of the first LEADER programme was to 'find innovative solutions which [would] serve as a model for all rural areas and ensure maximum integration between sectoral measures' (Commins and Keane, 1994, p.168). The Department of Agriculture, Food and Forestry issued invitations to groups interested in participating, to submit a 'business plan' for consideration in May 1991. The original Community Initiative offered assistance in the form of integrated grants to groups, which were to enjoy 'a substantial degree of flexibility' in implementing at local level the initiatives financed by national global grants. Seventeen groups (two were later amalgamated) in Ireland (Figure 6.2) were selected on the basis of their business plans. Each Local Action Group (LAG) entered into a formal contract with the intermediary body that set out the terms and conditions under which they would operate. The contract agreement included, *inter alia*, the funding schedule and terms for payment, reporting arrangements, and the other general operational and administrative conditions appropriate to the execution of the 'business plan' for each group (Kearney et al., 1994). The areas targeted were predominantly rural, suffering from population decline, a dependency on agriculture and peripheral disadvantage. The land area covered almost 61% of Ireland, with a population involving almost 30% of the country (population density varied from ten to forty persons per square km with an average of twenty-five). The nature of the tasks undertaken by the LEADER groups was diverse and included technical supports, vocational training, services and marketing of local products. The dominant three areas of activity were rural tourism, small enterprises and natural

The Emergence of Rural Governance in Ireland   185

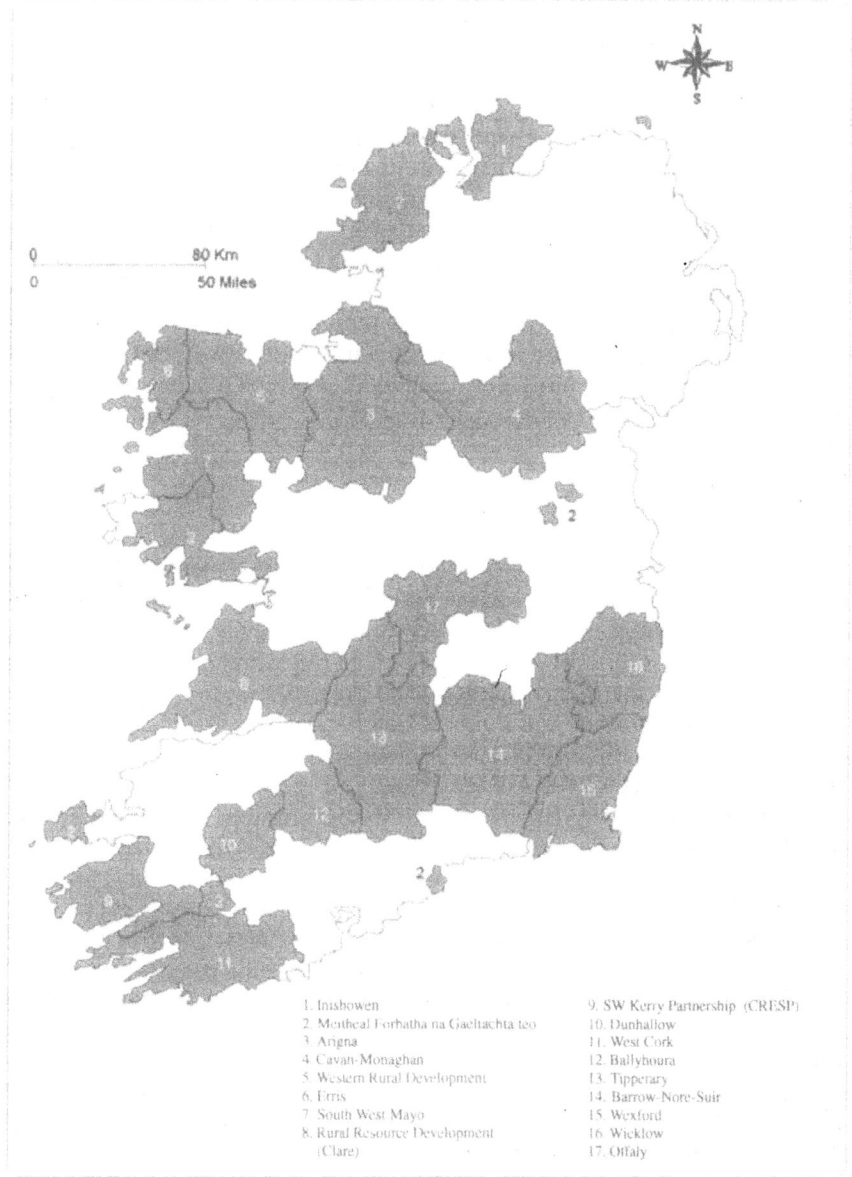

1. Inishowen
2. Meitheal Forbatha na Gaeltachta teo
3. Arigna
4. Cavan-Monaghan
5. Western Rural Development
6. Erris
7. South West Mayo
8. Rural Resource Development (Clare)
9. SW Kerry Partnership (CRESP)
10. Dunhallow
11. West Cork
12. Ballyhoura
13. Tipperary
14. Barrow-Nore-Suir
15. Wexford
16. Wicklow
17. Offaly

Figure 6.2   The spatial distribution of LEADER I areas in Ireland (Kearney *et al.*, 1994)

resources, with the allocations of funding being in the region of 44%, 11% and 15% respectively (ibid.).

In terms of finance, the EU contributed £20.083million, the Irish government £13.896million, with the combined amount being matched by the groups through their own resources (investments from entrepreneurs) making a total of approximately £70million. Although there had been a gradual growth in the setting up of community groups prior to LEADER I many of the groups (almost 75%) were established specifically for the purpose of attracting and administering LEADER funds (see Walsh, 1998). These groups supposedly represented a broad sector of interests in rural areas, such as co-operatives, community groups, tourism boards and other sectoral interests (for example, farming groups). Environmental concerns were for the most part excluded, as were the interests of the unemployed and trade unions.

LEADER II

LEADER II was to be the consolidation of the achievements of LEADER I. This programme was seen as a continuation of the earlier programme and involved double the number of community groups. LEADER II was established for the period 1994-1999. The lead Department for administering LEADER II was the then Department of Agriculture, Food and Forestry (now the Department of Agriculture, Food and Rural Development). The Operational Programme (OP) for the implementation of LEADER II was prepared when Ireland was still an Objective 1 region and subsequently all rural areas could apply/benefit from this programme. The objective of LEADER II was to 'stimulate innovative measures by those, whether public or private, engaged at local level, in all sectors of rural activity; to make known the results of these experiments throughout the Community; to assist rural operators in different Member States who wish to profit from the lessons learnt elsewhere, and, to work jointly on some projects' (Kearney and Associates, 2000, p.2). This programme was to be administered by local rural groups pursuing medium and long-term developmental projects for their own areas. The role of animation and capacity-building within the developmental phase was viewed as the foundation of the LEADER II initiative. Further, issues of innovation, transnational co-operation and transfer of know-how/best-practice were promoted as desired goals.

The differences between LEADER 1 and LEADER II initiatives include:

- Greater emphasis was placed on innovation and complementarity, the inclusion of a new measures concerned with the preservation and improvement of the environment and living conditions;
- More attention was paid to the structure of the local groups and establishment of performance indicators;

The Emergence of Rural Governance in Ireland 187

- The initiative was extended to all rural areas;
- LEADER II was operating alongside the Operational Programme for Local Urban and Rural Development and sub-programmes such as the County Enterprise Boards and Area Partnerships;
- The operating guidelines were much more focused, forcing groups to place more emphasis on the processes of fostering and supporting local development; and
- Funding was made available for a number of collective bodies representing sectoral interests (ibid., pp. 4, 5).

Assistance was granted from the Structural Funds for an amount not exceeding 67 Mecu with a National Exchequer contribution fixed at 28.582 Mecu. A further IR£18.3million were granted from the Community Initiative Reserve by the EC. As with LEADER I, advertisements for the initiative were placed (in national newspapers, at public meetings etc.) and interested groups invited to apply. The submission of a 'business plan' was again necessary and out of the forty-eight applications, thirty-six groups were funded (four in a pre-development category; thirty LAGs (seventeen of which had taken part in LEADER I with some having changed their spatial coverage) and two sectoral (collective) groups, with a third added in 1998. The two collective bodies, Irish Farmhouse Holidays and Irish Country Holidays, were funded to facilitate, promote and market the rural tourism concept particularly through the local group or cooperative approach (LEADER Atlas of Rural Development, 2000). The third addition to the collective bodies was Múintir na Tíre, a long-established community development association which sought to work with three pilot communities for two years in order to establish representative community council structures based on the Múintir na Tíre model (Kearney and Associates, 2000). From the eligibility criteria outlined by the Department, the structure of the groups, including Board membership, was to be representative of community, public and private interests. Boards tended to comprise between nine and twenty-six members with an average membership of around sixteen or seventeen. Representation came from communities, state agencies, local authorities and social partners. In those groups not involved in operating Area Partnerships, representation from the trade unions and the socially disadvantaged was again weak. On average, 40% of the board is from communities, 30% from state agencies/local authorities, with the balance made up by the social partners.

LEADER +

The most recent addition to this trilogy is LEADER +. The aim of LEADER + is 'to encourage and help rural actors to think about the longer-term potential of their area' (European Commission, 2000, p. 3). This, as a concept or

188 Renegotiating Rural Development in Ireland

objective, indicates nothing new, springing directly from LEADER I and II and their objectives of improving the lot of rural communities. Further, the time scale over which LEADER + is to operate is not significantly longer than its predecessors. Jointly funded by Member States and the European Community, LEADER + is intended to support pilot strategies (yet again) to develop the indigenous potential of rural areas. All rural areas will be eligible under LEADER +, however Member States may limit its application to certain rural areas (European Commission, 2000). This initiative seeks to encourage the implementation of integrated, high-quality, original strategies for sustainable development designed to encourage experimenting with new ways of:

- Enhancing the natural and cultural heritage;
- Reinforcing the economic environment, in order to contribute to job creation; and
- Improving the organisational abilities of their community (ibid., 2000).

Co-operation in the 'broad sense of the term' is seen to be a fundamental component of the programme. Financial assistance is again to be provided to the LAGs and at the decision-making level the economic social partners and associations are to make up at least 50% of the local partnership. The LEADER + initiative is to be structured around three actions:

- Action 1: support for integrated territorial development strategies of a pilot nature based on the bottom-up approach and horizontal partnerships;
- Action 2: support for inter-territorial and transnational co-operation; and
- Action 3: the networking of all rural areas in the Community, whether or not beneficiaries under LEADER + or not (ibid.).

Whither LEADER IV?

The LEADER Initiative would appear to have been successful. Under LEADER I, projects receiving assistance created almost 1,445 jobs, with close to 50% of those employed being previously unemployed. Kearney *et al.* (1994, p.41) suggested that a large majority of those involved in the LAGs perceived the initiative as providing an opportunity for local people to initiate development by harnessing local resources and generally in 'empowering' local groups to adopt a multi-sectoral approach to development. Some also perceived the initiative as the related concept of the 'bottom-up' approach, while a small minority considered it in the first instance, as a source of funds for local development and as a means of generating employment and value-added to the areas concerned (this relating to the original understanding of LEADER rather than its mode of operation).

The Emergence of Rural Governance in Ireland 189

While on first reflection the objectives behind the LEADER initiative seem to be a positive step, there are a number of fundamental weaknesses. These include:

- The selective nature of the groups. Not all sectors of society were included (for example, the unemployed); neither were all groups who applied for funding accepted. This would seem to indicate that those who were not successful were not in need of assistance, or more critically were not able to produce a professional business plan in order to obtain funding;

- The need for business plans. There was a rather narrow connotation of development implicit in the requirement that groups submit 'business plans' in their original applications to participate in the programme (Commins and Keane, 1994). The paradox here is that those least likely to have the resources to produce a 'business plan' were most likely those with the greatest need;

- The requirement of matching funds. While this seemed reasonable for commercial ventures, there were strong arguments that those community groups that were well organised, had a good level of economic development, a climate of enterprise and the human resources necessary, were in a greater position to take advantage of the funds available as opposed to those in the less mobilised regions who were perhaps more in need of funds. Commins and Keane (ibid.) commented in relation to the matching funds requirement, that it was significant that the budgets for education and training had been under-spent well into the time-frame of the programme; they suggested that undoubtedly part of the reason for this was the condition that 50% of cost must be provided from 'own funding';

- The short time frame in which the LEADER groups had to operate. This caused most problems to those groups which were newly established (to specifically attract LEADER funds) and which often suffered teething problems before being able to commence their operations (see Kearney et al., 1994). Ray (2000) also recognised the ill match between the funding times scale and that of the socio-economic changes that were being addressed. The focus on more short-term quantifiable goals overlooked the bigger picture that the LEADER programme professed to address (for example, capacity building, animation etc.). Ray (ibid.) further argued that in 'remote, disadvantaged rural areas, especially where the self-confidence of the local population has been undermined by centuries of cultural and political repression, the animation of endogenous, innovative development has to be seen as a medium and long term process of transformation in world views' (p.86). The short time frame (three years in the case of LEADER I, five years for LEADER II) did little to take this in to account;

- The desire to expedite the allocation of funds available within the allocated period. That is, the necessity of producing a tangible 'result' at the end of the programme's time frame;

- The lack of training that people were given in relation to local development and especially the partnership process that LEADER sought to engender (see NESC, 1994);

- The lack of flexibility. Despite their purported flexibility, LEADER groups were still very much constrained by the parameters and criteria set from the top-down;

- The chasing of funds. That almost 50% of the successful applicants for LEADER II were recipients of LEADER I funding raises a number of questions. The first question/observation is that this outcome positively reinforces the LEADER initiative, in that seventeen groups were capable of successfully applying for increased funding in a second initiative. On the other hand, more sceptically, it could also mean that the chasing of funds became an end in itself and that without another programme to apply to, theses groups (even after initial set-ups), were in themselves unsustainable. In other words, what LEADER II may be indicating is a desire for short term 'developments' at the expense of any longer-term sustainable outcomes;

- The type of development pursued. The LEADER II programme once again reinforced a specific type of development. The language used in outlining the objectives of these development plans, that is, these multi-dimensional and multi-sectoral programmes; bottom-up strategies and tripartite relationships, all followed the type of 'political speak' that is associated with rural development in Ireland. The fact that many of these action groups retained the services of external consultants (see Kearney and Associates, 2000) to prepare their applications once again outlined the 'professional' approach to this so-called 'bottom-up', inclusive development and the value-for-money criteria that was still imperative;

- The growing shift in responsibility from government to community. The specific aims that commonly arose from the different plans; those of creating employment, diversifying local economies, improving the lives of the disadvantaged and marginalised; improving the quality of life of rural communities and protecting the environment (among others), all indicated a shift in responsibility from national to local. Essentially a shifting of responsibility without the power, the democratic legitimacy, or the resources, necessary.

Overall, the strength of the LEADER initiatives is that they have very successfully promoted the idea of local participation in rural development, along with a desire for innovative (even experimental) ways of pursuing it. The weakness is that they have not gone far enough. The mobilising of local actors to become involved in, and take control of, the future of their communities is a significant start. However, such a shifting of responsibility is never likely to be a sustainable process without either the legitimacy or adequate resources. The initial steps on the ladder of a decentralised, integrated and bottom-up approach to territorial development are rendered all the more problematic by the tight framework dictated by the Structural Funds criteria. Rather than be bold in terms of innovation (as should be the core of pilot programmes) there is a more pressing need to conform to

The Emergence of Rural Governance in Ireland 191

certain categories, for example those of technical support, vocational training, rural tourism and small enterprises (as indicated in LEADER I). Further, it was recognised by Kearney and Associates (2000) that like other local development initiatives (for example, CEBs and Area-based partnerships) LEADER shows deficiencies in the information systems used to monitor local development activities, in particular, 'the lack of common client identifiers limits the potential to share data locally and hinders comprehensive evaluation of local development' (p.25). LEADER undoubtedly has helped to open up rural areas to other territories and experiences through the creation of new forms of networks. The conflict however between the timescale of the programmes and the desire for such things as capacity building and animation, does not allow for the longer-term and less quantifiable, objectives to be pursued as vigorously as they should. That LEADER I was essentially a pilot programme with a diverse implementation across the EU with varied outcomes, was highlighted by Ray (1998) who suggested that while this was the desired result, there was little by way of evaluation of these diverse programmes for the transferability of best practice. As LEADER I drew to a close those few evaluations that were carried out are described by Ray as 'not 'evaluations' commissioned by the local LEADER groups but, rather, a sociology of (LEADER) development' (ibid., p.79). The subsequent LEADER II and LEADER + (and possibly LEADER IV, V?) can thus be viewed rather sceptically in that they have emerged from a fundamentally underevaluated pilot programme. It would appear that while there have been positive outcomes to the LEADER initiatives thus far (and perhaps it is still too early to judge), the longevity of these outcomes is questionable. The development 'spectacle' and the chasing of EU funds seems set to continue under new headings.

The County Enterprise Boards (CEBs)

The establishment of the CEBs was one of the main features of the 1993-1997 Programme for a Partnership Government. In all, there are thirty-five Enterprise Boards,[6] with a support team, headed by a County Enterprise Officer who directs individual projects or channels community initiatives to the appropriate state agency. The main objective of the CEBs is 'to encourage local initiative by a greater devolution of functions, and through their establishment empower local communities to obtain local funding to develop their own areas' (Department of Finance, 1993, p.70). Through the remit of the CEB the Government suggests that it is seeking to fill a gap which has been identified in current support services for local enterprise initiatives, whereby the full potential of local enterprise for employment creation can be released through greater co-ordination between the efforts of the state agencies and those of other government departments in promoting local economic development (ibid.).

The Boards themselves are made up of between twelve and fourteen members drawn from elected members of the Local Authority, ICTU (trade unions), IBEC (employers), the farming organisations, the state development agencies, the County Manager and community and other representatives. The Boards have a multi-sectoral brief, and are co-ordinated at a national level in respect to the allocation of funds to the CEBs; the criteria for the evaluation of project applications to the CEBs, and the overall scope for complementarity in funding arrangements *vis-à-vis* other local development programmes (ibid.). The functions of the CEBs are to:

- Prepare a County Enterprise Plan with pro-active strategies for local enterprise, development and job creation;
- Identify local economic resources and how they may be developed;
- Encourage the development of a local enterprise culture;
- Assess applications for support and decide on the most appropriate level of assistance in the form of feasibility, employment and capital grants (the following grant levels apply - a maximum of 50% on the cost of capital and other investment, or £50,000 whichever is the lesser; and a maximum of 75% of the cost of preparing a feasibility study/business plan, subject to an overall limit of £5,000 in the case of a single project);
- Promote the development of small businesses through better access to business information, advice, counselling and management development, i.e. soft supports;
- Develop and strengthen collaboration between the local community, the private sector and the state agencies; and
- Help to co-ordinate local community effort and assist community groups to carry out economic assessments and analyses (CEBs, no date).

The Boards complement programmes such as LEADER and Area Partnership Companies and the initiative is built around co-ordinated action to help small businesses overcome their structural weaknesses. Funding is related to an annual performance agreement. In their first three years of operation the CEBs approved more than 6,000 local enterprise projects and £50million in grants with more than £50million paid out. For 1999, public funds of £80.773million were made available (ibid.).

Commins and Keane (1994, p.176) suggested that while it was difficult to assess the contribution of the CEBs to rural development, they nevertheless believed that 'they [CEBs] offer possibilities for an additional degree of funding for rural development, as well as a mechanism for achieving greater complementarity and horizontal co-ordination of actions at county level'. However the approach of the CEBs is as yet unproven, and one of the prominent shortcomings of the Boards is their lack of a multi-dimensional approach, their targets being mainly small enterprise and employment creation. Further, the ability of the CEBs to either attract or retain small businesses in the more peripheral rural areas has yet to be fully evaluated.

The Emergence of Rural Governance in Ireland 193

The County Development Boards (CDBs)

The CDBs were established in each of the twenty-nine County Councils and five County Borough Corporations to operate from 1 January 1999. The CDBs have been founded to pursue a horizontally integrated services delivery across separate groups and specialist agencies which deal with such matters as local development, industrial development, planning, social services and agriculture which would usually report vertically to their parent department. Membership of the County Development Board is made up of the following four groups; local government, local development bodies, state agencies and the social partners.

Table 6.1 County/City Development Board

Sector	Members	Number
Local Government	SPC Chairs Cathaoirleach/Mayor County/City Manager Urban Representative	Typically 7
Local Development	Two representatives for each of the following three types of local development bodies: County/City Enterprise Board LEADER II Group(s) ADM-supported Partnership Companies and ADM-supported Community Groups	6
State Agencies	As appropriate Health Board FÁS Teagasc VEC Enterprise Ireland IDA Regional Tourism Organisations D/CSFA regional officer SFADCo/Údarás	Typically 7
Social Partners	Employees and Business Organisations (one member) Trade Unions (one member) Agriculture and Farming Organisations (one member) Community and Voluntary Organisations (two members)	5
TOTAL		Typically 25

(Department of the Environment and Local Government, 1999)

In addition, there will also be work groups or committees linked to the CDBs which will deal with certain aspects of the CDBs work such as the Irish language, or traffic/rural transport. There will also be consultation through new community and voluntary organisation fora and County Council area committees. It is planned that the CDBs will work on the partnership principle with the Regional Assemblies. The primary function of the CDBs is to prepare and oversee the implementation of a new County/City Strategy for Economic, Social and Cultural development which, when finished, will provide a 'shared vision' for the development of an area for up to ten years (Department of Environment and Local Government, 1999). Within this plan the CBD will:

- Work towards and formulate an agreed county/city strategy for economic, social and cultural development;

- Develop a vision at local level to encompass the various local and sectoral plans;

- Provide the focus for co-operation on a continuing basis at county/city level in the work of the various agencies, promote co-ordination and avoid overlap at this level; and

- Seek to maximise the effectiveness of spending on programmes and projects at local level (Department of Finance, 1999, p.197).

The Western Development Commission

Yet another structure pertaining to regional governance is provided in the Western Development Commission. The Irish Government in 1997 formed the Western Development Commission (WDC) with the aim of developing the social and economic potential of the west region, comprising Counties Galway, Donegal, Sligo, Leitrim, Mayo, Roscommon, and Clare. Funded by central government the WDC had its origins in the DTWT initiative of the early 1990s (as described in Chapter 5). On 14 May 1996 the then government approved the establishment of the Western Development Commission and Western Investment Fund. On 1 February 1999, it was established as a statutory agency under the Development Commission Act 1998 (WDC, 1999a). The WDC is made up of twelve board members appointed at the discretion of the Minister of Agriculture, Food and Rural Development for a three-year period. The WDC has the following functions:

- Collaborate with the existing statutory and community-based agencies operating in the Region;

- Develop a strategy for achieving economic and social development and to set out priorities to be pursued;

- Promote and manage the WIF;

- Work closely with business and representative business organisations to create the necessary conditions for private investment;

The Emergence of Rural Governance in Ireland   195

- Encourage local, community and indigenous enterprise and job creation; and

- Work with government departments and their agencies to co-ordinate and refocus as necessary their expenditure plans, priorities and programmes in support of the Commission's central function (Department of Agriculture, Food and Rural Development, 2000).

The WIF is a £25million exchequer supported investment controlled by the WDC. It is not a grant-aided system and funding is provided through equity participation and loans. Investments range between £20,000 and £250,000 in 'commercially sound business/community projects with good growth potential' (WDC, 1999b). A total of £5million is to be made available each year over the next five years for investment in information technology, manufacturing and services and tourism and approval is being sought from the EU in the marine and agriculture and food sectors. A more detailed account of the emergence of this newly formed regional tier of governance and its limited ambitions as a regional actor is provided in Chapter 5.

The Gaeltacht and Údarás na Gaeltachta

> (T)he Gaeltacht weighs heavily on the conscience of the Irish. Their attitude toward it is much like that of a young couple in a city apartment who know they should be doing something for the old folks withering away on the broken down family farm, but who are too busy to do much more than send off a little money now and then (Connery, 1968, p.64).

No discussion on the devolving of power and the growth of regionalist structures could be complete without some mention of the Gaeltacht and particularly Údarás na Gaeltachta. The Gaeltacht region poses important questions in terms of cultural identity and language, but more significantly in terms of governance, decentralisation of policy making and the role of local communities in the development process. This section can only superficially deal with this complex issue. Nevertheless, the exploration of yet another tier of administration in Ireland adds to the overall complex mosaic of rural development and the constraints within which different actors and levels of governance operate.

The Gaeltacht region (Figure 6.3) is defined as those places in which the Irish language is still (at least in theory) the main spoken language. Located along the western seaboard, the Gaeltacht consists of parts of counties Galway (in Connemara), Northwest Mayo (and Achill island) and the west coast of Donegal (there are also some smaller pockets in counties Kerry and Cork in the south, and in Meath in the midlands). The total extent of the area is estimated at approximately 350,000 hectares and has a population c.85,000. In these areas, despite their somewhat

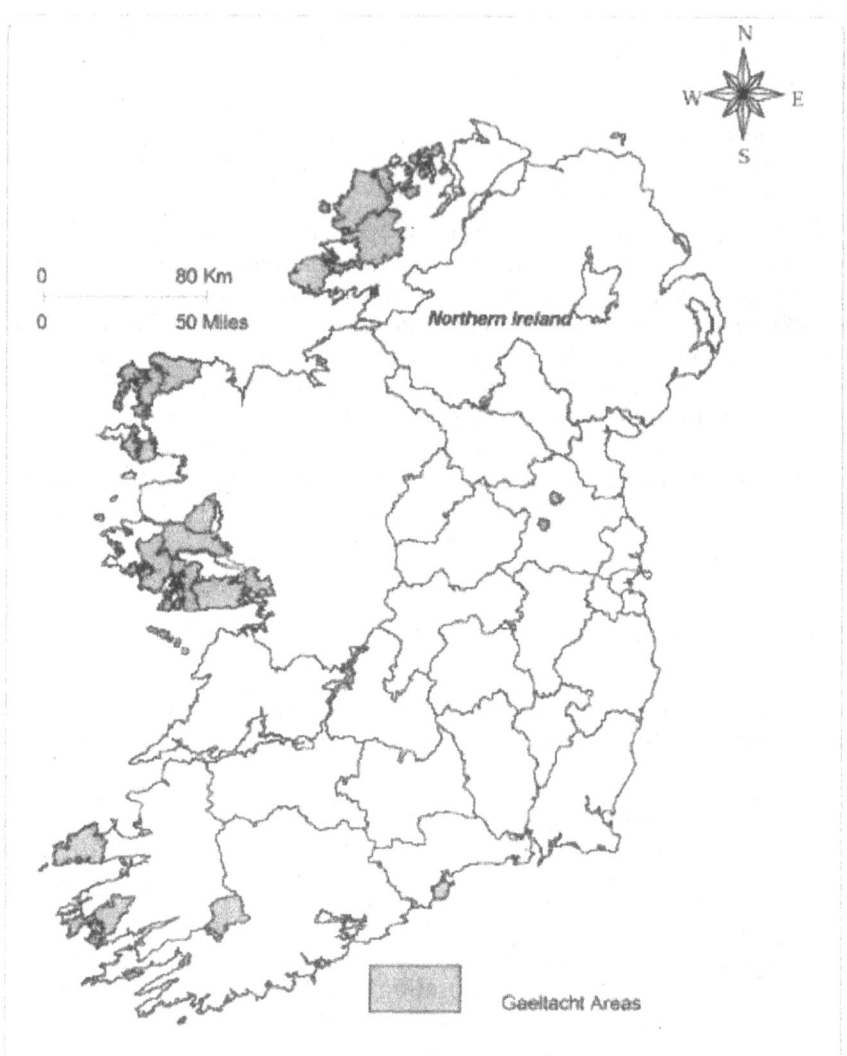

Figure 6.3 The Gaeltacht regions in Ireland

misleading boundaries (many areas classed as part of the Gaeltacht are not Irish-speaking and vice versa), the Irish language has survived various potent anglicising influences. Its use as a community language however, continues to decline, with the result that the genuinely Irish speaking communities may now be less than 10,000 in total (Hindley, 1990).

The growing attention given to the Irish language is significant not only to Irish culture and history, but also as an economic asset: 'if the language goes, then the region will lose more than its heritage, it will also lose an important economic asset' (Flanagan, 1994, p.108). For a number of years there have been continued efforts through special state-sponsored development initiatives to preserve the Gaeltacht. This is spearheaded by Údarás na Gaeltachta, eessentially a regional government agency, that is dedicated to the preservation of the Irish language in Gaeltacht areas. There are twenty members on the Board of Údarás na Gaeltachta, three of which are appointed by the Minister for Arts, Heritage, Gaeltacht and the Islands (O'Brien and Hijmans, 1999). Their task is to 'develop the economy of the Gaeltacht so as to facilitate the preservation and the extension of the Irish language as the principle language of the Gaeltacht community' (Údarás na Gaeltachta, 1998, p.4). Údarás seek to achieve this through:

- Promoting schemes of employment through the development of local natural resources, skills and entrepreneurial abilities;
- Promoting schemes of employment through attraction of mobile investment to the Gaeltacht; and
- Promoting community development and pursuing a range of language and cultural activities involving community groups and industries (Údarás na Gaeltachta, 1998, p.5).

Údarás na Gaeltachta carries out these particular functions with funding from several different areas including Oireachtas Grants (amounting to over 60% of total income), receipts from EU funds (amounting to approximately 13% of total income), rents from leased property, income from FÁS, and other income such as fees earned (Údarás na Gaeltachta, 1998). Of the several factors which constrain the development of the Gaeltacht, the most notable are: poor quality infrastructure; the weak industrial structure; remote geographical locations; high cost of transportation; a poorly developed research and development base; and an entrepreneurial climate not conducive to economic innovation (see Ó Cinnéide, 1992c).

It is through this need for 'development' in areas of declining agriculture and growing unemployment levels, that Údarás na Gaeltachta seem to have been placed in a catch-22 situation by those who determined the parameters of its powers and functions. O'hAolain (1983) argued that the 'promotion of a vigorous industrial development programme and the concomitant responsibility for the conservation and strengthening of the Irish speaking community in the Gaeltacht can only be achieved by an agency or institution which is as financially and organisationally equipped for the latter task as it is for the former ... Údarás is completely unequipped to tackle the very problem which accounts for its own existence - the decline of the language, or, as [it] has [been] described the shrinking language minority' (p.7). Successive governments have asserted the importance of development in the Gaeltacht areas but the provision of financial incentives to attract foreign investment has led to an industrial base which is mainly 'branch-plant', providing low skilled, low income factory floor jobs. Many of the Údarás policies have been successful, but the main criticism is that for the size of their annual budget, estimated at £20million (50% of which is from the state), the amount of employment created by the agency is relatively unspectacular (Ní Fhlatharta, 1996). This privileged position often proves a bone of contention for other agencies in the region, who feel aggrieved by the special status afforded to the Gaeltacht for linguistic reasons. In the present day, the range of incentives (tax breaks, grants, training schemes) available to the Údarás to attract foreign investment has been curtailed, but where those incentives are available they are by far the most significant factor in attracting foreign firms to the region (Ó Cinnéide and Keane, 1988).

Top-down or bottom-up: Where does the Gaeltacht go from here?

Despite the high profile of Údarás na Gaeltachta, the economy of the region is still not on a very sound footing. Recent reports have shown how the region has progressed from consisting of demoralised communities suffering from emigration, unemployment, and a large dependence on central government support and initiatives, to being an area where jobs have been created which compare with the national norm, where population decline had been stabilised, and where the standards of living and education have increased. The current question is, where can Údarás na Gaeltachta take the region from here? Many commentators (Flynn, 1983; O'hAolain, 1983; Ó Cinnéide and Keane, 1990; Ó Cinnéide, 1992a; Ó Cinnéide, 1992b; Ó Cinnéide, 1992c) suggest that the answer lies in concentrated community development and a change in the structures of governance. It is difficult to see the Gaeltacht reaching any stage of self-sustaining development, without a revival of initiative amongst the local population. The core 'mission' of the Údarás has always been to ensure the survival and strengthening of the Irish language; were it to fail in this, any other achievement would be regarded as a failure. With this in mind, the importance of integrating the local communities into the development processes becomes fundamental to any future policy implementation in the region. The Gaeltacht can be essentially seen as a microcosm of the larger problems facing rural Ireland (that is, those of legitimacy, accountability and governability). The lesson of the Gaeltacht experience is that getting the economy of a region right may not be the panacea for the ills of that region. A people-centred integrated approach seems the more attractive way forward. If the Gaeltacht experience signifies anything, then it must be that the notion of development centred purely on the economy, from a top-down perspective, is not the most efficient nor even successful approach. Thus the convincing argument is for a bottom-up, and people-focused approach, integrated with a top-down policy-driven programme.

Concluding remarks

Ó Cinnéide and Keane (1990, p.475) suggest that it is 'imperative that rural residents be centrally involved in the planning of their areas'. In order for this to occur, a strategic planning process is required which facilitates the participation of rural residents and key actors in developing plans for their own areas. This type of strategic plan was also proposed by Bryson and Einsweiler (1987) and contrasts with the former top-down approaches in that it is action-oriented; more broadly participative; more emphatic about the need to pay attention to the communities' and areas' strengths and weaknesses, as well as opportunities and threats (cited in Ó Cinnéide and Keane, 1990). With such a strategic approach, Kearney *et al.*, (1994) outlined a number of factors that would further influence the effectiveness of local participation, including:

- realistic expectations and an adequate division of responsibility between state and local community;
- local development plans taking into account the entire resource potential of an area, being multi-dimensional, co-ordinated and integrated throughout;
- information being easily accessible to local groups and individuals in order to help identify attainable goals and objectives;
- a strong emphasis placed on innovation rather than imitation; and
- the developing of networks between communities, and access to funding for local development initiatives.

Local development, therefore, not only involves 'key actors' but a complex process involving social, economic and geographical considerations. From the arguments raised here it would appear that in order for local development to be successful it must be based on the concepts of partnership, participation, animation and capacity building. While this may be logical in theory, putting into practice these concepts proves much more problematic.

This problematic become clear when exploring the developmental process. While those involved in rural development issues in Ireland talk and expound on the virtues of capacity building, local animation, providing training supports for local development and encouraging local entrepreneurs, the more tangible products of 'providing capital grants for specified investments, important that this undoubtedly is, have greater visibility and political appeal than creating human and social capital' (Commins and Keane, 1994, p.237). The concept of rural industrialisation, seen by many as the traditional lynchpin of regional/rural development policy in Ireland, would seem to have mistakenly concluded that the provision and dispersion of jobs in the remoter rural regions had successfully 'developed' these regions. Wilkinson (1992, p.29) suggested that there was a 'tendency for profit-seeking firms to move into and out of rural areas, taking with them the benefits of development but leaving behind many of the externalities to be endured by the rural community'. Further, it is perhaps Wilkinson (ibid., p.33) who best indicated where the future for rural communities lies, in his suggestion that '(t)he idea is to assist local development efforts by taking human needs and human capacities as the building blocks of a planned rural development programme. 'Human capital' implies that people are means, not ends of development. Putting people first means not only paying attention to their endowments and giving priority to the development of human capital, but actually putting people up front, in the driver's seat, in control of the process of development. It is a philosophy of empowerment through capacity building, of investing in people and not just in bricks and mortar'. In the limited scope available to this book, this brief investigation of the Pilot Area Programme for Integrated Rural Development; LEADER; Area-based Partnerships; CEBs; CDBs; Údarás na Gaeltachta, and the Western Development Commission, is by no means exhaustive, either in detail or coverage.[7] What these excerpts have highlighted is a move toward a new form of governance and a changing relationship between state and society. Further, it is also clear that there is a greater responsibility being shifted toward community and citizen. While this is welcome in the broader democratic process, it also raises questions of institutional and democratic legitimacy and what Stoker (1998) terms the 'blurring of responsibilities'. The lack of a multi-dimensional approach has been alluded to, and, despite the problematic of legitimacy, there is nevertheless an emergence within Ireland of a form of governance where the local has an impact on the national and where the community has a role to play in its future development and direction.

The government's recognition and commitment to 'encouraging, supporting and empowering active rural communities to plan and contribute to the development of their own areas' (Department of Agriculture & Food, 1999, p.49) are still debatable in view of the limited supports available. That the emphasis on local development and the partnership approach is questionable stems from the EU's promotion of local development through such initiatives as LEADER and the need to develop new structures to administer rural development programmes, rather than any great desire by the Irish government to devolve power from its centralist base. It can be recognised that regional actors in Ireland seem to lack the resources and organisational capacity to look at the EU stage as a 'new space of engagement' (Boyle, 2000) and the resulting tiers of administration (the two 'super' regions) conceded by the Irish

The Emergence of Rural Governance in Ireland 201

government are not only without any recognisable identity, but merely reflect the development 'spectacle' and the subsidy-shopping engaged in by the government. These 'super' regions are little more than 'a 'named' economic space which makes sense only in terms of the rules of the game established by Europe' (Boyle, 2000, p.765). The lack of recognition of the 'new space of engagement' afforded by the EU stage, highlights the historical weakness of the regional actors in Ireland (see Chapter 5) the dominance of a centralist mentality and the minimal enhancement of the existing base of regional governance.

Notes

1 An example of this is in the creation of the National Roads Authority (NRA) which is taking over much of the responsibility from local authorities in planning and designing the country's roads.
2 That is, arrangements in relation to staff, acceptance of tenders, making contracts, fixing rents, making lettings and deciding on applications for planning permission.
3 That is, adoption of annual estimate of expenses, fixing of annual rate to be levied to meet these, amount to be borrowed, making of development plans and by-laws, house building programmes and assisting other bodies in providing services and amenities.
4 For example, Teagasc (the national institute for agricultural research and training); Fobáirt (national agency for supporting indigenous industry); Coillte (national agency for developing forestry).
5 About 20% of the projects were social and cultural in character and while some built on existing activities, others did break new ground.
6 The thirty-five CEBs are: Cavan, Clare, Carlow, Cork City, Cork North, South Cork, West Cork, Donegal, Dublin City, Fingal County, South Dublin County, Dun Laoghaire/Rathdown, Galway, Kerry, Kildare, Kilkenny, Laois, Leitrim, Limerick City, Limerick County, Longford, Louth, Mayo, Meath, Monaghan, Offaly, Roscommon, Sligo, Tipperary North Riding, Tipperary South Riding, Waterford City, Waterford County, Westmeath, Wexford and Wicklow.
7 Other areas that could have been explored in this section include Shannon Development; the Community Development Programme; Forum; the Global Grant for Local Development - see Commins and Keane (1994) for a more detailed account of some of these programmes.

7 Recasting the Rural in Ireland

Rural areas clearly have a 'geography'. Some expand and prosper while others decline through depopulation, unemployment and emigration. This 'geography' of rural change has moved the arena of rural development firmly into the political, social, economic and cultural domains of regional, national and EU policies. This study has explored discourses of rural change through the transition from top-down rural development strategies to the more locally designed and integrated frameworks more recently being promoted. While there is no clear strategy or direction for rural development in Ireland (bar responding to EU directives), it is increasingly apparent that there are changes taking place in how society is governed and these changes, with their spatial variations, require considerable analysis and debate. In rural Ireland the current debate is moving toward an exploration of the changing relationship between state and citizen represented by the emergence of (and demand for) new forms of rural governance and the recognition of the role of local actors in rural development discourse.

There are also a number of contestations arising in rural areas, Irish and otherwise, that centre on the dichotomies of 'consumption versus production; development versus preservation; deregulation versus reregulation; global versus local processes; the service classes versus the 'locals' and the farm lobby versus environmentalists' (Ilbery, 1998, p.258). Hence, the issue of rural development has generated considerable literature. Despite this volume of writing however, the understanding of development in general and rural development in particular, remains a mire of varying interpretations. Development is shown to be many different things to different people, rendering the establishment of development goals a very problematic issue (Storey, 1995). What is clear, is that development often means creating 'new' attitudes, and that the changing of 'old' attitudes is a slow process (Andersson, 1992). Rural areas are dynamic, they have become arenas for conflict and tension, sites for consumption as well as production activities. However not all rural areas have the same capacities or undergo change at the same time or pace. Consequently, different development trajectories (Ilbery, 1998) create increasingly uneven development and large-scale differentiation across rural space.

The main problem with rural development policy in the EU, and consequently in Ireland, is that none exists. While rural development is described in terms of its crucial importance, there is no common policy; each member state devises and implements its own often rather complicated and *ad hoc* version. A wide range of policies have been pursued by countries to achieve 'rural development' objectives, including; agricultural policies, leadership and training, technical support, environmental policies, health and education programmes, infrastructure grants, subsidised credit and direct investments. Rural development can not therefore be classed as short term, or inexpensive, in its demands. Further, as this critique of rural development has shown, there is a need for a 'fuller understanding of the distribution of power and of the operation of allocative mechanisms which impact on rural areas' (Cloke, 1986, p.245). The call for discourses on rural development to be routed through lay discourses, so that policies can be influenced by non-experts (see Halfacree, 1993), is therefore becoming more widespread. Consequently interpretations and critiques of rural development are moving away from the theoretically undifferentiated approach to what is 'rural' to one that explores its differences across rural space.

The key to an ample understanding of rural areas is avoidance of easy assumptions of homogeneity. Rural areas must be seen to have multiple meanings and not characterised in this way. The assumptions and philosophies which have influenced rural development strategies (see Chapters 3 and 4), have shown how rurality can be constructed and deployed in a variety of contexts (see also Murdoch and Pratt, 1993). It is paramount, therefore, to avoid the mistake of 'trying to adapt unique situations and problems to universal norms, irrespective of how simple and direct these norms may be' (Keane, 1992, p.193). A supply of training along sectoral lines, such as agriculture and forestry or town and country planning, is no longer sufficient. The integrative nature of rural development needs to be acknowledged, particularly in terms of education and training provision. The conflict that has emerged between the desire to preserve the 'traditional' Ireland in the face of the increasing pressures of modernisation has led to new insights and new roles being created and played out in rural areas. The broad strategies that have been pursued, both the centrally controlled sectoral approach (top-down) and the locally designed community approach (bottom-up), have begun to move towards an intermediate model - a shift from government to governance. The validity of this intermediate model and the capacity of rural areas to respond to the new development discourses involved are still debatable. The foregoing analysis shows that while progress has been made, effective local development with co-ordinated efforts from the voluntary and state sectors is not prominent.

Despite the modernising influences which have contributed to the changing of rural Ireland, ranging from the decline in importance of agriculture, the increase in the non-farming population, to the ensuing demolition of the idea that rural events have rural causes (Cloke, 1985),

Ireland still remains in the grip of the traditionalists. New entrepreneurial opportunities are being promoted in rural areas with the growth of tourism and recreation. New trends in new product specialisation and farm diversification have also given rise to a more commercially viable style of farming, and rural lands, including forestry, are being viewed more in terms of recreation and amenity purposes. The perseverance with pilot projects and short-term development plans, while being informative in a developmental sense, can not however 'represent an equitable or optimum response to the needs and aspirations of rural society' (Murray and Dunn, 1995, p.96). The argument is that rural development should not be viewed through project or sector specific mediums, nor as a continuum (Asby and Midmore, 1993) from the base of developing the human capacity through to the sustainable creation of enterprise. Instead, there is a need for an alternative circular model for development which provides the scope for maximum participation and capitalisation of human capacity; this positive move would, in turn, enhance enterprise creation, further contributing to human capacity development. The success of such a model rests on the existence of meaningful participative democracy. Consequently, little progress will be made in Ireland in this respect without change to the current system of centralisation. If the government is to support such development initiatives, then it must do so from a holistic and decentralised approach, and not as has been the case, along centralised sectoral lines.

The lack of a sufficiently democratic local government (Shortall, 1994) has led to a questioning of the Irish government's commitment to rural development. The search for new forms of governance, relevant to the lives of rural dwellers and the circumstances of rural areas, calls for the transition from a centrally controlled development strategy, to a locally designed, co-ordinated and integrated framework. The participatory development process, and the democratic ideals promoted in Irish rural development discourse to date, are not lived up to in practice. Thus, rural development in Ireland must undergo a significant reorientation. Fundamental to this reorientation is to make local communities the focus of rural development policies by creating the opportunities for meaningful participation so that communities can identify their own problems and priorities, and thus develop their own strategies for development. Against a tradition of paternalism and cultural conservatism, the real challenge is to put such a system in place. New forms of rural governance and organisation are therefore required 'to break out of the entrenched patterns of patronage and exclusion and focus collective efforts on problems common to all groups' (Wilkinson, 1992, p.34). The strategies employed to date, based on sectoral measures, have only partially been successful; policies need to be targeted at different types of rural areas (Ilbery, 1998). The potential for rural development in any given region must be based on an assessment of the opportunities and weaknesses of that region. To this end there is a notable lack of co-ordination of policies, training and education of local communities, which might enable them to participate. A new approach, characterised by a 'territorial approach to development; emphasis on the mobilisation of indigenous human and natural resources; high degrees of local participation in all stages of the development process; sectoral integration and co-operative action' (Ó Cinnéide, 1992b, p.11) is necessary. This approach, while receiving much lip service, has received very little funding, in comparison to the project-oriented top-down strategies.

Development discourse, despite enormous continuity over time, changes its language, strategies and practices. While it provides an important conceptual framework for evaluating rural change, in Ireland development discourse has been shown to be too often associated with words such as 'under' or 'over' or 'balanced'. The use of this type of terminology 'suggests that development has a structure and that the speaker has some idea about how this structure ought to be developed' (Welch, 1984, p.2). The significant divide between stated policies of rural development agencies, and what actually happens on the ground has been illustrated in this work. This gulf between theory and practice contributes to the growing debate on integrated rural development and the nature of community involvement within this context. Local development strategies are increasingly being viewed as a radical response aimed at combating exclusion, with the development process 'focusing on concepts such as multi-dimensionality, integration, co-ordination, subsidiarity and sustainability' (Walsh, 1996, p.159). Locally based development initiatives are depicted as having the potential to make a significant and positive contribution to the economic and social well being of their communities. In order for such initiatives to be successful however, more needs to be understood about the process of local development, and the kinds of education and training required. The terms, partnership, participation and integration, used widely in rural development rhetoric, are bandied about superficially without adequate attention being given to their underlying meanings and connotations. Partnership arrangements between community, state and private sector will only make an impact if the constraints of centralised control are lifted. The trend for local development plans to be fund-driven or rushed to meet some programme submission deadline, needs to be addressed, as do the 'quick-fix' or tangible outcomes which are being dispensed. While much has been made of the alleged change from a project-oriented, sector-specific approach, to one of developing the human capacity and the collective initiative, in terms of action, little has been done.

Rural agencies also have to change. Previous approaches to rural development in Ireland have not been successful because of insufficient co-ordination, a lack of local participation, and a lack of regional specificity (Ó Cinnéide, 1992b). There must be a dispelling of the notion that financial intervention and infrastructural provision will overcome the problems of rural areas, and defuse growing devolutionist pressures (Buller and Wright, 1990). What is required is a move away from macro-planning initiatives to development based on a small-scale, community-oriented approach. While Walsh (1996) outlines the undoubted importance of animation, facilitation and capacity building to such an approach, the recognition of facilitation as critical to assisting 'project promoters in the preparation of their proposals so that they have a good chance of being approved' (ibid., p.163), does raise a further issue. Clearly such local development should not be about finding the best way to satisfy certain criteria laid down by the professionals. As such, despite the integrated ethos which the Irish government promotes, the reality is somewhat different. Its administering of LEADER and the OPRD, through the Department of Agriculture, Food and Forestry, and INTERREG, through the Department of Finance for example, with sub-programmes handled by differing authorities, seems anything but integrated (Shortall, 1994). The absence of any single institution with sole responsibility for rural development leads to an uncoordinated and fragmented approach. The capacity of locally-based development agencies needs 'considerable upgrading in order to meet the challenges posed by an area-based approach to development' (Ó Cinnéide, 1992b, p.5). Creating a proper framework for rural development should be regarded as part of the process of development, and not just a means to an end. The Irish system does not recognise this vital component, calling isolated or disjointed projects or programmes "development" ("spectacle"), without acknowledging the benefits of a proper framework to long-term sustainable rural life. Consequently, contemporary governance in Ireland tends to deal with rural development through a multiplicity of government departments, with often conflicting development aspirations. The need for institutional development to be part of the development process itself (Stern, 1992) is therefore crucial.

The role of community-based rural development is set to increase in the future. Keane (1992, p.197) has suggested that rural communities are trying to force change and respond to their lack of development by 'addressing their situations, questioning their options in a relatively systematic manner, and taking various forms of action'. It is also important however, to understand that local communities can not be expected to assume responsibility for developing their own local economies without adequate training, authority and resources. Care needs to be taken in assessing how much local communities can achieve, and safeguards introduced against increasing community responsibility without the corresponding resources. Further, community involvement in rural development can not be categorised as a broad homogenous grouping. Instead, greater links must be fashioned between rural and urban areas economically, socially and politically and mediated through changing

Recasting the Rural in Ireland 207

constructs of history, culture and tradition. Community sector involvement is therefore but one means to an end, and can not be 'regarded as the most appropriate policy vehicle for tackling the problems of rural areas' (McLaughlin, 1987, p.364 original emphasis).

The role of community and voluntary organisations however restricted, is an important domain in rural development. In order for it to be of even limited success, there must be a loosening of top-down structural control and a greater exchange of information and dialogue between the community sector and state. In this respect, the gulf between those with ready access to policy makers and those without is creating a new type of deprivation in rural development discourse. Marginalised groups of this kind are not deprived in economic terms but suffer from a 'governance deprivation' which denies them the kind of local structures so vital to local communities, voluntary groups and community development initiatives (like DTWT).

Community participation is increasingly acclaimed as the most important ingredient in future rural development. This, however, can also be more spectacle than reality. There is no straightforward relationship between state and community and often, there can be confusion about the development goals desired. Kearns (1974) recognised this when speaking of the Gaeltacht areas; he suggested that no efforts to resuscitate these communities, regardless of how well motivated or financially supported, could be successful unless they were paralleled by a revival of the human spirit (cited in Ó Cinnéide, 1993a). The findings in the study of DTWT (Chapter 5) also clearly demonstrate the need to formulate and implement development policies to match local needs with a prerequisite for greater co-ordination between the various actors, and the development of the local capacity. To this end, the move towards developing the human capacity to instigate, lead, and control development (Ó Cinnéide, 1996), and the need to dispel feelings of powerlessness and hopelessness, through programmes of social animation is recommended (Melo, 1992). The so-called populist organisation, DTWT was also shown to be a microcosm of the larger political situation. This group ended up being centrally run with the community-government partnership serving as merely a spectacle for legitimising government policies and proposals. The participative ideals promoted were given little practical effect, and while it was easy to espouse the principle of participative development, the reality was somewhat different. The ability of the local communities to deal with the 'top-down', without losing their ability to represent the grassroots was shown to be particularly problematic and highlighted the significant issues of institutional and democratic legitimacy and also that of accountability.

Nevertheless, DTWT did highlight a need for radical structural changes, on a local and national scale. These included: alterations in organisational frameworks; changes in the mind-set of those people who create and administer policies in rural areas; and changes in those who are affected by these policies. The major implication that this raises for rural development in Ireland, is that while there may currently be difficulty in achieving any degree of devolution of powers to the regional and local scales, it may become easier as the rest of Europe devolves. Despite increasing centralisation of functions (Greer, 1984; Carey, 1995a; McAllister, 1995), devolution of responsibility to the regions is becoming a key element for future European development. The recent changes to the regional status of Ireland, with the introduction of two regions in order to retain Objective 1 status (in at least part of the country) will provide a significant test for the Irish government and their steadfast reluctance to devolve power from the centre. Hence community-led development and partnerships are assuming a considerably raised profile. Increased dissatisfaction, and a growing tendency towards self-reliance, has forced the bottom-up approach to development to become an accepted and necessary ingredient for development in the majority of rural communities (Ó Cinnéide, 1986; O'Cearbhaill, 1992a&b; Murray and Dunn, 1995). Consequently, the move towards new forms of governance, greater decentralisation and regionalisation seems inevitable.

On a larger scale, the significance of the 'region' in the future of the European political economy and the concept of a 'Europe of the regions' is also gaining currency. The emergence of the region as a powerful political and economic actor has brought with it a 'new space of engagement'. A movement away from the traditional regional conceptualisation of a sub-national administrative unit, to one of a more innovative capacity, is increasingly promoted. The common place of the 'global village', and the increased integration of politics and economics within Europe, demands a change in centralised administrations. Shifts in power structures within regions, and increasingly, from national governments to the EU, widen the gap between the ordinary citizen and the policy maker. There is a pressing need for subsidiarity where 'decisions [can] be taken, and policies formulated and implemented at the lowest possible level [which] will become ... a fundamental element in the political health of the country' (Hume, 1997, p.5). The case of DTWT highlighted this slow, but recognisable shift in the power structures of rural Ireland. In its efforts to organise from below, and to resist and challenge the government, the DTWT almost found an ally in a place where the voluntary sector in Ireland had not looked before – Europe. Voluntary and community groups are now realising that there is a need to form alliances at a European rather than at a national level. Such a shift in focus to the institutions of the European Community, is most unlikely to be reversed (Mazey and Richardson, 1993), and as such, local development organisations are now more in need of familiarity with the power structures in place at Brussels and Strasbourg, than with those in Dublin. This move toward greater regionalisation must however have a co-ordinated strategy, backed up by a programme of capacity building within local communities. For the successful animation of local communities, there is a need to provide not only the requisite hardware (communications, infrastructure, and housing), but also the software (skills, knowledge, and attitudes). The argument for a programme of social animation (Ó Cinnéide 1993b) consequently gains force. However, there continues to be a tendency by the Irish government to overlook the inherent potential of regions. The attitude of the Irish state to the role of the regions, particularly in national economic policy, is largely one of indifference. While Ireland has made effective use of its EU resources, some areas have benefited more than others. There is therefore a need to recognise not just one Ireland, nor even two, but many Irelands (see Chapter 1) which have similar problems, similar hopes, but need different strategies for development. With this in mind, the foremost need is to establish regional institutions with a clear mandate for development. The continued march towards a 'Europe of the regions' indicates that this will happen sooner rather than later. Significantly, only as recently as 1997, there has been a move by the UK towards regionalisation in its consideration of the Scottish and Welsh devolution proposals (albeit national rather than regional devolution). Britain's shift from its tradition of centralisation will enter it into the 'European mainstream where it is taken for granted that strong regional institutions are necessary' (Hume, 1997, p.1). A similar path for Ireland would seem to be not far behind. The emergence of new forms of rural governance, while slow, indicates a move toward a more radical and challenging concept of integrated planning and partnership that will determine the future of rural areas in Ireland.

With such changes taking place in rural Europe it is not surprising that there is renewed interest in rural development despite its fragmented, pragmatic, and individualistic make-up. Rural issues are now among the major concerns of policy makers, and, despite the absence of a common rural development policy, there is a slow shift in the thinking, structures and programmes designed to combat problems in Ireland's rural areas. There is a movement away from agricultural modernisation and rural industrialisation, to an emphasis on rural diversification and alternative work practices. Bottom-up approaches are now receiving increased attention, with local initiatives being fostered, and encouraged, in association with top-down approaches. Rural lifestyles and rural communities are been seen not in terms of a cost-benefit tabulation, or in terms of economic viability, although this is not to dismiss economic development entirely, but more so in terms of the social and cultural character of the community which may be both vital, and viable (Matthews, 1977). With this shift in emphasis, rural lifestyles are faced with significant debates that will determine its future. At the heart of these debates are such questions as:

- What do people want from rural areas?

- What do people want to do with rural areas?
- Can everybody have the same access to services?
- Do we expect trade-offs between rural and urban living?
- Are problems in rural areas essentially those of rural areas?
- Can problems in rural areas be dealt with exclusively through some specifically regional or rural-oriented planning?

These questions (amongst others) are being posed in a moment of significant economic change, and against rapidly changing physical and social environments. To further our understanding of this change a number of interesting areas for further research can be identified from this work. These include:

- the area of people participation in rural development;
- the role of the established institutions in rural Ireland;
- the extent to which community participation can become part of the rural development process;
- the forms of bargaining and mediation which are dominant in rural policy arenas (see Cloke, 1986);
- the area of policy makers and community proposals, and the complex and contradictory interactions between the state and local community. An analysis of such relationships is required, to help determine the degree of consensus or conflict that arises between the policy makers, and the people they seek to serve.

Finally, within this book, the logic of allowing people to have greater control over their lives, with increased participation and partnership between citizen and state, has been easily argued. Clearly, the call for integrated multisectoral approaches with an eye to future sustainability is warranted. The challenge however lies in the ability and willingness of Irish government and citizens to sign up to these ideals and create the egalitarian institutions and levels of governance that would make these ideals a more attainable reality. Finally, it is hoped that this book has brought to the forefront the current challenges facing rural development and highlighted the need for a broad understanding of the complex and multidimensional nature of rural development, by policy makers and community alike.

Bibliography

ADM (1997), *Partnerships: Making a difference in people's lives*, Area Development Management Ltd, Dublin.
Advisory Committee to the Western Bishops Conference on Development (1991), Meeting Minutes, 15 March, 1991, Unpublished.
Agazzi, E. (1988), 'Philosophical Anthropology and the Objectives of Development', in UNESCO, *Goals of Development*, UNESCO, pp. 13–30.
Amdam, J. (1996), Planning for Rural and Local Development in Ireland and Norway. Paper presented at the Conference of Irish Geographers, UCG Ireland 10–12 May, 1996.
An Foras Taluntáis (1963), *West Cork Resource Survey*, An Foras Taluntáis, Dublin.
Andersson, L. (1992), 'Relations between functional organisations and local territorial life, some key words for local development in the nineties', in M. Ó Cinnéide and M. Cuddy (eds.), *Perspectives on Rural development in Advanced Economies*, SSRC, University College Galway, pp. 173–184.
Anon (1994a), 'Half-hearted commitment to stemming West decline', *Connacht Tribune*, 19 August.
Anon (1994b), 'Plea for bottom-up approach by Council', *Connacht Tribune*, 28 October.
Anon (1995a), 'Holiday home owners are top planning objectors', *Connacht Tribune*, 17 February.
Anon (1995b), 'Galway Focuses on the Emigrant Experience', *Galway Advertiser*, 18 May.
Arensberg, C. and Kimball, S.T. (1940), *Family and Community in Ireland*, (2nd revised edition, 1968), Harvard University Press, Cambridge.
Asby, J. and Midmore, P. (1993), *Human Capacity Building and Planning: Old Ideas with a Future for Marginal Regions*, Aberystwyth Rural Economy Research Papers, No. 93–03, Wales.

Babbie, E.R. (1979), *The Practice of Social Research* (2nd edition), Wadsworth, Belmont, California.
Barbier, E. (1989), *Economics, Natural Resource Scarcity and Development*, Earthscan Publications, London.
Barrington, T.J. (1980), *The Irish Administrative System*, Institute of Public Administration, Dublin.
Bell, C. and Newby, H. (1971), *Community Studies*, Allen and Unwin, London.
Best, J. (1983), 'What is Rural Development?', *RRDC Bulletin*, University of Reading.
Best, S. (1989), 'The Commodification of Reality and the Reality of Commodification: Jean Baudrillard and Post-Modernism', *Current Perspectives in Social Theory*, Vol.9, JAI Press, pp. 23–51.
Bohan, H. (1994), Can the West be Saved! Paper presented at the Merriman

Summer School, 20 August, Ballyvaughan, Co. Clare.
Bowler, I., Bryant, C. and Nellis, M.D. (eds.), (1992), 'Contemporary Rural Systems in Transition', *Economy and Society*, Vol. 2, C.A.B, International.
Boylan, T.A. (1992), 'Paradigms in Rural development: From Critique to Coherence?', in M. Ó Cinnéide and M. Cuddy (eds.), *Perspectives on Rural Development in Advanced Economies*, SSRC, University College Galway, pp. 13-23.
Boyle, M. (2000), 'Euro-regionalism and struggles over scales of governance: the politics of Ireland's regionalisation approach to Structural Fund allocations 2000-2006', *Political Geography*, Vol. 19, pp. 737-769.
Bradley, T. and Lowe, P. (eds.), (1984), *Locality and Rurality*, Geobooks, Norwich.
Brady, B. and NíChuinn, U. (1995), Irish Rural Link Newsletter, October, Issue No.8.
Breathnach, P. (1984), 'Community Participation in Rural development: Examples from the Scottish and Irish peripheries', in M. Blacksell and I. Bowler (eds.), *Contemporary Issues in Rural Planning*, South West Papers in Geography, Occasional Series No.6, pp. 105-122.
Breathnach, P. (1986), 'State and Community in Rural Ireland', in P. Breathnach and M. Cawley (eds.), *Change and Development in Rural Ireland*, Geographical Society of Ireland, Special Publications No.1, pp. 77-81.
Breathnach, P. (1995), 'Uneven Development and Irish Peripheralisation', in P. Shirlow (ed.), *Development Ireland*, Pluto Press, London, pp. 15-26.
Breathnach, P. (2000), The National Development Plan: Institutional and Governance Structures for Regional Development. Paper presented at the seminar on the National Development Plan 2000-2006: Spatial and Social Implications for the West of Ireland, Clarenbridge, Galway, Ireland, 16 June, 2000.
Breathnach, P. and Cawley, M. (eds.), (1986), *Change and Development in Rural Ireland*, Geographical Society of Ireland, Special Publications, No .1.
Breen, R., Hannan, D.F., Rottman, D.B., and Whelan, C.T. (1990), *Understanding Contemporary Ireland*, Macmillan, London.
Brody, H. (1973), *Inishkillane: Change and Decline in the West of Ireland*, Penguin Press, London.
Brookfield, H. (1975), *Interdependent Development*, University of Pittsburgh Press, Pittsburgh, PA, Meuthuen, London.
Brown, T. (1985), *Ireland: A Social and Cultural History, 1922 to the Present*, Cornell University Press, Ithaca and London.
Brunt, B. (1988), *The Republic of Ireland*, Paul Chapman Publishing.
Brunt, B. (1993), 'Ireland as a Peripheral Region in Europe: Structural Funds and Regional Economic Development', in R. King (ed.), *Ireland, Europe and the Single Market*, Geographical Society of Ireland, Special Publications No.8, pp. 30-43.
Bruton, H. (1985), 'The Search for a Development Economics', *World Development*, Vol.10.
Bruton, J. (1996), Address given at the launch of 'The Challenge: A Positive Future through Action', 16 May, Athenry, Co. Galway.
Bryant, C. (1992), 'Community Development and Changing Rural Employment in Canada', in I. Bowler, C. Bryant and M. Nellis (eds.), *Contemporary Rural*

Bibliography 213

Systems in Transition, Economy and Society, Vol.2, C.A.B, International, pp.265-278.
Bull, C., Daniel, P. and Hopkinson, M. (1984), *The Geography of Rural Resources*, Oliver & Boyd.
Buller, H and Wright, S. (eds.) (1990), Rural Development: Problems and Practices, Avebury, England and USA.
Buller, H. and Wright, S. (1990), 'Introduction: Concepts and Policies of Rural Development', in H. Buller and S. Wright (eds.), *Rural Development: Problems and Practices,* Avebury, England and USA, pp. 1-23.
Bunce, M. (1994), *The Countryside Ideal,* Routledge, London and New York.
Burkey, S. (1993), *People First*, Zed Books Ltd, London and New Jersey.
Bury, J.B. (1955), *The Idea of Progress*, Dover Publications, New York.

Caffrey, D (2000), *White Paper on Rural Development: Statements.* Seanád Debates Official Reports, 9 March.
Cara (1995), Cara Magazine, Vol.28, No.4, July/August 1995, Aer Lingus Publication.
Carey, D. (1995a), Address given by the Minister of State Dónal Carey at a seminar on Rural Renewal at the European Communities Economic and Social Committee Conference on the Citizens Europe, 4 May, University College Galway.
Carey, D. (1995b), Address given by the Minister of State Dónal Carey at a seminar on 'Rural Renewal: An Integrated Approach to the Provision of Public Services', 24 May, Roscommon.
Carey, D. (1995c), Address given by the Minister of State Dónal Carey at the final seminar on 'Rural Renewal: An Integrated Approach to the Provision of Public Services', Ennis, 25 May, Clare.
Carter, R.W.G. and Parker, A.J. (1989), 'Introduction', in R. Carter and A.J. Parker (eds.), *Ireland: A Contemporary Geographical Perspective*, Routledge, London and New York, pp. 1-8.
Casey, E. (1992), Proposal to the Commission of the European Community to undertake a major study of the West of Ireland, Developing the West Together, April 1992, Unpublished.
Cassidy, J. (1994a), 'A Pinch of Incense: The Importance of Developing The West', Speech delivered at the launch of 'A Crusade For Survival' Sligo, February 1994.
Cassidy, J. (1994b), 'Elbows At The Ready', Speech delivered at the launch of the Council for The West, Sligo, October, 1994.
Causer, G. and Jones, C. (1993), 'Responding to 'skill shortages': recruitment and retention in high technology labour markets', *Human Resource Management Journal*, Vol.3, No.3, pp. 1-20.
Cawley, M. (1999), 'Poverty and Accessibility to Services in the Rural west of Ireland', in D.G. Pringle, J. Walsh and M. Hennessy (eds.), *Poor People, Poor Places*, Oak Tree Press, Dublin, pp. 141-156.
Chubb, B. (1992), *The Government and Politics of Ireland* (3rd edition), Longman, London and New York.
CIE Tours (1995), Ireland: CIE Tours International, Holiday Brochure, CIE Tours.
Cloke, P. (1985), 'Whither Rural Studies?' *Journal of Rural Studies*, Vol.1, No.1, pp. 1-9.

Cloke, P. (1986), 'Implementation, Intergovernmental Relations and Rural Studies: A Review', *Journal of Rural Studies*, Vol.2, No.3, pp. 245-253.
Cloke, P. (1987a), 'Rurality and Change: Some Cautionary Notes', *Journal of Rural Studies*, Vol.3, No.1, pp. 71-76.
Cloke, P. (1987b), 'Concept, Theory and Rural Geography: A Special Issue', *Journal of Rural Studies*, Vol.3, No.4, pp. 295-296.
Cloke, P. (1989a), 'Rural Geography and Political Economy', in R. Peet and N. Thrift (eds.), *New Models in Geography*, (Vol. 1), Unwin Hyman, London, pp. 164-197.
Cloke, P. (1989b), 'Land-Use Planning in Rural Britain', in P. Cloke (ed.), *Rural Land-Use Planning in Developed Nations*, Unwin Hyman, London, pp. 18-46.
Cloke, P. (1993), 'The Countryside as Commodity: New Spaces for Leisure', in S. Glyptis (ed.), *Leisure and the Environment*, Belhaven Press, London and New York, pp. 53-70.
Cloke, P. (1995), '(En)culturing Political Economy: A life in the day of a 'rural' geographer', in P. Cloke, M. Doel, D. Matless, M. Phillips and N. Thrift, *Writing the Rural: Five Cultural Geographies*, PCP, London, pp. 149-190.
Cloke, P. (ed.) (1987), *Rural Planning: Policy into Action?* Harper & Row, London.
Cloke, P. (ed.) (1989), *Rural Land-Use Planning in Developed Nations*, Unwin Hyman, London.
Cloke, P. and Goodwin, M. (1992), 'The Changing Function and Position of Rural Areas in Europe', in P. Huigen, L. Paul and K. Volkers (eds.), *The Changing Function and Position of Rural Areas in Europe*, Utreacht, pp. 19-33.
Cloke, P. and Goodwin M. (1993), Rural Change: Structured Coherence or Unstructured Incoherence? *Terra*, Vol. 105, No. 3, pp. 166-174.
Cloke, P. and Milbourne, P. (1992), 'Deprivation and Lifestyles in Rural Wales II, Rurality and the Cultural Dimension', *Journal of Rural Studies*, Vol.8, No.4, pp. 359-371.
Cloke, P. and Park, C. (1985), *Rural Resource Management*, Croom Helm, London.
Clout, H. (1972), *Rural Geography: An Introductory Survey*, Pergamon Press, Oxford.
Clout, H. (1984), *A Rural Policy for the EEC?* Methuen, London and New York.
Clout, H. (ed.), (1987), *Regional Development in Western Europe*, David Fulton Publishers, London.
Clout, H. (1993), *European Experience of Rural Development*, Topic Paper 5, Rural Development Commission.
Cole, J. and Cole, F. (1993), *The Geography of the European Community*, Routledge, London and New York.
Collins, T. (1992), 'Participation and Marginalised groups', in B. Reynolds and S. Healy (eds.), *Power, Participation and Exclusion*, Justice Commission, Dublin, pp. 100-120.
Commins, P. (1983), Community-Based Co-operatives and Rural Development in the West of Ireland. Paper presented at the Regional Studies Association Conference on, 'Changing Problems and Regional Responses in Rural Development', 23-24 May, Powys, Wales.

Bibliography 215

Commins, P. and Keane, M. (1994), *Developing the Rural Economy: Problems, Programmes and Prospects*, NESC Report No. 97, NESC, Dublin.

Commins, P. and O'Hara, P. (1991), 'Starts and Stops in Rural development: An Overview of Problems and Policies', in B. Reynolds and S. Healy (eds.), *Rural Development Policy: What Future for Rural Ireland?* Justice Commission, Dublin.

Community Workers Co-operative (1992), *Structural Funds: The Challenge to Address Social Exclusion*, Community Workers Co-Operative, Dublin.

Connaughton, P. (2000), Rural Development White Paper, Dáil debates Official Report, 13 February.

Connery, D.S. (1968), *The Irish*, Simon & Schuster, New York.

Connolly, N. (1995), A Study on the Role of the Catholic Church in Rural Community Development. Unpublished Masters in Rural Development Dissertation, University College Galway.

Conway, A. (1991), 'Developing the Rural economy', in B. Reynolds and S. Healy (eds.), *Rural Development Policy: What Future for Rural Ireland?* Justice Commission, Dublin, pp. 68–82.

Coogan, T.P. (1975), *The Irish: A Personal View*, Phaidon, London.

Coogan, T.P. (1987), *Disillusioned Decades – Ireland 1966–1987*, Gill and Macmillan, Dublin.

Cook, I. and Crang, M. (1995), *Doing Ethnographies, Concepts and Techniques in Modern Geography*, Norwich.

Copp, J.H. (1972), 'Rural Sociology and Rural Development', *Rural Sociology*, Vol. 37, pp. 515–533.

Coughlan, D. (2000), 'National Plan could Jolt Cosy Relationships' *The Irish Times*, 2 May, 2000.

Council for the West (1994), Launch of the Council for the West, Press Release, 22 October.

County Enterprise Boards (no date), Information Leaflet.

Coward, J. (1989), 'Irish Population Problems, in R. Carter and A. Parker, (eds.), *Ireland, A Contemporary Geographical Perspective*, Routledge, London and New York, pp. 55–86.

Coyle, C. (1996), 'Local and regional Administrative Structures', in C. Curtin, T. Haase, and H. Tovey, (eds.), *Poverty in Rural Ireland*, Oaktree Press, Dublin, pp. 276–305.

Craig, S. (1995), *Making Partnership Work*, Combat Poverty Agency, Dublin.

Cresta (1995), Ireland. Holiday Brochure, Cresta.

Crotty, R. (1993), 'A system that cannot deliver', in C. Keane (ed.), *The Jobs Crisis*, The Thomas Davis Lecture Series, Mercier Press, Cork and Dublin, pp. 64–74.

Crouch, D. (1994), 'Home, Escape and Identity: Rural Cultures and Sustainable Tourism', *The Journal of Sustainable Tourism*, Vol. 2, Nos. 1&2, (Special Issue on Rural Tourism and Sustainable Rural Development), pp. 93–101.

Crush, J. (1995), 'Introduction: Imagining Development', in J. Crush (ed.), *Power of Development*, Routledge, London, pp. 1–27.

Cuddy, M. (1991), 'Rural Development in Ireland: An Appraisal', in T. Varley, T. Boylan and M. Cuddy (eds.), *Rural Crisis: Perspectives on Irish Rural Development*, SSRC, University College Galway, pp. 28–47.

Cuddy, M. (1992), 'Rural Development: The Broader Context' in M. Ó Cinnéide and M. Cuddy (eds.), *Planning and Development of Marginal Areas*, SSRC, University College Galway, pp. 65–77.

Cuddy, M., and Ó Cinnéide, M. (1990), 'Critical Issues in Rural Development', in M. Cuddy, M. Ó Cinnéide and M. Owens (eds.), *Revitalising the Rural Economy*, Centre for Development Studies, University College Galway, pp. 12–21.

Curtin, C. and Varley, T. (1991), 'Populism and Petit Capitalism in Rural Ireland', in S. Whatmore, P. Lane and T. Marsden (eds.), *Rural Enterprise*, Fulton Press, London, pp. 97–119.

Danson, M.W. (2000), 'Debates and Surveys: The Sustainability of Industrial Development in Ireland', *Regional Studies*, Vol. 34, No. 3, pp. 277–290.

Davern, N. (2000), White Paper on Rural Development: Statements, Seanád Debates Official Report, 9 March 2000.

Debord, G. (1983), *Society of the Spectacle*, Red and Black, Detroit.

DeBuitléir, D. (1992), 'Institutional Reform: A Participation perspective', in B. Reynolds and S. Healy (eds.), *Power, Participation and Exclusion*, Justice Commission, Dublin, pp. 34–59.

Delors, J. (1990), Rural Development and the Common Agricultural Policy. Paper presented at the European Conference on Rural Society, Brussels.

Department of Agriculture & Food (1999), *Ensuring the Future – A Strategy for Rural Development in Ireland*. Stationary Office, Dublin.

Department of Agriculture, Food and Rural Development (2000), Western Development Commission, www.irlgov.ie, accessed 23 May, 2000.

Department of Education (1998), *Adult Education in an Era of Learning – A Green Paper*, Government Publications, Stationary Office, Dublin.

Department of Enterprise, Trade and Employment (1998), Ireland – Employment Action Plan, Government Publications, Stationary Office, Dublin.

Department of Finance (1958), *The Programme for Economic Expansion*, Government Publications, Stationary Office, Dublin.

Department of Finance (1993), *National Development Plan 1994–1999*, Government Publications, Stationary Office, Dublin.

Department of Finance (1999), *The National Development Plan 2000–2006*, Government Publications, Stationary Office, Dublin.

Department of the Environment (1996), *Better Local Government: A Programme for Change*, Government Publications, Stationary Office, Dublin.

Department of the Environment (1997), *Sustainable Development – A Strategy for Ireland*, Government Publications, Stationary Office, Dublin.

Department of the Environment and Local Government (1999), Preparing the Ground: Guidelines for the progress from Strategy Groups to County/City Development Boards, Task Force on the Integration of Local Government and Local Development Systems, Dublin.

Department of the Environment and Local Government (2000), The National Spatial Strategy: Some Key Questions and Answers. www.irlgov.ie, accessed 2 June, 2000.

Department of the Environment and Local Government (2000), The National Spatial Strategy: What are the Issues? www.irlgov.ie accessed 8 February, 2000.

Department of the Environment and Local Government (2000), The National Spatial Strategy: Scope and Delivery. www.irlgov.ie, accessed 8 February, 2000.

Bibliography 217

Derounian, J. (1993), *Another Country*, NcVo Publications.
Developing the West Together (1992), Tender Information Brief, Unpublished.
Developing the West Together (No Date), Circular, Unpublished.
Dewey, R. (1960), 'The Rural-Urban Continuum: Real but Relatively Unimportant', *American Journal of Sociology*, Vol. 66, (1960–66), pp. 60–66.
Dillon, B. (1989), 'Community Participation – Avoiding the pitfalls and maximising the benefits', in Community Workers Co-Operative, *Whose Plan? Community Groups and the National Development Plan*, Community Workers Co-Operative, Dublin, pp. 40–43.
Donovan, K. (1996), 'You can't go home again', *The Irish Times*, 24 April.
Dooney, S. and O'Toole, J. (1998), *Irish Government Today*, 2nd Edition, Gill & Macmillan Ltd, Dublin.
Dorr, D. (1983), *Option For The Poor, Catholic Social Teaching*, Gill and Macmillan, Dublin.
Duffy, P. (1994), 'Conflicts in Heritage and Tourism', in U. Kockel (ed.), *Culture, Tourism and Development: The Case of Ireland*, Liverpool University Press, pp. 77–86.

Edwards, B. (1998), 'Charting the discourse of community action: perspectives from practice in rural Wales', *Journal of Rural Studies*, Vol. 14, No. 1, pp. 63–78.
Eipper, C. (1986), *The Ruling Trinity*, Gower, England.
Escobar, A. (1995), 'Imagining a post development era', in J. Crush (ed.), *Power of Development*, Routledge, London, pp. 211–227.
Euradvice (1992), Study of the West of Ireland: Technical Proposal and Financial Tender, Unpublished.
Euradvice (1994), *A Crusade for Survival*, Developing The West Together, Galway.
European Commission (1988), *The Future of Rural Society*, COM(88), 501, Brussels.
European Commission (1993a), *Regional Development Programmes 1992*, Office for Official Publications of the European Communities, Luxembourg.
European Commission (1993b), *The ERDF in 1991*, Office for Official Publications of the European Communities, Luxembourg.
European Commission (1994), *Competitiveness and Cohesion: Trends in the Regions*, Office for Official publications of the European Community, Luxembourg.
European Commission (1995), *Teaching and Learning: Towards the Learning Society*, White Paper on Education and Training, Office for Official publications of the European Community, Luxembourg.
European Commission (1995), *The implementation of the reform of the Structural Funds in 1993*, Office for Official publications of the European Community, Luxembourg.
European Commission (2000), Commission Notice to the Member sates Laying Down Guidelines for the Community Initiative for Rural Development (LEADAR+), C(2000), 946, www.europa.eu.int.

Falk, W. and Pinhey, T. (1978), 'Making Sense of the Concept Rural and Doing Rural Sociology: An Interpretive Perspective', *Rural Sociology*, 43, pp. 574–

588.
Fallon, J. (1995), 'One stop shop bid to end the services loss to rural areas', *Connacht Tribune*, 9 June.
Farrington, J., Bebbington, A., Wellard, K. and Lewis, D.J. (1993), *Reluctant Partners? Non-Governmental Organisations, the State and Sustainable Agricultural Development*, Routledge, London and New York.
Faughnan, P. and Kelleher, P. (1992), 'Participation by the Voluntary Sector – A study of Voluntary and Community Organisations', in B. Reynolds and S. Healy (eds.), *Power, Participation and Exclusion*, Justice Commission, Dublin, pp. 60–99.
Fay, R. (1989), 'Campaigning Issues', in Community Workers Co-operative, *Whose Plan? Community Groups and the National Development Plan*, Community Workers Co-operative, Dublin, pp. 47–51.
Fineman, S. (1994), 'Organizing and emotion: towards a social construction', in J. Hassard and M. Parker (eds.), *Towards a New Theory of Organizations*, Routledge, London, pp. 75–86.
Finnegan, R.B. (1983), *Ireland-The Challenge of Conflict and Change*, Westview Press, Colorado.
Finnegan, T. (1994), 'Developing The West Together', in N. Collins (ed.), *Unemployment North & South: The Major Social Ill*, Publisher unknown, pp. 129–140.
Finnegan, T. (1995), Developing The West Together. Paper presented to the National Planning Conference, Killarney.
Fitzgerald, G. (1993), 'Growth and Jobs: The Politics of Public Ambivalence', in C. Keane (ed.), *The Jobs Crisis*, Mercier Press, Dublin and Cork, pp. 38–51.
Flanagan, S. (1994), 'Tourism and the Regional Economy: The Gaeltacht Experience', in P. Breathnach (ed.), *Irish Tourism Development*, Geographical Society of Ireland, Special Publication, No. 9, pp. 103–123.
Flynn, F. (1983), 'Gaeltacht Development: A View', in P. Breathnach (ed.), *Rural Development in the West of Ireland*, Occasional Paper No. 3, St. Patricks College, Maynooth, pp. 23–36.
Forfás (1996), *Shaping our Future: A Strategy for Enterprise in Ireland in the Twenty-First Century*, Forfás, Dublin.
Frazer, H. (1994), The Role of Community Development in Local Development. Paper presented at the conference on 'New Relationships in the Nineties: The Role of Community Development', October 1994, Kilkenny.

Galbraith, J.K. (1993), 'The Larger World Economy', in C. Keane, (ed.), The Jobs Crisis, The Thomas Davis Lecture Series, Mercier Press, Cork and Dublin, pp. 168–176.
Gibbon, P. (1973), 'Arensberg and Kimball Revisited', *Economy & Society*, pp. 479–498.
Gilg, A. (1985), *An Introduction to Rural Geography*, Edward Arnold, London.
Gillmor, D. (1986), 'Rural Industrialisation', in P. Breathnach and M. Cawley (eds.), *Change and Development in Rural Ireland*, Geographical Society of Ireland, Special Publications No.1, Dublin, pp. 25–33.
Girvin, B. (1993), 'Social Change and Political Culture in The Republic of Ireland', *Parliamentary Affairs: A Journal of Comparative Politics*, Vol. 46,

No. 3, pp. 380-98.
Goodwin, M. (1998), 'The governance of rural areas: some emerging research issues and agendas', *Journal of Rural Studies*, Vol. 14, No. 1, pp. 5-13.
Goulet, D. (1971), *The Cruel Choice*, Atheneum, New York.
Government Task Force (1994), Report on a 'Crusade for Survival', Stationery Office, Dublin.
Gray, J. (2000), 'The Common Agricultural Policy and the Re-Invention of the Rural in the European Community', *Sociologia Ruralis*, Vol. 40, No. 1, pp. 30-52.
Greer, J. and Murray, M. (1993), 'Rural Ireland – Personality and Policy Context', in M. Murray and J. Greer (eds.), *Rural development in Ireland*, Avebury, England and USA, pp. 3-20.
Greer, J. V. (1984), 'Integrated Rural Development: Reflections on a Magic Phrase', *Pleanail*, Vol. 1, pp. 10-15.
Greer, R. (1971), *Countryside Planning: The Future of the Rural Regions*, Manchester University Press.
Grimes, S. (1992a), 'Information and communication Technologies: the Prospects for Rural Areas', in M. Ó Cinnéide and M. Cuddy, (eds.), *Perspectives on Rural Development in Advanced Economics*, SSRC, University College Galway, pp. 123-135.
Grimes, S. (1992b), 'Fostering Indigenous Entrepreneurship in the European Periphery', in M. Ó Cinnéide and S. Grimes (eds.), *Planning and Development of Marginal Areas*, SSRC, University College Galway, pp. 59-70.

Halfacree, K.H. (1993), 'Locality and Social Representation: Space, Discourse and Alternative Definitions of the Rural', *Journal of Rural Studies*, Vol. 9, No. 1, pp. 23-27.
Harkin, M. (1998), 'Decline of the West', *The Irish Times*, 20 January.
Harriss, J. (1982), 'Introduction', in J. Harriss (ed.), *Rural Development*, Hutchinson & Co. (Pub.), Ltd, pp. 1-16.
Haughton, J. (1998), 'The Dynamics of Economic Change', in W. Crotty and D.E. Schmitt (eds.), *Ireland and the Politics of Change*, Addison, Wesley Longman Ltd., Harlow, pp. 27-50.
Hayes, T. (2000), White Paper on Rural Development: Statements, Seanád Debates Official Report, www.irlgov.ie, accessed 13 September, 2000.
Hazelkorn, E. (1986), 'Class, Clientelism and the Political Process in the Republic of Ireland' in P. Clancy, S. Drudy, S. Lynch and L. O'Dowd (eds.), *Ireland: A Sociological Profile*, Institute of Public Administration in association with The Sociological Association of Ireland.
Healy, J. (1968), *No One Shouted Stop!* (formerly *The Death of an Irish Town*), The House of Healy, Achill, Ireland.
Healy, S.J. and Reynolds, B. (1991), 'Towards an Integrated Vision of Rural Ireland', in B. Reynolds and S. Healy (eds.), *Rural Development Policy: What Future for Rural Ireland*, Justice Commission, Dublin, pp. 41-67.
Healy, S.J. and Reynolds, B. (1992), 'Participation: A Values Perspective', in B. Reynolds and S.J. Healy (eds.), *Power, Participation and Exclusion*, Justice Commission, Dublin, pp. 9-33.
Heelas, P. and Morris, P. (1992), 'Enterprise culture: its values and value' in P. Heelas and P. Morris (eds.), *The Value of the Enterprise Culture: The Moral*

Debate, Routledge, London, pp. 1–15.
Hettne, B. (1990), *Development Theory and the Three Worlds*, Longman, London.
Hewison, R. (1987), *The Heritage Industry*, Methuen, London.
Higgins, J. (1986), 'The Distribution of Income on Irish Farms', *Irish Journal of Agricultural Economics and Rural Sociology II*, pp. 73–91.
Higgins, J. (1995a), The future of the West: The Need to Change Our Thinking. Paper presented on the occasion of the Connacht Exhibition, 9 September, Foxford, Co. Mayo.
Higgins, J. (1995b), Address given at the Fine Gael Trade Union Conference Euro Seminar on 'Islands of Poverty: Breaking the Circle', 14 October, Galway.
Higgins, M.D. (1982), 'The Limits of Clientelism: Towards an Assessment of Irish Politics' in C. Clapham (ed.), *Private Patronage and Public Power: Political Clientelism in the Modern State*, Francis Printers, London, pp. 114–141.
Hindley, R. (1990), *The Death of the Irish Language: A Qualified Obituary*, Routledge, London.
Hogan, J. (1994), Opening Address given at the Council for The West, Press Conference, Sligo, 22 October.
Hoggart, K. (1990), 'Let's do Away with Rural', *Journal of Rural Studies*, Vol. 6, No. 3, pp. 245–257.
Hoggart, K. and Buller, H. (1987), *Rural Development: A Geographical Perspective*, Croom Helm, London.
Hoggart, K., Buller, H. and Black, R. (1995), *Rural Europe*, Arnold, Great Britain.
Hume, J. (1991), Address given at the Developing the West Together seminar sponsored by the Catholic Western Bishops' Conference, 4–5 November, Galway.
Hume, J. (1993), Keynote Address delivered at the Conference on Local Economic Development in Ireland, Business Innovation Centre, March, Galway.
Hume, J. (1997), Address given at the Council for the West Conference, 24 May, Westport.
Hussey, G. (1993), *Ireland Today*, Townhouse Viking, Dublin.

IBEC (1998), *National Survey of Labour and Skills Needs in the Services Sector*, Irish Business and Employers Confederation, Dublin.
IDA Ireland (2000), 'Pharmaceuticals', IDA web Page, www.idaireland.com, accessed 6 July, 2000.
Ilbery, B. (1998), 'Conclusion', in B. Ilbery (ed), *The Geography of Rural Change*, Longman, Essex, UK, pp. 257–261.
Imrie, R. and Raco, M. (1999), 'How new is the new local governance? Lessons from the United Kingdom', *Transactions of the Institute of British Geographers*, Vol. 24, No. 1, pp. 45–63.
Ingham, B. 'The Meaning of Development: Interactions Between 'New' and 'Old' Ideas', *World Development*, Vol. 21, No. 11, pp. 1803–1821.
Inglis, T. (1987), *The Monopoly of the Church in Modern Irish Society*, Gill and MacMillan, Dublin.
Ireland Today (1999), 'Success or failure', *Ireland Today*, 22 March.
Irish LEADER Network (no date), *Rural Communities in Action*, James O'Keefe Institute, Cork.

Johnson, J.H. (1987), 'Republic of Ireland' in H. Clout (ed.), *Regional*

Bibliography 221

Development in Western Europe (Third Edition), David Fulton, London, pp. 285–305.
Johnson, J.H. (1994), *The Human Geography of Ireland*, John Wiley & Sons, England.
Jones, G. (1973), *Rural Life*, Longman Group, London.
Jouen, M. (1999), LEADER's Contributions: An Overview of National Differences, LEADER European Observatory, www.europa.eu.int.
Kavanagh, P.J. (1996), 'A land brimful of riches', *Irish Post*, Vol. 27 No. 22, 1 June.
Keane, M. (1990), 'Economic Development Capacity Amongst Small Rural Communities', *Journal of Rural Studies*, Vol. 6, No. 3, pp. 291–301.
Keane, M. (1992), 'New directions in the Formulation and Implementation of Rural Development Policy', in M. Ó Cinnéide and M. Cuddy (eds.), *Perspectives on Rural Development in Advanced Economies*, SSRC, University College Galway, pp. 185–198.
Keane, M. (1996), Rural Development: The Theory-Practice Interface. Paper presented at the Conference on 'Rural Development: Striking the Proper Balance', 29–30 March, Kilfinane, Co.Limerick.
Keane, M., Griffith, B. and Dunn, J.W. (1993), 'Regional Development and Language Maintenance', *Environment and Planning A*, Vol. 25, pp. 399–408.
Kearney, B. and Associates (2000), Operational Programme for LEADER II Community Initiative: Ex-Post Evaluation, Interim Report, www.leaderii.ie.
Kearney, B., Boyle, G.E. and Walsh, J.A. (1994), *EU LEADER I Initiative in Ireland:Evaluations and Recommendations*, Department of Agriculture, Food and Forestry, Dublin.
Keeble, D., Tyler, P., Brown, G. and Lewis, J. (1992), *Business Success in the Countryside: The Performance of Rural Enterprise*, HMSO, London.
Kelleher, C. and O'Mahony, A. (1984), *Marginalisation in Irish Agriculture*, An Foras Talúntais.
Kennedy, K.A., Giblin, T. and McHugh, D. (1988), *The Economic Development of Ireland in the 20th Century*, Routledge, London.
Kennedy, R. (1973), 'The Irish: Emigration, Marriage and Fertility', in R. Carter and A.J. Parker (eds.), *Ireland: A Contemporary Geographical Perspective*, Routledge, London and New York.
Kennedy, S. (1981), *Who Should Care?* Turoe Press.
Keogh, D. (1988), 'Catholicism and the Formation of the Modern Irish Society', in The Princess Grace Irish Library (eds.), *Irishness in a Changing Society*, Colin Smythe, Gerrards Cross, pp. 152–177.
Kiberd, D. (1990), 'Autumn of the Patriarch', *The Irish Times*.
Kirby, P. (1988), *Has Ireland a Future?* Mercier Press, Dublin and Cork.

Lea, D. and Chaudhri, D. (1983), 'The Nature, Problems and Approaches to Rural Development' in D. Lea and D. Chaudhri (eds.), *Rural Development and the State*, Methuen, London, pp. 1–32.
LEADER Atlas of Rural Development (2000), Ireland/Eire, www.rural-europe.aeidl.be/rural-en/, accessed 19 July, 2000.
Lee, J.J. (1989), *Ireland 1912–1985*, Cambridge University Press.
Lee, R. (1994), 'Definition' in R.J. Johnston, D. Gregory and D. Smith (eds.),

The Dictionary of Human Geography, Blackwell, Oxford, MA, p.128.
Lincoln, C. (1993), 'City of Culture: Dublin and the Discovery of Urban Heritage', in B. O'Connor and M. Cronin (eds.), *Tourism in Ireland: A Critical Analysis*, University Press, Cork, pp. 203–232.
Lloyd, M.G. (1988), 'Rural Economic Development Initiatives', in P.H. Selman (ed.), *Countryside Planning and Practice*, Stirling University Press.
Lorendahl, B. (1996), 'New Cooperatives and Local Development: A Study of Six Cases in Jamtland, Sweden', *Journal of Rural Studies*, Vol. 12, No. 2, pp. 143–150.
Lowe, P., Cox, G., MacEwen, M., O'Riordan, T and Winter, M. (1986), *Countryside Conflicts*, Gower/Maurice Temple Smith.
Lowe, P., Marsden, T. and Munton, R. (1990), *The Social and Economic Restructuring of Rural Britain: A Position Statement*, Economic and Social Research Council.
Lyons, M. (1999), 'Department moves to combat skills shortage', *The Irish Times*, 14 May.

MacConnell, S. (1996), 'Funding of plan for the West defended by Taoiseach', *The Irish Times*, 17 May.
MacDubhghaill, U. (1996), 'Plan to save West calls for defined regional policy and 20-year commitment from state', *The Irish Times*, 16 May.
MacDubhghaill, U. and O'Sullivan, K. (1996), 'Plan to create 15,000 jobs in West agreed by Cabinet', *The Irish Times*, 15 May.
MacSharry, R. (1990), 'Rural Development', in M. Cuddy, M. Ó Cinnéide and M. Owens (eds.), *Revitalising the Rural Economy, How can it be done?* Centre for Development Studies, University College Galway, pp. 28–30.
Marsden, T., Lowe, P. and Whatmore, S. (1990), 'Introduction: Questions of Rurality', in T. Marsden, P. Lowe and S. Whatmore (eds.), *Rural Restructuring: Global Processes and their Responses*, David Fulton Publishers, London, pp. 1–20.
Marsden, T. and Murdoch, J. (1998), 'The shifting nature of rural governance and community participation', *Journal of Rural Studies*, Vol. 14, No. 1, pp. 1–4.
Matthews, A. (1995), 'Agricultural Competitiveness and Rural Development', in J. O'Hagan (ed.), *The Economy of Ireland*, Gill & MacMillan, Dublin, pp. 350–355.
Matthews, R. (1977), 'I'd Sooner Be Here Than Anywhere: Economic viability versus social vitality in Newfoundland, in S. Wallman (ed.), *Perceptions of Development*, Cambridge University Press, pp. 119–135.
Mazey, S. and Richardson, J. (1993), Pressure Groups and the EC, *Politics Review*, Vol.3, No.1, pp. 20–24.
McAllister, L. (1995), Local Community Participation in the design and delivery of services. Paper presented at the seminar on 'Rural Renewal: An Integrated approach to the provision of public services', 24 May, Roscommon.
McCafferty, D. and Walsh, J. (1999), Local partnership in Local Governance: the sub-regional dimension of devolution. Paper presented at the European Congress of the Regional Science Association International, University College Dublin, 23–27 August, 1999.
McConnell, F. (1993), 'The death of an Irish Village', *The Irish Times*, 11 April.

Bibliography 223

McCreevy, C. (1998), Dáil Debates, 10 November.
McDonagh, J. (1997), The (Re)negotiation of Rural Development in the West of Ireland, Unpublished PhD Thesis, Bristol University.
McDonagh, J. (1998), 'Rurality and Development in Ireland – the need for debate?' *Irish Geography*, Vol. 31(1), pp. 47–54.
McDonagh, J. (2000), 'Partnership and Integrated Development in Rural Ireland', *Administration*, Vol. 48, No.1, pp. 69–86.
McDonald, F. (1989), Local Government in Ireland: A Comment', in Community Workers Co-operative, *Whose Plan? Community Groups and the National Development Plan*, Community Workers Co-Operative, Dublin, pp. 35–39.
McDyer, J. (1982), *Fr. McDyer of GlenColmkille, An Autobiography*, Brandon Publishers.
McGreil, M. (1998), *Quo Vadimus, cá bhfuil ár dtriall? Where are we going?* Report on the Pastoral Needs and Resources of the Archdiocese of Tuam, Unpublished.
McGuiness, M. (No Date), 'Impressions of LEADER', in Irish LEADER Network, *Rural Communities in Action*, James O'Keeffe Institute, Cork, p.23.
McInerney, C. (1992a), Developing The West Together, What Local Communities Are Saying. Paper presented to the Annual Conference of the Irish Planning Institute.
McInerney, C. (1992b), 'Discussion Document on the Role of the Church in Development in the West of Ireland', Developing the West Together, Unpublished.
McInerney,C. (1995), 'Poverty in Rural Ireland', *The Irish Reporter*, No.17, pp. 26–27.
McIver Consulting (1995), *Managing Strategic Change: Vision 2010*, Education and Training Study, Forfás, Unpublished.
McLaughlin, B. (1986a), 'Rural policy into the 1980s: The Revival of the Rural idyll', *Journal of Rural Studies*, Vol. 2, No. 2, pp. 81–90.
McLaughlin, B. (1986b), 'The Rhetoric and the Reality of Rural Deprivation', *Journal of Rural Studies*, Vol. 2, No. 4, pp. 291–307.
McLaughlin, B. (1987), 'Rural policy into the 1990s – Self-Help or Self Deception', *Journal of Rural Studies*, Vol. 3, No. 4, pp. 361–364.
Meager, N. (1986), 'Skill Shortages Again and the UK Economy', *Industrial Relations Journal*, Vol. 17, No. 3, pp. 236–248.
Melo, A. (1992), 'Education and Training for Rural development', in M. Ó Cinnéide and M. Cuddy (eds.), *Perspectives on Rural Development*, SSRC, University College Galway, pp. 199–207.
Mernagh, M. and Commins, P. (1997), *In from the Margins*, Research and Development Unit, SICCDA, Dublin.
Millan, B. (1992), Correspondence with Bishop John Kirby, 21 May, unpublished.
Mingay, G.E. (ed.), (1989), *The Rural Idyll*, Routledge, London.
Mormont, M. (1990), 'Who is Rural? Or How to be Rural: Towards a Sociology of the Rural', in T. Marsden, P. Lowe and S. Whatmore (eds.), *Rural restructuring, Global Processes and their Responses*, David Fulton, London, pp. 21–43.
Moynihan, M. (ed.), (1980), *Speeches and Statements by Eamon DeValera 1917–1973*, Gill and Macmillan, Dublin.
Munck, R. and Fagan, M. (1995), 'Development Discourses: Conservative,

Radical and Beyond', in P. Shirlow (ed.), *Development Ireland*, Pluto Press, London, pp. 110–121.
Murdoch, J. and Day, G. (1995), What is a Rural Community? Paper presented at the Conference on the Migration Issues in Rural Areas, March 1995, Swansea.
Murdoch, J. and Pratt, A. (1993), 'Rural studies: Modernism, Postmodernism and the 'Post-Rural'', *Journal of Rural Studies*, Vol. 9, No. 4, pp. 411–428.
Murdoch, J. and Pratt, A. (1994), 'Rural Studies of Power and the Power of Rural Studies: a Reply to Philo', *Journal of Rural Studies*, Vol. 10, No. 1, pp. 83–87.
Murphy, J.A. (1988), 'Religion and Irish Identity', in The Princess Grace Irish Library (eds.), *Irishness in a Changing Society*, Colin Smythe, Gerrards Cross, pp. 132–151.
Murphy, J.A. (1991), *Ireland: Identity and Relationships*, Publisher unknown, pp. 79–89.
Murray, M. and Dunn, L. (1995), 'Capacity Building for Rural Development in the United States', *Journal of Rural Studies*, Vol. 11, No.1, pp. 89–97.
Murray, M. and Greer, J. (1992), 'Rural Development in Northern Ireland: Policy Formulation in a Peripheral Region of the European Community', *Journal of Rural Studies*, Vol. 8, No. 2, pp. 173–184.
Murray, M. and Greer, J. (eds.) (1993) *Rural Development in Ireland*, Avebury, Athenaeum Press, Newcastle upon Tyne.

Nash, C. (1993), 'Embodying the Nation: the West of Ireland, Landscape and Irish Identity', in B. O'Connor and M. Cronin (eds.), *Tourism in Ireland: A Critical Analysis*, Cork University Press, pp. 86–114.
NESC (1982), *Policies for Industrial Development, Report No. 66*, National Economic and Social Council, Dublin.
NESC (1986), *A Strategy for Development 1986–1990, Report No. 83*, National Economic and Social Council, Dublin.
NESC (1991), *The Economic and Social Implications of Emigration, Report No. 90*, National Economic and Social Council, Dublin.
NESC (1993), *A Strategy for Competitiveness, Growth and Employment, Report No. 96*, National Economic and Social Council, Dublin.
NESC (1994), *New Approaches to Rural Development, Report No. 97*, National Economic and Social Council, Dublin.
Ní Fhlatharta, B. (1994), 'Tourism strategy for Gaeltacht is launched following new report', *Connacht Tribune*, 23 December.
Ní Fhlatharta, B. (1995), 'Údarás industry jobs now rising to 2,020 in country', *Connacht Tribune*, 3 February.
Ní Fhlatharta, B. (1996), 'Údarás set new record in 1995 for employment', *Connacht Tribune*, 2 February.
Ní Laoire, C. (1995), The Migration Experience of People and Places in Rural Ireland. Paper presented at the Migration Issues in Rural Areas Conference, March 1995, Swansea.
Nicholls, D.C. (1976), 'Agencies for Rural Development in Scotland', in P. J. Drudy (ed.), *Regional and Rural Development*, Alpha Academic, Great Britain.

O'Brien, T. and Hijmans, A. (1999), 'Fianna Fáil wins in Údarás elections', The

Irish Times, 6 December.
O'Cearbhaill, D. (1982), 'Development through Self-help – The achievements of Killala Community', in J. Sewel and D. O'Cearbhaill (eds.), *Co-operation and Community Development (A Collection of Essays)*, SSRC, University College Galway.
O'Cearbhaill, D. (1992a), 'Creatures of the Centre? The Uneasy Relationship of Central Government with Regional and Local Authorities in Ireland', in M. Tykkylainen (ed.), *Development Issues and Strategies in the New Europe*, Avebury, England, pp. 211–220.
O'Cearbhaill, D. (1992b), 'Ireland's Integrated Rural Development Pilot Project 1988–90: Process, Performance and Prelude', in M. Ó Cinnéide and S. Grimes (eds.), *Planning and Development of Marginal Areas*, SSRC, University College Galway, pp. 123–134.
O'Cearbhaill, D. and Varley, T. (1993), 'Gaeltacht and Galltacht Community Councils in Ireland: A Comparison', in T. Flognfeldt, J.C. Hansen, R. Nordgreen, and J.M. Rohr, (eds.), *Conditions for Development in Marginal Regions*, Oppland College, Norway, pp. 143–154.
Ó Cinnéide, M. (1986), 'Organising Community Involvement in the Development Process', in P. Breathnach and M. Cawley (eds.), *Change and Development in Rural Ireland*, Geographical Society of Ireland, Special Publications, No. 1, pp. 82–89.
Ó Cinnéide, M. (1992a), 'Some spatial dimensions of tourism in Ireland', in M. Ó Cinnéide, and M. Cuddy (eds.), *Planning and Development of Marginal Areas*, SSRC, University College Galway, pp. 37–58.
Ó Cinnéide, M. (1992b), 'Introduction', in M. Ó Cinnéide, and S. Grimes (eds.), *Perspectives on Rural Development in Advanced Economies*, SSRC, University College Galway, pp. 1–12.
Ó Cinnéide, M. (1992c), 'Approaches to the development of peripheral rural areas: Some lessons from the Irish experience', in M. Tykkylainen, (ed.), *Development Issues and Strategies in the New Europe*, Avebury, England, pp. 77–88.
Ó Cinnéide, M. (1992d), 'Restructuring of Rural Areas in Ireland', in P. Huigen, L. Paul, and K. Volkers, (eds.), *The Changing Function and Position of Rural Areas in Europe*, Utrecht. pp. 87–98.
Ó Cinnéide, M. (1993a), 'An Innovative Approach to Local Economic Development in Inishowen, Republic of Ireland', in T. Flognfeldt, J. Hansem, R. Nodgreen and H. Rohr (eds.), *Conditions for Development in Marginal Regions*, Oppland College, Norway, pp. 239–248.
Ó Cinnéide, M. (1993b), 'Ways to Develop the Competitiveness of the Periphery: The example of Ireland', in L. Lundqvist, and L.O. Persson, (eds.), *Visions and Strategies in European Integration*, Springer-Verlag, Berlin, pp. 209–224.
Ó Cinnéide, M. (1995), 'Keynote Address', delivered at a Conference on The West – The Economic Way Forward, Irish Management Institute, 9 June, Galway.
Ó Cinnéide, M. (1996), Rural Development: the Critical Issues. Paper presented at the Conference on Rural Development – Striking the Proper Balance, 29–30 March, Kilfinane, Co. Limerick.
Ó Cinnéide, M. and Cuddy, M. (eds.), (1992), *Perspectives on Rural Development*

in *Advanced Economies*, SSRC, University College Galway.

Ó Cinnéide, M. and Grimes, S. (eds.), (1992), *Planning and Development of Marginal Areas*, SSRC, University College Galway.

Ó Cinnéide, M. and Keane, M. (1988), *Local socio-economic impacts associated with the Galway Gaeltacht*, Research Report No. 3, SSRC, University College Galway.

Ó Cinnéide, M. and Keane, M. (1990), 'Applying Strategic planning to Local Economic Development', *TPR*, Vol. 61, No. 4, pp. 475–486.

O'Connor, B. (1993), 'Myths and Mirrors: Tourist Images and National Identity', in B. O'Connor and M. Cronin (eds.), *Tourism in Ireland: a Critical Analysis*, Cork University Press, pp. 68–85.

O'Connor, B. and Cronin, M. (1993), 'Introduction', in B. O'Connor and M. Cronin (eds.), *Tourism in Ireland: A Critical Analysis*, Cork University Press, pp 1–12.

O'Connor, P.J. (1992), *Living in a Coded Land*, Irish Landscape Series No.1, Oireacht na Mumhan Books.

O'Donohue, K. (1989), 'Towards more effective local development – some proposals and issues', in Community Workers Co-operative, *Whose Plan? Community Groups and the National Development Plan*, Community Workers Co-operative, Dublin, pp. 44–46.

O'Faolain, N. (1993a), 'The West Awakes', *The Irish Times*, 6 April.

O'Faolain, N. (1993b), 'A beef sandwich without the beef', *The Irish Times*, 7 April.

O'Faolain, N. (1993c), 'Partners with their people', *The Irish Times*, 8 April.

O'Gráda, C. (1997), *A Rocky Road: The Irish Economy since the 1920's*, Manchester University Press, Manchester.

O'hAolain, P. (1983), 'Gaeltacht Development: A View', in P. Breathnach (ed.), *Rural Development in the West of Ireland*, Occasional Papers, No.3, Maynooth College, pp. 1–22.

O'Hara, P. (1998), *Partners in Production? Women, Farm and Family in Ireland*, Berghahn Books, New York, Oxford.

O'Hara, P. and Commins, P. (1991), 'Starts and Stops in Rural development: an Overview of Problems and Policies', in B. Reynolds and S. Healy (eds.), *Rural development Policy: What Future for Rural Ireland?* Justice Commission, Dublin, pp. 9–40.

O'Hearn, D. (1998), *Inside the Celtic Tiger: The Irish economy and the Asian model*, Pluto Press, London.

O'Leary, E. (1999), 'Regional Income Estimates for Ireland, 1995', *Regional Studies*, Vol. 33, No. 9, pp. 805–814.

O'Malley, E. (1992), *The Pilot Programme for Integrated Rural Development, 1988–1990*, Broadsheet Series, No. 27, ESRI, Dublin.

O'Morain P. (2000), 'Irish Child Poverty Among Worst in EU', *The Irish Times*, 4 July.

O'Nuanain, S. (1992), 'Marginal areas development in Ireland: a Bottom-up Top-down Framework for Integration', in M. Ó Cinnéide and S. Grimes (eds.), *Planning and Development of Marginal Areas*, SSRC, University College Galway, pp. 81–86.

O'Raghalaigh, F. (1993), 'Ireland: End of the Rainbow for Multinationals', *Sunday Business Post*, 3 October.

O'Riain E. (1997), 'An Offshore Silicon valley? The Emerging Irish Software Industry', *Competitiveness and Change*, Vol. 2, pp. 175–212.
O'Sullivan, J. (1999), 'Employment reaches record 1.5m plus', *The Irish Times*, 14 May.
O'Sullivan, K. (1996), 'West Plan', *Connacht Tribune*, 17 May.
O'Tuathaigh, G. (1993), 'The Regional Dimension', in C. Keane (ed.), *The Jobs Crisis*, Mercier Press, Dublin and Cork, pp. 87–105.
Oakley, P. and Marsden, D. (1984), *Approaches to Participation in Rural Development*, United Nations, International Labour Organisation, Geneva.
OECD (1990), *Partnerships for Rural Development*, OECD Publications, Paris.
OECD (1993), *What Future for Our Countryside?* OECD Publications, Paris.
OECD (1995), *Creating Employment for Rural Development – New Policy Approaches*, OECD Publications, Paris.
OECD (1998), *Education at a Glance: OECD Indicators*, OECD Publications, Paris.
OECD (1999), *OECD Economic Surveys: Ireland*, OECD Publications, Paris.
Osborne, D. and Gaebler, T. (1992), *Reinventing Government – How the entrepreneurial spirit is transforming the public sector*, Addison-Wesley, Reading, MA.

Pacione, M. (1985), *Rural Geography*, Harper and Row, London.
Pahl, R.E. (1966), 'The rural-urban continuum', *Sociologia Ruralis*, No. 6, pp. 299–329.
Peillon, M. (1982), *Contemporary Irish Society*, Gill and Macmillan, Dublin.
Perroux, F. (1983), *A New Concept of Development*, Croom Helm, London.
Phillips, A. and Tubridy, M. (1994), 'New supports for Heritage Tourism in Ireland', *Journal of Sustainable Tourism*, (Special issue on Rural Tourism and Sustainable Rural Development), Vol.2, Nos. 1&2, pp. 112–129.
Philo, C. (1992), 'Neglected Rural Geographies: a Review', *Journal of Rural Studies*, Vol. 8, No. 2, pp. 193–207.
Poostchi, I. (1986), *Rural Development and the Developing Countries*, Alger Press, Canada.
Pratt, A. (1996), 'Discourses of Rurality: Loose Talk or Social Struggle?', *Journal of Rural Studies*, Vol. 12, No.1, pp. 69–78.
Programme for Competitiveness and Work (1994), Government Publications, Dublin.
Pyke, B. (1991), Developing The West Together. Paper presented at the Developing The West Together Seminar, 4 November, Galway.

Rafferty, M. (1992), 'The Colour of the Cat', in *Co-options*, Journal of the Community Workers Co-Operative, pp. 60–69.
Ray, C. (1998), 'Territory, structures and interpretation – two case studies of the European Union's LEADER I Programme', *Journal of Rural Studies*, Vol. 14, No. 1, pp. 79–88.
Redfield, R. (1970), *A Village that Chose Progress: Chan Kom Revisited*, University Press, Chicago.
Regan, C. and Breathnach, P. (1981), *State and Community: Rural Development Strategies in the Slieve League Peninsula, County Donegal*, Occasional Paper Series No. 2, St. Patrick's College Maynooth, County Kildare.

Rhodes, R.A.W. (1996), 'The new governance: governing without government', *Political Studies*, XLIV, pp. 652–667.

Rice, S. (1996), '£200 million fund for west aims to create 15,000 jobs', *Connacht Tribune*, 24 May.

Robinson, G. M. (1990), *Conflict and Change in the Countryside*, Belhaven Press, London.

Rodriguez, E. R. (1990), 'Main Policies and Strategies for the Development of Objective (1), Regions in Spain', in M. Cuddy, M. Ó Cinnéide and M. Owens (eds.), *Revitalising the Rural Economy, How can it be done?*, Centre for Development Studies, University College Galway, pp. 60–63.

Rogers, A. (1987), 'Voluntarism, Self-Help and Rural Community Development: Some Current Approaches', *Journal of Rural Studies*, Vol. 3, No. 4, pp. 353–360.

Rolston, B. (1992), 'Image without substance: the rhetoric of State/Voluntary partnership in the North of Ireland', in *Co-options*, Journal of the Community Workers Co-operative, pp. 34–37.

Rural Development News (1992), *Rural Development News*, Issue No. 5. Rural Development Graduates Association, University College Galway.

Sabel, C. (1996), *Ireland – Local Partnerships and Social Innovation*, OECD, Paris.

Scott, D., Shenton, N. and Healey, B. (1991), *Hidden Deprivation in the Countryside*, A Report commissioned by the Peak Park Trust, Department of Social Policy and Social Work, University of Manchester.

SFA (1999), *Fifth National Employment Survey*, Small Firms Association, Dublin.

Sheeran, P. (1988), 'The Idiocy of Irish Rural Life Reviewed', *The Irish Review*, Vol. 5, pp. 27–33.

Short, J. (1991), *Imagined Country*, Routledge, London.

Shortall, S. (1994), 'The Irish Rural Development Paradigm – An Exploratory Analysis', *Economic and Social Review*, Vol. 25, No. 3, pp. 233–260.

Smyth, P. (1998), 'Corporation tax deal could lose us EC goodwill.' *The Irish Times*, 30 November.

Smyth, W.J. (1986), 'Geographical perspectives on the nature of change in rural Ireland', in P. Breathnach and M. Cawley (eds.), *Change and Development in Rural Ireland*, Geographical Society of Ireland, Special Publications, No. 1, pp. 4–10.

Sorenson, T and Epps, R. (1996), 'Leadership and Local development: Dimensions of Leadership in Four Central Queensland Towns', *Journal of Rural Studies*, Vol. 12, No. 2, pp. 113–125.

Stern, E. (1992), 'Institutional Frameworks for Rural Development' in M. Ó Cinnéide and M. Cuddy (eds.), *Perspectives on Rural Development in Advanced Economies*, SSRC, University College Galway, pp. 161–171.

Stiefel, M. and Wolfe, M. (1994), *A Voice for the Excluded, Popular Participation in Development: Utopia or Necessity?*, Zed Books, London.

Stohr, W. (1989), 'Regional Policy at the Crossroads: An Overview', in L. Albreachts, F. Moulaert and P. Roberts (eds.), *Regional Policy at the Crossroads: European Perspectives*, Kingsley Publications, London, pp. 191–197.

Stohr, W. (1990), *Global Challenge and Local Response: local initiatives for economic regeneration in contemporary Europe*, Mansell Publishing, London.

Bibliography   229

Stoker, G. (1997), 'Public-Private Partnerships and Urban Governance', in J. Pierre (ed.), *Public-Private Partnerships in Europe and the United States*, Macmillan, London.
Stoker, G. (1998), *Governance as theory: five propositions*, UNESCO, Oxford, MA.
Strijker, D. (2000), 'Agriculture: still a key to rural identity?' in T. Haartsen, P. Groote and P. Huigen (eds.), *Claiming Rural Identities*, Van Gorcum, The Netherlands.
Sweeney, P. (1998/1999), *The Celtic Tiger: Ireland's continuing Economic Miracle*, Oaktree Press, Dublin.
Syrett, S. (1995), 'Local Economic Development in Peripheral Rural Areas: The Case of Portugal', in S. Hardy, M. Hart, L. Albrechts and A. Katos (eds.), *An Enlarged Europe*, Regional Studies Association and Jessica Kingsley Publishers, London, pp. 281–294.
Szuchewycz, B. (No date), 'The Meanings of Silence in the Irish Catholic Charismatic Movement', in C. Curtin and T.M. Wilson (eds.), *Ireland From Below*, Galway University Press, pp. 46–69.

Teigen, H. (1995), Creating Agglomeration or Deglomeration Economies? Development strategies in rural areas? Paper presented at the XIII International Seminar on Marginal Regions, Maynooth/Kerry, Ireland, 15–22 July, 1995.
Tobin, F. (1984), *The Best Of Decades*, Gill and Macmillan, Dublin.
Tovey, H. (1992), 'Rural Sociology in Ireland: a Review', *Irish Journal of Sociology*, Vol. 2, pp. 96–121.

Údarás na Gaeltachta (1998), Annual Report, Údarás na Gaeltachta.
Uphoff, N. (1988), 'Assisted Self-Reliance: Working with rather than for the poor', in J.P. Lewis (ed.), *Strengthening the Poor: What Have We Learned?*, New Brunswick, NJ, Transaction Books.
Uphoff, N. (1993), 'Grassroots Organizations and NGOs in Rural Development: Opportunities with Diminishing States and Expanding Markets', *World Development*, Vol. 21, No. 4, pp. 607–622.

Varley, T. (1991a), 'Power to the People? Community Groups and Rural Revival in Ireland', in B. Reynolds and S.J. Healy (eds.), *Rural Development Policy: What Future for Rural Ireland?* Justice Commission, Dublin, pp. 83–110.
Varley, T. (1991b), 'On the Fringes: Community Groups in Rural Ireland', in T. Varley, T. Boylan and M. Cuddy (eds.), *Rural Crisis*, Centre for Development Studies, University College Galway, pp. 48–76.
Varley, T. (1992), 'Partnership in Poverty 3', *Co-Options*, The Journal of the Community Workers Co-operative, pp. 47–53.
Varley, T., Boylan, T. and Cuddy, M. (eds.), (1991), *Rural Crisis*, Centre for Development Studies, University College Galway.
Varley, T. and Curtin, C. (1992), 'Co-operation in Rural Ireland: An Approach in Terminal Crisis?' in M. Ó Cinnéide and M. Cuddy (eds.), *Planning and Development of Marginal Areas*, SSRC, University College Galway, pp. 111–121.

Wallman, S. (ed.), (1977), *Perceptions of Development*, Cambridge University Press.
Walsh, J. (1989), 'Regional Development Strategies', in R. Carter and A.J. Parker (eds.), *Ireland: A Contemporary Geographical Perspective*, Routledge, London

and New York, pp. 441–472.

Walsh, J. (1992a), 'Economic Restructuring and Labour Migration in the European Periphery: The Case of the Republic of Ireland', in M. Ó Cinnéide and S. Grimes (eds.), *Planning and Development of Marginal Areas*, SSRC, University College Galway, pp. 23–36.

Walsh, J. (1992b), 'The Republic of Ireland', in R. Martin and P. Townroe (eds.), *Regional Development in the 1990s*, Jessica Kingsley Publishers, Regional Studies Association, London and Philadelphia, pp. 127–137.

Walsh, J. (1993), 'Demographic and Labour Force Adjustments in the Context of Economic restructuring: The Experience of Ireland', in T. Flognfeldt, J.C. Hansen, R. Nordgreen, and J.M. Rohr, (eds.), *Conditions for Development in Marginal Regions*, Oppland College, Norway, pp. 31–44.

Walsh, J. (1995), *Regions in Ireland: a Statistical Profile*, Regional Studies Association, Dublin.

Walsh, J. (1996), 'Local development Theory and Practice: recent experience in Ireland', in J. Alden and P. Bolan (eds.), *Regional Development Strategies*, JKP, London, pp. 159–177.

Ward, N. and McNicholas, K. (1998), 'Reconfiguring rural development in the UK: objective 5b and the new rural governance', *Journal of Rural Studies*, Vol. 14, No. 1, pp. 27–40.

Waters, J. (1994), 'Bishops Report dead and awaiting burial', *The Irish Times*, 8 February.

Watts, N. (1997), 'Army of navvies crosses Irish sea in search of riches', *The Irish Times*, 24 February.

Welch, R.V. (1984), 'The Meaning of Development: Traditional Views and more Recent Ideas', *New Zealand Journal of Geography*, April, pp. 2–4.

Western Development Commission (1999a), *Blueprint for Investing in the West; Promoting foreign direct investment in the West*, Western Development Commission, Roscommon.

Western Development Commission (1999b), *Blueprint for Success: A development plan for the West 2000–2006*, Western Development Commission, Roscommon.

Western Development Partnership Board (1996), *The Challenge: A Positive Future Through Action*, Western Development Partnership Board, Sligo.

Whitebloom, S. (1994), 'How Ireland's West Hopes To Be Won', *The Guardian*, 10 December.

Wilkinson, K.P. (1992), 'Social Stabilisation: The Role of Rural society', in M. Ó Cinnéide and M. Cuddy (eds.), *Perspectives on Rural Development in Advanced Economies*, SSRC, University College Galway, pp. 25–35.

Williams, A.M. (1991), *The European Community*, Blackwell, Oxford.

Williams, R. (1973), *The Country and the City*, Chatto and Windus, London.

World Commission on Environment and Development (1987), *Our Common Future*, Oxford University Press.

Wulf-Mathies, M. (1998), 'The problems of divisions', *The Irish Times*, 16 September.

Yeates, P. (1996), 'Survey finds major change in trend of emigration', *The Irish Times*, 10 April.

Index

Accessibility, 39
Agriculture, 1, 18–21, 24, 26, 36, 53, 108, 143
  agri-tourism, 89
  Common Agricultural Policy (CAP), 19, 89, 90, 91, 92
  decline of, 19
  diversification, 19, 204, 209
  income, 19
  mechanisation of, 22
Amsterdam Treaty, 36
Animation, 113, 118, 121, 159, 199
  (see also animators)
Animators, 124
  (see also animation)
Area Development Management (ADM), 95, 179
Arensberg and Kimball (1940), 59
Authoritarianism, 164

Berlin Summit, 170, 171
British Isles, 12
  Great Britain, 12

Capacity building, 113, 159, 199, 208
Céide Fields, 17
Celtic Tiger, 1, 14, 25, 31, 42
Centralisation, 208
Centralist policy, 143
Church, role of, 111–161
Clientelism, 5, 163, 164
  patronage, 164
  brokerage, 164
Collective action, 178
  (see also partnership)
Collective benefit, 5
Commercialisation, 50
Community development, 3
  community development programme, 175
  community enterprise schemes, 175
  community enterprise, 3
  community participation, 157, 207
  community-based development, 178
  empowerment, 112–122, 155, 175
  grassroots organisations, 118
  (see also development)
Comparative advantage, 39
Competitiveness, 37
Congested Districts Board 1891, 19, 134
Connemara, 17
Consumption, 202
Council for the West, 140, 143, 147–149, 151, 157
Counter-urbanisation, 72
County Development Boards (CDBs), 94, 95, 96, 193–194, 200
County Enterprise Boards (CEBs), 95, 122, 144, 168, 187, 191–192, 200
County Enterprise Plan, 192
Culture, 15
  cultural conservatism, 49
  cultural integrity, 59
  dependency culture, 23

Dáil Eireann, 167
de Valera, Eamonn, 19, 44, 52
Decentralisation, 84, 111, 114, 115, 160, 208
Democracy, 1, 4, 5, 151, 164
  democratic legitimacy, 182, 200, 207
  local democracy, 158
  participatory democracy, 5, 151, 159
Demography, 25, 35, 42
Depopulation, 14, 45, 93, 143
  (see also population decline)
Deregulation, 84, 111, 202
Developing the West Together (DTWT), 32, 111, 123, 128, 129–159, 195, 207, 208
  (see also community development, pressure groups, populist movement)
Development, 1, 74–110
  agencies, 4, 85, 108
  area-based, 177
  bottom-up, 4, 84, 110, 111, 128–159, 198, 209
  community approach 203
  definitions of, 75–77
  discourses of, 1, 5, 17, 83, 86, 87, 155, 159, 173, 112, 118, 205

231

232   Renegotiating Rural Development in Ireland

functional approach to, 4, 122,
leadership and local development,
    124
local development, 121
multi-sectoral, 20
participatory, 4
people-centred approach, 117
practice of, 74
process of, 74, 77–80
rural, 80–110, 148
spectacle of, 3, 74, 86, 106, 108, 172,
    201, 206, 207
sustainable, 38
territorial approach to, 4, 122, 205
top-down, 4, 84, 91, 92, 112, 122,
    143, 198, 199, 202, 209
sectoral approach, 203
Devolution, 109, 110, 160
of power, 164, 208, 209
of responsibility, 208
Diaspora, 33
Discourse,
    academic, 6, 71
    changing, 10–46, 202
    lay, 6, 71
    (see also development, rural)

Eco-auditing, 97
Economy, 22–31
    agglomeration, 41
    branch-plant, 41
    Corporation Tax Rate, 25
    deglomeration, 41
    economic autarky, 22
    economic efficiency, 82, 114
    GDP, 22
    GNP, 77
    indigenous, 23
    mobile investment, 23
    of scale, 27
    protectionist policy, 22
    self-sufficiency, 22, 59
Emigration, 20, 22, 31–33, 45, 61, 66
Employment and Human Resources
    Operational Programme, 102
Entrepreneurship, 36, 124
Environmental management, 166
Equity, 82, 114
European Union (EU), 3 114, 120, 121,
    169, 182, 183, 184, 186, 201, 208
European Union funding, 163
    Cohesion Fund, 168
    Community Support Framework,
    (CSF), 137, 139

European Regional Development
    Fund (ERDF), 90, 169
    Structural Funds, 25, 29, 141, 146,
    168, 171, 183, 190

FÁS, 33, 42, 181, 197
Fianna Fáil, 19, 123
Food and Agricultural Organisation
    (FAO), 118
Foreign Investment, 22, 25, 102

GAA, 12, 68
Gaeltacht, 64, 112, 115, 195–199, 207
General Agreement on Trade and Tariffs
    (GATT), 92
Glencolumbkille, 17, 127
Governance, 1, 2, 4, 79, 85, 96, 110, 111,
    114, 115, 203, 204, 208
    collective regulating of society, 163,
    new forms of governance, 160
    the emergence of rural governance,
    162–201
Government programmes
    BMW Operational Programme, 100,
    101
    National Anti-Poverty Strategy, 96
    National Development Plans (NDP),
    92, 93, 94, 98, 99–106, 109, 115,
    117, 120, 144, 168, 171, 182
    National Employment Plan for
    Ireland 1998, 37
    National Spatial Strategy (NSS), 92,
    105, 106–107, 109
    OPRD, 206
    Programme for Competitiveness and
    Work 1994, 100
    Programme for Economic and Social
    Progress (PESP) 1991, 99, 120
    Programme for Economic Expansion
    1958, 22
    Programme for Prosperity and
    Fairness, 29
    South and East Operational
    Programme, 100, 101, 103
Government Task Force, 146–147

Hayes, Canon, J., 124, 126
    (see also Muintir na Tíre)
Heritage, 63, 68, 106
    authentic, 63
    constructs of, 69, 71
    local scales of, 71
    management of, 76
    manufactured, 63

regional scales of, 69–70
scales of, 65–71
Highlands and Islands Development Board (HIDB), 85, 108
Highlands and Islands Enterprise (HIE), 85
Horan, Monsignor, J., 124, 125
Human capacity, 45, 205, 207
Human Development Index (HDI), 77
Human Resource development, 122

IBEC, 192
Iconography, 64
ICTU, 192
Identity, 10, 15, 16, 49, 68
  constructions of, 10, 50
  cultural, 10, 17, 44
  language, 65, 68
  national, 10, 51, 63, 68
  regional, 15, 44, 65
  religious, 65
  rural, 17, 18, 20, 21
  symbolic, 15, 44, 65
Immigration, 32, 50
Industrial Development Agency (IDA), 12, 90, 91, 102
Information Technology (IT), 25, 39
In-migration, 60, 61
Institutional legitimacy, 182, 207
Integrated planning, 160, 162, 209
Integrated Rural Development, 92, 205
Integration, 205
Integration of policies, 143
Inter-Departmental Committee on the Problems of Small Western Farms, 88
INTERREG, 206
Intervention, 20, 82
Ireland,
  alternative nomenclatures, 12

Land-use planning, 165
LEADER, 3, 83, 87, 95, 96, 119, 122, 145, 147, 163,168, 173, 176, 183–191, 192, 200, 201, 206
  LEADER +, 187–188
  LEADER I, 183–186,
  LEADER II, 186–187
Less Favoured Areas (LFAs), 24, 90, 91
Local Action Group (LAG), 184, 188
Local Authorities, 164, 165–168,174
  Boroughs, 166
  County Councils, 166
  Local Authority Area Committees, 96
  Town Commissioners, 166

Index   233

Urban District Councils (UDCs), 166
Local Development Programme, 147
Local development, 164, 199, 200, 201, 205
Local Enterprise Networks (LENS) 153, 155
Local Government Act 1963, 12, 89
Local government, 163, 174, 204
Local planning, 164
Locality, 113

Macro-scale planning, 112
Market forces, 3
McDyer, Father J., 124, 127
  (see also Glencolumbkille)
Mechanistic view, 3
Migration, 93
Mobility, 3
Modernisation, 112
Modernity, 66, 68, 113
Muintir na Tíre, 126, 187
  (see also community development)
Multi-National Corporations, 25, 26
Multi-sectoral programmes, 190

National Car Test, 97
Nationalism, 64, 164
Nature conservation, 21
Non-governmental organisations (NGOs), 5, 84, 118
  (see also community development)

Participation, 111, 113, 117, 118, 119, 120, 121, 141–142, 159, 165, 181, 204, 205
  participative democracy, 204
Partnership, 1, 4, 5, 28, 86, 87, 111, 112, 113, 118, 128, 150, 159, 162, 165, 205, 178–183, 209
  Area-based initiatives, 99, 175
  Area-based partnerships, 3, 96, 122, 178, 187, 191, 200
  (see also collective benefit)
Paternalism, 84
Peripherality, 10, 23, 83, 156
PILOT, 153, 155
Pilot Area Programme for Integrated Rural Development (IRD), 176–178, 200
Pilot Programmes, 1, 27, 204
Pluralism, 50
Pluri-activity, 19
Population decline, 50, 51
  (see also depopulation)

Populism, 84
Populist movements, 147, 157
  (*see also* community development,
    Developing the West Together)
Positionality, 48
Poverty Programme, 176
Poverty-proofing, 97
Pre-development, 178
Pressure groups, 114
  (*see also* Developing the West
    Together, populist movement)
Product specialisation, 204
Proportional representation, 163

Reductionist view, 3, 52
Regional Assembly, 94, 163, 168, 169–173, 194
Regional Authorities, 94, 163, 168–169
Regional Development Organisations, 89
  (*see also* Údarás na Gaeltachta,
    Western Development Commission,
    Highlands and Island Enterprise,
    Highland and Islands Development
    Board)
Regionalisation, 160, 208
  BMW region, 98, 101, 102, 103, 105, 171
  commodified regions, 70
  constructs of, 70
  Education Board, 13
  Health Board, 13
  NUTS II region, 171
  NUTS III region, 168
  Objective 1 in transition, 169
  Objective 1 region, 160, 169, 171
  Regional Authority Areas, 13
  regional development, 24, 29, 109
  regional devolution, 169
  regional governance, 195
  regional policy, 4, 105
  regional-oriented planning, 3, 109, 169, 210
  South and East Region (S&E), 171
  Tourist Board, 13
Regional Social Development Unit, 153, 155
Rural, 1–6, 58–61
  alternative uses of, 1
  as lived experience, 60–63
  brain-drain, 66
  commodification of, 45, 51, 52
  constructs of, 51, 52
  crisis, 1, 2
  custodian, 20

decline, 6, 18, 19, 20, 27
depopulation, 14, 34
deprivation, 49, 62
descriptive definition of, 54
development discourse, 202, 204
development, 1, 2, 162
dichotomies, 202
discourse, 122, 128
functional definition of, 54
heritage, 63–71
idyll, 37, 51, 52, 60–63, 111
imagery, 62, 69
isolation, 49
literature, 58–60
new rural dwellers, 3, 6, 45, 48, 57, 112
political-economic interpretations, 72
poverty, 14, 28, 29,
  (*see also* deprivation)
regeneration, 10, 17
rural-oriented planning, 3, 210
rural-proofing, 97, 104
rural-urban continuum, 52
rural-urban dichotomy, 58
rural-urban relationships, 58
rural-urban variable, 58, 59
service provision, 26, 27, 53
services, 27, 118
socio-cultural definition of, 54
specific products, 21
theoretical insight to, 51
Rural Development Commission, 85
Rural Development Forum, 94, 96
Rural Environmental Protection Scheme
  (REPS), 21, 103
Rurality, 3, 17, 47–73
  changing approaches to, 47
  changing definitions of, 47
  constructs of, 3, 48, 66, 72, 203
  discourses of, 71
  Irish, 61
  phases of, 55–58
  representations of, 71, 79
  social construction of, 55–58, 71
  symbolic importance of, 72

Sectoral strategies, 99
Self-determination, 78, 79
Self-reflection, 47
Semi-state organisations, 166
Skill shortage, 28, 31, 34–44
  labour shortage, 28, 40
  human resource deficit, 33, 34, 37, 45, 53, 72

skills deficit, 40
Small and Medium Sized Enterprises (SMEs), 45
Small-scale development, 112
Small-scale planning, 112
Social
  animation, 159, 207, 209
  exclusion, 29
  inclusion, 95
Spatial diversity, 3
State agencies, 168
  (*see also* FÁS, Industrial Development Agency, Údarás na Gaeltachta)
Strategic Planning, 122, 163
Subsidiarity, 205, 208
Subsidy shopping, 172
Sustainability, 37, 205
Symbolism, 47, 64

Teilifís na Gaeilge, 65
Tokenism, 117
Tourism, 64
  cultural, 64

Údarás na Gaeltachta, 33, 42, 195–199, 200
Underdevelopment, 10, 83, 112
Unemployment, 14, 25, 28, 34, 35, 36, 42
URBAN, 176

Vehicle Registration Tax (VRT), 97
Voluntary sector/organisations, 4, 27, 84, 113, 114, 115, 117, 118, 157, 163, 175, 207, 208
  (*see also* community development)

Western Development Commission (WDC), 153, 155, 194–195, 200
Western Development Partnership Board (WDPB), 140, 143, 150–159
Western Investment Fund (WIF), 153, 155, 194, 195
Western Package, 134
White Paper on Industrial Policy 1984, 24
Wolf-Mathies, M., 171
  (*see also* regionalisation)